ROCK 'N' RADIO

ROCK 'n' RADIO

When DJs and Rock Music
Ruled the Airwaves

IAN HOWARTH

Véhicule Press

Published with the generous assistance of the Canada Council for the Arts, the Canada Book Fund of the Department of Canadian Heritage, and the Société de développement des entreprises culturelles du Québec (SODEC).

Funded by the Government of Canada
Financé par le gouvernement du Canada | Canadä

Cover design: David Drummond
Photo of author: Benjamin Dobutovic
Typeset in Minion and Bodoni by Simon Garamond
Printed by Marquis Printing Inc.

LIBRARY AND ARCHIVES CANADA CATALOGUING IN PUBLICATION

Howarth, Ian, 1951-, author
Rock'n' radio : when DJs and rock music ruled the airwaves / Ian Howarth.

Issued in print and electronic formats.
ISBN 978-1-55065-469-1 (softcover). – ISBN 978-1-55065-475-2 (EPUB)

1. Radio and music. 2. Disc jockeys – Canada.
3. Rock music – Canada – History and criticism.
I. Title. II. Title: Rock and radio. III. Title: Rock 'n' radio.

ML68.H853 2017   782.42166   C2016-907369-6
C2016-907370-X

Published by Véhicule Press, Montréal, Québec, Canada
www.vehiculepress.com

Distributed by LitDistCo
www.litdistco.ca

Printed in Canada on FSC certified paper

For my wife Mary Anne
and daughter Jessica, both of whom had
a hand in making this book complete.

Contents

Introduction

Music, it is said, is good for the soul. And whether it was soul music, rhythm and blues, or straight-up rock 'n' roll, it was radio – specifically Top 40 radio – that delivered those sounds to a hungry post-WWII audience that would be witness to a rapidly changing popular music scene in North America.

Baby Boomers grew up in the golden age of rock, the days of Elvis, Little Richard, the Beach Boys, the Beatles, the Rolling Stones, Led Zeppelin, and Pink Floyd. In the late 1950s and early '60s, radio stations across the U.S. and Canada moved to keep up with the times, dumping their middle-of-the-road programming to meet the needs of an increasingly powerful and demanding youth demographic. By the mid-60s, Top 40 radio was an increasingly well-oiled machine pumping out rock songs using a simple jukebox formula: play the same songs that kids are putting a dime in the jukebox to hear, then play them again.

If Top 40 radio made stars out of some unlikely rock 'n' rollers, it also made stars out of the young men behind the microphone with a pile of 45-rpm records and energy to burn. Their fast-paced patter between songs was a trademark of Top 40 DJs, most of whom took their cues from pioneering U.S. Top 40 DJs like Alan Freed on WINS in New York, WABC's Cousin Brucie, and Charlie Tuna in L.A. at KHJ, who became the standard upon which any aspiring top DJ modelled himself.

The Canadian Top 40 market was no different than it was in the U.S. Though CHUM-AM in Toronto may lay claim to being the first Top 40 radio station in Canada, the Montreal radio market was easily as dynamic. These are the stories of the Golden Age of Montreal rock radio, told first-hand by the men – and yes, there were some women – in front of the mic, and the people behind it: the newscasters, the traffic reporters, the program directors, the general managers, promoters, and the local bands that launched their almost-famous careers with the help of Top 40 radio.

Their stories are recalled through the lenses of some 40 to 50 years past, heady times for all involved who are now scattered across Canada and the U.S., mostly retired from the biz, but still with sharp memories and colourful stories to share. A little sex, some drugs, disappointments and triumphs, all with a soundtrack from the greatest decades in rock music playing in the background. It was a time when rock radio was growing up alongside significant and dynamic socio-political change. The fledgling civil rights struggle in the U.S., the Vietnam War, campus unrest and the subsequent peace movement all percolated behind the musical soundtrack of the '60s and early '70s. In Canada, we had our first populist star prime minister in Pierre Elliot Trudeau, who would lead the country through one of its most difficult and violent times during the October Crisis of 1970 in Quebec. It was the beginning of a youth-driven cultural revolution inextricably entwined with the art and music of the day.

Dozens of DJs came and went in the always-fragile employment world of Top 40 radio, but few were still the same shirt-and-tie-wearing DJs by the time late '60s rolled around. Some left more of a mark than others. Top 40 forerunner Bob Gillies broke new ground with his *Campus Club* show on CKGM. In 1964, CFCF's Dave Boxer and Buddy Gee (a.k.a. George Morris) on CKGM became Montreal's first Top 40 DJ stars. A year later, there was the ascendency of CFOX, the first AM station in Montreal to go completely Top 40, with Dean Hagopian and his cast of characters changing the face of AM rock radio. At the beginning of the next decade, under the leadership of the charismatic and quirky owner Geoff Stirling, CKGM would become the new rock radio contender in the city. With the combination of deal-maker general manager Jim Sward and genius program director John Mackay, CKGM ended CFOX's five-year domination in the Top 40 ratings. Two years later, with Ralph Lockwood as their morning man, Lockwood and DJs like Marc "Mais Oui" Denis were part of CKGM's remarkable run as the No. 1 English-language Top 40 station in Montreal until the late '70s.

While Top 40 DJs were more content to let the music talk politics, it was not the same when CKGM-AM and FM owner Geoff Stirling decided in October 1969 to let radio neophyte Doug Pringle transform his FM station from an easy-listening format to an "underground" alternative radio station, a musical experiment that signalled a significant shift in the radio hierarchy and one which ultimately would contribute to the undoing of the Top 40 radio era. CHOM-FM, as CKGM-FM came to be called in 1971, would become Montreal's new mantra, where DJs were announcers with more than just time, temperature and weather on their agendas.

Reuniting with these voices and personalities over the phone and in person was a long journey back to my adolescence and early adulthood – and theirs, too. The exact dates may be a bit blurred by time, but the memories are still sharp. These were the voices of my past, the ones that I had close to my ear growing up. Some, like Steve Shannon, now a virtual one-man radio station in Barriere, B.C., still carry on a love affair with radio. Doug Pringle manages five radio stations in western Canada and George Morris is the voice behind Lotto 6/49 commercials; rock promoter Donald Tarlton (a.k.a. DKD) is more-or-less retired; and J. B. & the Playboys' Bill Hill and the Haunted's Bob Burgess have not given up the guitar.

This is a celebration of those halcyon days of Montreal rock radio when DJs were personalities, celebrities even, on stage for four hours a day. It was a time when Montreal was red-hot, a time when the hits – good and bad – just kept on comin'. This book is my tribute to that golden era, to preserve and share great stories, to give them their deserved place in our cultural history.

A Boy and His Rocket Radio

SLEEPING WITH RADIO

My first radio was a rocket-shaped crystal with one slippery, plastic
earbud and a cord with a claw-like attachment that I hooked up
to the nearest metallic object – usually at night while lying in bed
when the signals were strongest. Any station that was surging over
the night's airwaves won my attention until the signal faded. I was in
charge, not spinning the records, but the next best thing: the dial.
I was a natural-born dial spinner. It was the early '60s, and
finding something good on the radio was a crapshoot, the airwaves
clogged with a lot of adult talk and sanitized middle-of-the-road
music. But every once in a while I'd hit on a station playing something that struck a chord in me. In 1961, a group called the Marcels
had a No. 1 hit called "Blue Moon," a doo-wop version of a Rodgers
and Hart song written in 1934, covered by Frank Sinatra, then re-
worked by Elvis in 1956. I had no idea the Marcels were black or that
this was a doo-wop-styled song. I was 10 years old and it sounded
great. I was hooked on radio.

OUR PARENTS' MUSIC

Most Baby Boomers know who Perry Como is and can probably
hum a few bars of "Catch a Falling Star." Released in 1957, the song
made history when it became the first single to be certified gold
by the Recording Industry Association of America, and, in 1959, it
garnered Como a Grammy. It was his last No. 1 hit. For much of the

1950s, he was the most popular singer behind Elvis, but by the end of the '50s his popularity had waned. My father was a big Perry Como fan and, as with thousands of other white North American men in their mid-30s, Como's signature buttoned-up cardigan and white shirt was the wardrobe-du-jour that went perfectly with a post-workday martini. I was six years old when "Catch a Falling Star" came out, and I can still sing the first verse and chorus six decades later. I'm not sure how this happened, but research on the brain has subsequently labelled this phenomenon "reminisce bumps," the power of music to make memories.

Como and other pop singers like Pat Boone, Patti Page and Andy Williams played major roles in the soundtrack of the mid-50s. Page's "How Much is That Doggie in the Window?" was so ubiquitous on the radio and TV, it was impossible to ignore. The new post-WWII demographic was not quite consumer-qualified, but when we did come into some money – our allowance – we weren't buying Perry Como singles. That was what our parents listened to. Sure, our parents' music seeped into our consciousness and stayed there like the first two lines of a popular Christmas carol, but it wasn't by choice. As children, we weren't in charge of the music we listened to. It was delivered by the radio stations older people listened to and by the records in the modest collections of our middle-class parents, which, in any case, we weren't allowed to put on a turntable without supervision. Nevertheless, we were little sponges.

My parents' record collection was mostly a motley assortment of 78-rpm records probably passed on to them by their parents. They broke easily, my three brothers and I discovered. The home collection was occasionally updated, however, with some records bought by my mother in a valiant effort to educate her four sons. I was the third, born in 1951. I remember being quite taken by one particular record my mother introduced me to, *Peter and the Wolf*, a narration of the famous story told using various musical instruments, each representing a different character. The record has been re-released several times over the years with an astonishing array of narrators like Sting, David Bowie, Patrick Stewart, and one in 1960 with Captain Kangaroo. I have warm memories of listening to it in

13

front of our heavy wood-encased radio and turntable unit, typical of those days. I played it over and over again. Only later in life would I realize that my mother must've liked it particularly for the 25 minutes it kept me out of her hair. It was the equivalent of sticking a young child in front of the TV today – with PBS on, of course.

DISCOVERING MY LOVE FOR RADIO

While the family turntable may have been off limits, the radio was not, since it wasn't nearly as delicate as those 78s. My generation was very radio-centric, though the TV would eventually become radio's entertainment companion and competitor. The radio, like a campfire, drew families together. The dials were nice and big for little hands, and I fired that red needle from one end of the dial to the other and back again, trying to find something that held my attention.

With four kids and two adults crammed into a small suburban Toronto bungalow, I didn't get much alone time. Though I did have the radio to myself for brief moments, it was located in the living room, a heavy traffic area, so it was hit or miss for my burgeoning love affair. I finally asked my parents for one of my own, so I could do my dial spinning uninterrupted in the privacy of the room I shared with my younger brother.

My little rocket-shaped crystal was my connection to the outside world. Late at night, I would lie in my bed manoeuvring the dial tuner with the precision of a surgeon, except my best work was done in total darkness, lying on one side so the earplug wouldn't slip out.

As I fiddled with the station dial, the strongest signal always won out, of course, but nevertheless I turned it back and forth repeatedly to see what I could bring in. Some U.S. stations with strong signals faded in and out as if on the whim of the wind. If conditions were right, I heard WABC in New York City – which, on a good night, could be picked up in 38 states and Canadian border towns – WKBW in Buffalo, WBZ in Boston, WJR in Detroit, CHUM-AM in Toronto, and CKLW in Windsor, Ontario. They all blew in and out as if orbiting the Earth.

Unfortunately, the AM stations with the strongest signals played mostly easy listening late at night. It seemed they actually wanted their listeners to fall asleep. Still, every once in a while, I would get a radio station that had more of the "Blue Moon"-type music I loved. At night, I was in my own private radio world.

Then my parents sprung for a transistor radio – a definite upgrade – which opened up even more possibilities. That transistor had its own cachet, much superior to my little rocket radio that sadly found itself on the downside of a technological revolution. In addition to spinning a new dial, my nightly bedtime activity included turning the radio in various directions to capture the signal of a good station. I fell asleep every night to my radio, after I grew weary of switching stations. In the morning, the radio still on, I'd awaken to find I'd pushed my transistor batteries to their limit. I left it to resuscitate itself during the day, though I discovered worn-out batteries did not fully recover with rest. After school and on weekends, that transistor went everywhere with me, including on my bike, where I locked it to my handlebars with my thumb. Each turn of the bike required a radio-position adjustment so I could listen while I pedalled. Neighbours could hear me coming from blocks away.

New City, New Frequencies

My family life (and my radio-listening habits) took a sudden turn to the east in the summer of 1962 when my father was transferred to Montreal. It was not an easy exit since my parents' roots were in Ontario and my two older brothers had an established network of friends they didn't want to leave behind. When the movers came, my older brother tied himself to his lower bunk bed, refusing to go. My parents tried quiet persuasion at first, but after a few too many refusals they cut him loose and he sulked all the way in the car ride to Montreal. I thought of it as an adventure. I'll be damned if I even knew where Montreal was, but I was a co-operative family hostage, sitting beside my brooding brother for the drive to a bigger house and bigger money for my father.

We moved into a brand new two-storey house in what looked like a construction frontier town, the second family to move into a suburban work in progress. It was the beginning of the early-60s movement towards the suburbs that came about as post-WWII families outgrew the humble, cramped bungalows; their income increased and the burgeoning Canadian middle class explored the suburbs as a better place to bring up their kids. I had brought my portable friend with me and a whole new world of dial-turning opened up. New frequencies to discover, new voices and music to take in.

A City in Transition

Though I was marooned in the 'burbs, the radio kept me in touch with other places and worlds. Montreal was putting itself on the map as a vibrant, happening city, with a larger population than Toronto. It was in the midst of an early '60s building boom, a place where major corporations, also in expansion, had their head offices, which is what brought my father to Montreal.

In 1962, the 45-storey Canadian Imperial Bank of Commerce (now CIBC) building opened as the tallest in Canada. This is where my father would start his new job with Allied Chemical Canada. The first time I was allowed a downtown visit, I was impressed by the view from my father's 22nd-floor office. (Not so enthusiastic, however, were the employees on the higher floors who were reluctant to go anywhere near the windows. As legend has it, a brave soul who was apparently tagged to show employees that they were in no danger, went from floor to floor hurling himself at the windows to pacify paranoid office staff.) As for my father, he was probably feeling the vibe of the times, which was that the taller the building, the more bragging rights the city had.

Only a few months later the CIBC building lost its tallest-in-town tag – by one storey – to Place Ville Marie. In just one year Montreal had opened the two tallest buildings in Canada. The province, meanwhile, led by a new Liberal premier, Jean Lesage, was also flexing its new sense of identity and pride with the opening of a 27-storey head-office building for Hydro Quebec in Montreal. This was part of

American DJ Alan Freed is generally given credit for coining the term "rock 'n' roll."

same. He died in 1964 – a broke and broken man – of kidney failure due to complications from alcohol. But Freed had introduced R&B to white America, and in 1989 received his due as one of the first inductees into the Rock and Roll Hall of Fame.

The Alan Freed payola scandal was a setback for the fledgling rock radio business, which was run by conservative radio executives, some of whom believed rock 'n' roll was the devil's music and who seized on the scandal as an excuse to tone things right down. R&B was too sexual. Even the term rock 'n' roll mentioned in some black artists' songs was code for sex. It was "jungle music" to radio programmers, too risky to play for fear of alienating present or potential sponsors. For a few years, rock radio went with safe, white, sanitized rock music.

Most mainstream radio stations in the U.S. and Canada took to playing the Bobbys: Curtola, Vinton, Vee, Rydell and Darin. Pat Boone made a whole lot of money with his pasteurized version of Chuck Berry's "Tutti Frutti." Perry Como was still hanging in there along with TV teen-throbs like Ricky Nelson. And then there was Elvis. Nobody touched Elvis. He got away with his gyrations and jungle sounds. He was, after all, a good-lookin' white boy from the south who used to sing in church with his mama. But Elvis, in the prime of his rock 'n' roll ascendency, was drafted into the U.S. Army in 1958. When he came back two years later, it seemed that experience had knocked the Jailhouse Rock right out of him. Presley, though he no longer rocked the way he had early in his career, turned out to be a durable performer, still charting into the 1970s. Meanwhile, in another example of a derailed rock star, Richard Wayne Penniman, a.k.a. Little Richard, decided in 1957 to forego his rock music career to join the ministry. It would be five years before he came back to his music, but he never again regained the momentum he'd had in the early 50s.

With those two rock pioneers gone, radio stations looked in other directions to fill the airwaves. There were plenty of musicians ready to step up to the plate and hit a No. 1 record out of the park. Artists like Chubby Checker, Ray Charles, the Everly Brothers, Roy Orbison, Ben E. King, Lesley Gore, the Four Seasons, and the Beach Boys, along with the beginning of a wave of girl groups like the Shirelles, the Chiffons and the Ronettes (who introduced the legendary Wall of Sound, the brainchild of a young producer, Phil Spector) edged their way onto the early 1960s *Billboard* charts.

I ate up all that music, when I could find it, on my trusty transistor. I didn't have anything to play 45s on; though they were only 99 cents, that was beyond my prepubescent budget, but my older brothers seemed to have more purchasing power and if the timing was right, I could sneak into my oldest brother's bedroom and play his 45s on his portable red and white RCA Victor record player. There would be repercussions if I left any trace of my presence in his bedroom or was caught in the act of trespassing. Ultimately, I inherited that RCA player and played the hell out of my meagre collection of 45-rpms. A few years later, in 1967, when I could spring for an album, I wore out Jimi Hendrix's *Are You Experienced* with frequent plays. Cuts like "Hey Joe"' and "Manic Depression" were in heavy rotation. Finally, I was spinning my own music.

THE ARRIVAL OF TOP 40 RADIO

In 1964, two Montreal AM stations, CFCF and CKGM, took a chance with rock 'n' roll radio, delivering evening rock music shows hosted by Dave Boxer and Buddy Gee respectively. Boxer's show, especially, became the talk of the town. CKGM and CFCF ran up against one another in virtually the same time slot each night and on Saturday, competing for the hungry-for-rock teenage audience. Now my nighttime dial flipping was back and forth between 600 and 980 AM. In 1965, another rock radio variable was thrown into the mix when 1470 CFOX trumped everyone by going to a full Top 40 format. Throughout my high school life, these three stations were my connection to the world of rock music, one that was in a period of great transition. In the high school hallways, the talk was more about the latest singles and who was listening to whom and on which station than it was about TV. Brand new Montreal rock bands played the high school dance circuit.

There was a plethora of '60s dance crazes: the Monkey, the Watusi, the Jerk, the Swim, the Hully Gully, the Freddie, and the Pony.

On the floor I was mostly an improviser; the girls, however, seemed to have all the dance moves down. Some songs proved more of a challenge; the Troggs' "Wild Thing" made for some awkward dancefloor moments. By the time rock's psychedelic music came around, it was everyone for himself on the dance floor. Every Friday night there was a dance, where the evening would close out with a slow song like the Animals' version of "House of the Rising Sun" – an almost three-minute single – long enough for couples to do some serious groin-grinding in their best pair of tight Friday-night jeans before the harsh gymnasium lights abruptly came up.

[CHAPTER ONE]

Top 40 Radio Nights

CFCF DJ Dave Boxer and CKGM DJ Buddy Gee Battle for the Teen Audience

When Dave Boxer hit the airwaves on CFCF-AM 600 in July 1964, he single-handedly took a staid and moribund station – the oldest in Canada – from middle-of-the-road mediocrity to Top 40 radio excitement, if only for four-and-a-half hours a day. His timing, though somewhat accidental, couldn't have been better. Competitor CKGM was the only station in town experimenting with a Top 40 format, but soon Boxer's 6:30 to 11 p.m. show became the number-one show for a youth demographic that heretofore had never heard of CFCF. Until then, the station might have been only background noise on their parents' home radio. (There was also CJAD's Mike Stephens' *Club 800* show, but if teens didn't hurry home from school, they'd likely miss the 4 to 5 p.m. bite of rock.) In less than a year, Boxer's daily Top 40 show took flight and enjoyed a glorious four-year run. Boxer became arguably Montreal's first legitimate rock-radio star.

The management brain trust at CFCF, including general manager Dave Wright and programming director Gerry Bascome, decided the station needed a boost. They took a chance on a journeyman DJ who had toiled in the small markets of Sudbury, Timmins, Cornwall, Oshawa, and St. John's.

Boxer was a driven man. Pretty much every radio station in Canada had a Dave Boxer audition tape. When he circled back to

Montreal, after a futile search for employment in L.A., he was hardly an unknown quantity. After stints at the CBC, CKGM, and CJAD – none of which offered him his own show – CFCF came calling.

"The rest is history," Boxer wrote in his 174-page autobiography *Bubee's Book for Boxer Buddies OR You Can't Please All of the People All of the Time.* The book, now a collectors' item, is the only historical document written by and about Boxer, albeit written only one year into his successful four-year run at CFCF. The book illustrates Boxer's popularity and robust ego; however, it also displays his vulnerability. During his show's heyday, he received hundreds of letters from fans every week. A good portion of his book is given over to fan letters, and to his credit, not all of them are flattering. That so many fans would take the time to write these letters and mail them seems so foreign today. Their ferocity and frank nature speaks to Boxer's impact on a young audience hungry for something different.

Smitten fans, mostly girls, wrote from the heart: "I listen to 'CF radio every night, and I honestly think your show is great. You're a pretty good egg, too. I just love you. I like the real swinging records you play, and I really don't have any Beatles records or any of the other swinging ones. My parents only have organ or piano music. That's why I turn to you." There were also some malcontents, such as one young wordsmith who wrote: "Your voice reminds me of Frankie Stein or Drak Cula. You have about as much musical appreciation as a tone-deaf cow and are as bright as a half-watt light bulb." This was probably not the kind of letter Chuck Berry was thinking about when he wrote "Roll Over Beethoven." "Gonna write a letter, gonna mail it to my local DJ / It's a rockin' Little Richard I want my jockey to play." Top 40 DJs got plenty of cards and letters before stations would eventually set up request phone lines.

It's unlikely any of Boxer's young listeners knew he was a veteran radio man by the time he caught fire on CFCF. He had been on the radio road since 1954 and had honed his skills doing all kinds of radio and even a bit of TV. He came from humble Montreal roots, often working alongside his father, who owned a butcher shop. There was no post-secondary education for Boxer. He was out pursuing his radio

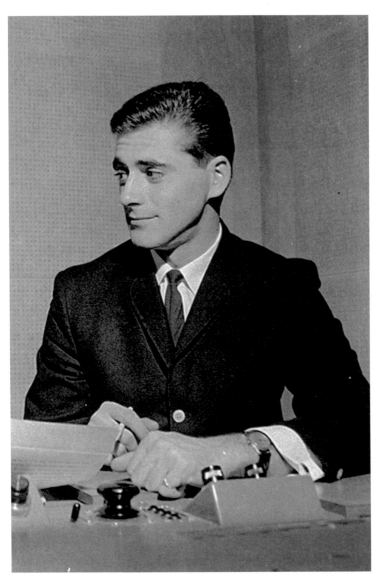

Dave Boxer's nightly CFCF show broke new ground on Montreal radio in 1964 as the first devoted solely to Top 40 hits.
Courtesy of Dan Kowal.

dreams at an early age, with a strong work ethic passed on through the long days his father put in. By the time Boxer got his own show on CFCF, he was not a young man by Top 40 DJ standards. Born in 1934, he was old enough to remember listening to World War II adventure shows like *Dick Tracy*, *Superman*, WWII ace fighter-pilot *Hop Harrigan*, and *The Green Hornet*, on his parents' radio. By the time Boxer turned 10, he was hooked on radio.

"From that time on," he wrote in his book, "I paid particular attention to everything happening on the radio. I studied each different voice, the many kinds of programs, the thousands of ways a guy could deliver commercials, station IDs, the weather forecast. I could tell any voice on the air." After finishing high school, he took a radio course in Montreal and sent out a whack of tapes. One of these landed on the desk of CHNO in Sudbury in 1954, his first radio job.

Gerry Bascome was hired at CFCF 600 as programming director in 1963. "The station was seventh in a market of six stations," Bascome jokes. "My mandate was to change the whole thing and have it making some money." Hiring Boxer and giving him a four-hour-long rock show every weekday night was a big step toward injecting some life into a tired old station. At announcers' meetings, Boxer had plenty to contribute, Bascome recalls. At first, leery that the whole rock 'n' roll programming gamble would go sideways, CFCF management tried to keep Boxer on a short leash, but after a few months of seeing the response his show was getting, they backed off and let him rock to his own agenda. "We just let Dave do his thing," says Bascome.

Boxer put his heart and soul into his show. "He had enthusiasm, spirit, and he was very competitive," Bascome recalls. "He liked the music he was playing, so it wasn't just an on-air guy doing what he was told. He was a big portion of where the whole thing [Top 40 radio] was going. He bought into it 100 percent. And we bought into him by the same amount."

Boxer's on-air style wasn't that of a prototypical fast-talking huckster, the Top 40 U.S.-style DJ, locked into a tight formula of time, temperature, weather and music, known as the Drake format (named after Bill Drake, one of the most sought-after Top 40 radio programmers in North America.) Instead, Boxer had a smooth, even mature approach to Top 40 radio. No yelling. No over the top rapid-fire hype. But he could sure sell himself and his radio show. His show featured "Boxer's Best Bet," "Boxer's Bomb," and "Boxer's Buddies" – a teeming army of adolescent loyalists. Boxer was out in the community, at dances, sock hops, record stores, concerts, and advertisers' events. Beyond using his own name in various ways to put his personal stamp on his radio show, he set about concocting a hodgepodge of hip language known as Boxerspeak – invented or altered words, some of them actually adopted by his growing legion of listeners. To punctuate something funny or a contest winner on the air, he would blow into a dime-store sliding whistle, his "fennortinzer." If something he said was funny, it "tickled your welkabubblizer." Boxer must have seemed a little unhip to some teen listeners. His show ended at 11 p.m. or "elevensville," when he would roll out his signature sign-off tune, "The Shadow of Your Smile," by saxophonist Boots Randolph. He would softly wind down his listeners with his voice over the song. "It's elevensville," he would say. "Time to send you off into the land of the giant marshmallows to sleep deliciously … dee-lis-cious-ly," stretching the word out like a pre-sleep yawn, as if he was tucking all his Boxer Buddies into bed.

The addition of the "ville" to certain words, like "splitsville" (as in, I'm outta here) or "germsville" (another Boxerism for hospital) were all terms that came out in the late 1950s and early 1960s beatnik culture that put Boxer precariously close to being an over-the-hip-hill DJ locked in a kind of 1950s time warp. (He was 30 when his popular stint at CFCF kicked off in 1964.) These were expressions that young TV viewers were more likely to hear springing from the mouth of the Gerald Lloyd "Kookie" Kookson III character (played by Ed Byrnes) on the show *77 Sunset Strip*.

In his book, which he sold via the CFCF Top 60 charts that were widely distributed in Montreal record stores, Boxer didn't mind reprinting letters from fans who thought he was clearly behind the times. "Dear Hopeless," wrote one disenchanted listener, "I know and you know that all, and I do mean ALL, the phrases you use are at least five years old. Please refrain from the 1957 vintage radio and get up with the times and you won't have such a dorky show."

He exhorted his listeners to "spread the word, birds." And spread the word about his show they did, word-of-mouth being the Twitter of the day. Boxer had his own pronunciation for CFCF, "Cuff-Cuff," a pronunciation that stuck for years, even after he left the station. His listeners were dubbed "movers and groovers."

Boxer may have straddled the '50s and early '60s, but his quirky nomenclature was both endearing and unifying. He was unabashedly "the cool dadd-io-on-the-radd-io." He was building an on-air persona that would bring him and his often-neglected teen audience together in a kind of cloven conspiracy of membership. All his listeners went to bed happy, having heard at least one Beatles single per hour, along with newly released singles, and the chance to participate in contests. Some parents, however, were not happy, and battles over use of the one phone at home were frequent from 6:30 to 11 p.m. "My mom won't let me phone you anymore," one teen told Boxer in a letter. "I spent four hours speed dialling and she put the kibosh on that."

Boxer had a feature he called "Beatles Bubbles" – three or four back-to-back Beatles hits. There were also new singles that got tested on air, some destined to become "Boxer Bombs," while others made the cut to the CFCF Top 60. It was Top 40 radio, but Boxer's Top 60 Hit List was a nod to the station's 600 AM frequency.

Boxer, along with every Top 40 DJ in North America, rode the Beatles phenomenon for all it was worth. It was worth plenty in terms of ratings, when the group launched their first North American tour in 1964, playing *The Ed Sullivan Show* in NYC in February, then releasing the film *A Hard Day's Night* in August. They were red-hot when they made their Montreal stop on September 8 at the Forum. Boxer shared emcee duties with CKGM Top 40 rival DJ Buddy Gee and popular CJMS jock Michel Desrochers, all of whom were newcomers to the rock radio biz. The night before, Boxer had been at Montreal's Dorval Airport to greet the band, his appearance making something of a splash with his already devoted Boxer Buddies fan club members in a state of high anticipation.

Of course, after the Beatles' two Montreal concerts, Boxer got letters. "Dear Dave, on September 8, you were really fabulous. At the

The Beatles were not keen to return to Montreal after their September 8, 1964 appearance. Boxer travelled to their London studios with a petition he presented to John Lennon and Paul McCartney to convince them otherwise.
Courtesy Ted Brennan.

performance, I took a bottle and captured some Beatles and Boxer air. I have that bottle tightly capped, and I've pasted Beatles pictures all over it. Right now, the bottle is on the shelf over my bed and every night before going to sleep, I look at it and remember the time John, Paul, George, and Ringo came to Montreal. It was such a night and I will never forget it."

No other city on that Beatles 1964 North American tour gave the group the same kind of toxic reception, however. There were bomb threats and a pointedly anti-Semitic attack on drummer Ringo Starr, who some mistakenly thought was Jewish. Manager Brian Epstein made good on his promise to never return to Montreal, despite the fact that in 1965 Boxer turned up in England to present the group with a petition signed by thousands of Montreal (and Boxer) fans who wanted the group to include Montreal in their 1965 itinerary. He wanted the group to know that Montreal was a Beatles city, and not the way the fringe elements that soured their Montreal experience had made it appear. Though acknowledging the petition, Epstein held his ground. Nevertheless, he allowed Boxer to interview the group as a kind of consolation. It was a noble effort, boosted by the fact that Boxer ran clips of his Beatles interviews on his show for weeks after he got back to Montreal, solidifying his reputation as a major Beatles insider and Montreal's version of the Fifth Beatle, a spot claimed by WINS Top 40 DJ Murray the "K" (Kaufman) in New York.

In a Montreal *Gazette* article that he wrote in 1980, after John Lennon's death, Boxer recalled that concert he emceed as something of a disappointment. "I had asked the audience to be quiet so I could hear whether the Beatles were as good as everyone said, and I found they weren't. I listened carefully and they were off-key many times. They couldn't seem to duplicate on stage what they had been doing in the recording studio. Maybe it was the noise and they couldn't hear themselves." At the time, Boxer kept this observation to himself – a wise move, since the Beatles continued to be a hit machine for years. To badmouth them on air would have been high treason and bad for business. As it was, his 1965 encounter with the group would stay with him forever. When Lennon died, he remembered him as "a very complicated guy, an intellectual nut, a very creative guy who was the oddball of the group."

As Boxer was helping CFCF obtain a whole new listener demographic, the station was looking to further improve its profile. Programming director Bascome and general manager Wright decided to offer popular Toronto CHUM and CKEY DJ Al Boliska the morning slot. Credited as a pioneer of early Top 40 radio, Boliska was a breath of fresh air for CFCF morning listeners who got to hear his famous "World's Worst Jokes" – a bit he made famous in Toronto and later converted into two comedy albums and a joke book. Thanks to Boliska and Boxer, CFCF was making a bit of a comeback in the ratings. However, Boliska's stay at CFCF was considerably shorter than Boxer's, and he returned to the Toronto market after less than a year.

Both CFCF radio and television were home to a number of legitimate Montreal entertainment personalities who, like Boxer, enjoyed star status in the city. At the age of 19, a somewhat star-struck Bill Haugland found himself working alongside seasoned professionals like Jimmy Tapp, Jack Curran, Dean Kaye, and Don McGowan. On the TV side, Magic Tom Auburn and Ted Zeigler as Johnny Jellybean had a huge number of loyal viewers. Starting out as a radio news announcer, Haugland would occasionally draw the 6 to 11 p.m. news shift when Boxer was on the air from '64 to '68. "Like a lot of the other guys working at CFCF, they all seem to me to have personalities larger than life," says Haugland. "[Boxer] enjoyed his notoriety, though at staff parties he was socially shy." When Haugland would arrive at the CFCF studios in Montreal's Park Extension area, he'd see girls hanging around the entrance looking for a glimpse of their radio idol. To the rookie news guy, Boxer once jokingly said, "Stick around, kid, I'll make you a star." Haugland did stick around – for 45 years – anchoring CFCF's *Pulse News* (before it became *CFCF News*, then *CTV News*) from 1977 until his retirement in 2006.

While at CFCF, Boxer used the time-tested publicity stunt to great advantage. A&W Restaurants, home of the Teen Burger (the Baby, Mama, and Papa Burger, too), was one of Boxer's main sponsors. Drive-in-style A&Ws were a major hangout for teens, especially on weekends, when they would pile into the car of one of their licensed friends, who had access to the family vehicle, and head off to the local "Dubs." There they would park the car, turn up the radio, roll down the window, and bark their orders into a drive-in-movie-style speaker. The waitress would bring the order out on a tray that hooked onto the rolled-down window.

For his stunt, Boxer chose a centrally located A&W franchise and, for three days, he lived and did remote reports from a suspended wooden hut in the parking lot. He became an instant curiosity, drawing hundreds of fans who came to check out the crazy DJ. That particular A&W franchise did a booming business, while Boxer hovered over the parking lot – great publicity for his advertiser and his show. Always big on rhymes and slogans, he called himself the "Nut in the Hut."

Backing Boxer up in the studio during his regular shift was announcer Keith Randall, dubbed "the deputy nut in the hut" for the duration of the A&W stunt. "I was a kind of journeyman radio guy," says Randall. "I could do news, sports, anything, except hockey play-by-play. Filling in for Boxer was a fun gig. I knew what he did. I would just do my interpretation of that. It was another way to make a few bucks of overtime." As for the "deputy nut in the hut" billing, "I think the emphasis should be on the deputy," Randall says. "I think Dave was like many guys in the radio business who were basically introverts and very closed up . . . Boxer was of that breed. He was a shy, introverted guy who managed to put on a show. I remember going to a party at his apartment one time with all of the big guns of Montreal music. Dave just sat in the corner playing disc jockey all night."

Boxer was a businessman as much as he was a DJ. He made regular personal appearances for advertisers and did the high school dance circuit to make extra money and raise his profile. As a local Montreal rock band supporter, he often invited bands like the Haunted and J.B. and the Playboys in studio, where he interviewed them and played their latest singles. His Top 60 charts were the barometer of success for some local bands, who managed to occasionally poke their way into the Top 10, thanks to Boxer putting their newest 45 into regular rotation.

Boxer teamed up with entrepreneurial musician Jurgen Peter of the rock group The Haunted, and together they formed the booking agency GASS (Groups and Sound Services). They also issued a bi-weekly music newspaper *Music Trend,* and put together shows at the Bonaventure Curling Club – the biggest music venue in the city at the time. Not surprisingly, the Haunted were often the headliners. As he did with show sponsor A&W, Boxer used his advertisers as vehicles to elevate his profile and that of local bands. He once hosted a "Boxer's Bash" at Grover's, a Montreal men's clothing store. He did remotes from the store and featured the Haunted, the Munks, and the Pussycats playing live. He was breaking new ground on the Montreal radio and concert scene, and he was making good money. "He was quite a businessman," says Randall. "And he was certainly, I would guess, one of the key players, if not the key player in the rise of the Montreal rock music scene. He was not shy about playing local bands, promoting them and using them at his dances."

Growing up in Montreal in the late '50s and early '60s, Michael

Godin was a huge fan of radio. It was the music, the production, the jingles, the patter of the DJs, the excitement of what they were doing on the air. "That [radio] just completely resonated with me, to the point that I never had to think about what I was going to do when I grew up," he says. "I wanted to be a DJ." Godin made good on this, first launching a high school radio station, then moving professionally to CFQR (CFCF's FM station), and later as a DJ at Quebec City's only English-language Top 40 station, CFOM.

Godin is a long-time Dave Boxer fan and perhaps one of the very few who has regular contact with him on the West Coast. Boxer has not kept in touch with his Montreal past, though some of his family still live in the area. Every month or so, Godin and Boxer get together to compare notes and swap a few old stories. Though separated by almost 20 years, Godin and Boxer share a lifelong love of radio, and both knew from an early age that radio was their calling.

Godin still has an Esquire shoeshine kit he won after calling in to CKGM. Dialling radio stations during contest time was a lot like spinning a roulette wheel. After winning once, he was an inveterate contest dialler and, when Boxer's show took over the airways in 1964, he was among hundreds trying to dial the one and only contest line. Boxer's show was built on audience participation, with contests second only to the music.

In one of his meetings with Boxer, Godin shared a particular contest phone-in moment. "I told him I remembered when he actually blew out the telephone exchange," says Godin. "Boxer was way ahead of the times in terms of audience participation. In those days it was still mechanical switchers at the telephone exchange. Once when I dialled in," (Godin still remembers the number), "there were about a half-a-dozen people all on the same line. It was like a party line just because the calls were overlapping. Dave blew out the exchange twice! After that, radio stations that ran contests had special numbers for participants." Decades later, Godin is still an unabashed Boxer booster, their occasional assignations an acknowledgment of a time when they both lived and breathed radio.

Now 80, Boxer is suitably impressed by Godin's sharp memory, an oral connection to his glory days. Boxer is no doubt flattered by the attention and has become a big fan of Godin's online "Treasure Island Oldies" show, even engaging ex-pat Montreal listeners in the program's chat room. Many of them remember the Dave Boxer show on CFCF. After 17 years on the air, Godin has his regulars in the chat room whom he calls "Nuts in the Hut" – a gesture that moved Boxer.

"Dave, ever since he got off the air, has been extremely private. He has no interest in reliving that era and that past. That's his prerogative, his personality," says Godin, who was sworn to secrecy about Boxer's contact information in Vancouver. Divorced and never remarried, Boxer has two sons living in the Vancouver area. He opened a Montreal-style smoked-meat deli right in the heart of Vancouver, serving the thousands of Quebec language refugees who settled in Vancouver. As sole owner and operator, he worked the same long hours as his father did at his butcher shop back in the '30s and '40s. After a number of years, he closed the restaurant and simply walked away from it.

Boxer's departure from CFCF in 1968 marked the end of the four-year rock 'n' roll experiment at the station. Boxer moved on to a brief stint at CKGM, then into sales for Standard Broadcasting, which owned CJAD and its FM partner CJFM. After a few Sunday-afternoon oldies specials on CJFM, Boxer left Montreal for good.

"Canada's First and Canada's Finest" was what CFCF liked to call itself. The station had some golden years but, when Boxer left, it started on a steady decline. Boxer's Top 40 show had run its course, bounced by competition from CFOX, which by 1968 became the new go-to Top 40 AM station in town.

As for CFCF, it almost made it to its 90th birthday. But by 2010, after numerous format changes, and a frequency change to 940, it finally collapsed. Boxer's Buddies are still around, though not quite as old as the venerable CFCF, and not too old to remember the "dadd-io-on-the-radd-io."

GEORGE MORRIS: THE MAN WHO LOVED MANTOVANI BECOMES THE BOSS WITH THE HOT SAUCE

At the end of World War II, there were millions of displaced people in Europe who had been prisoners of war or inmates in Nazi prison camps, or in labour camps, many of them children. Between 1946 and 1952 Canada opened its borders to some 200,000 displaced persons, mostly from Eastern European countries, including 39,000 Poles. By 1953, some 800,000 new Canadians, fleeing the post-war misery, arrived in Canada. The Sztaidelman family was among the new arrivals.

The Poland of 1948 must have been a difficult place to imagine a future. So Mrs. Sztaidelman and her six-year-old son Jerzy worked their way by train to Germany, before sailing off to a fresh start in Canada, a country they knew little about. Docking in Halifax, they made their way by train to Winnipeg, where an already established community of Poles would welcome them. After two years in Winnipeg, Jerzy's mother remarried and now Jerzy had a stepbrother and a stepfather, John Tully Morris. Jerzy Sztaidelman became George Morris, a ready-for-radio name if there ever was one. In 1950, the family packed up and moved to Montreal.

Some kids have a natural inner "ham." They're not afraid of adults, and precociousness comes naturally. So it was with 12-year-old George Morris, now a newly minted Montrealer, who applied to be a contestant on a CBC-TV show called *Small Fry Frolics*, a quiz and party program for kids. Morris proved to be a charades charmer, and he revelled in the amusement of the adults and the live studio audience. The show's producers liked him so much, they asked him back for repeat performances. He had the ability to "turn it on" like a second skin. Like the comedian getting his first laugh, Morris enjoyed the adrenalin surge and flush of triumph – and he wanted more.

Not a keen student, Morris left home at 15, hitching a solo ride to Toronto, where he stayed with family friends. Browsing the Toronto newspapers, he spotted an ad for a job demonstrating yo-yos for Cheerios. He applied, then trained and eventually travelled the country entertaining shoppers in grocery and department stores. Morris was back working his inner ham. Wearing a fedora to make himself look older, he would show up in stores for demonstrations promoted by local radio stations. His sleeper, creeper, loop-the-loop and around-the-world tricks helped sell countless boxes of Cheerios. The yo-yo, of course, was inside the box.

While in Toronto, Morris decided that radio was in his future. He fired off audition tapes to several stations across Canada, and he eventually landed a gig at a St. Jerome, Quebec, radio station that lasted all of one day. Then he bluffed his way into a job in Blind River, Ontario. "I lied my way into the job," Morris remembers. "I didn't really know what I was doing. But I had to eat." It was only three days into the Blind River gig when the manager discovered Morris didn't come as advertised – not to mention that he was not of legal working age. The fedora was not a convincing cover.

It was a rough start to his radio dream. Undaunted, Morris trudged on and landed other radio jobs in Hamilton, Sudbury, Thunder Bay, Peterborough, Kitchener, Victoria, and Vancouver – where he got fired for playing an entire side of a Lenny Bruce comedy album. All these stops were typical of the nomadic DJ life back in the day. By the time Morris turned 21, he had one cross-country yo-yo tour, 10 cities, and 10 radio jobs under his belt. It was time to ditch the fedora. He landed back in Montreal in 1963 where his radio career would take a sharp left turn into the brand new territory of the Top 40 AM rock radio experiment.

Morris settled in at CKGM-AM's all-night show, calling it *The GM Affair*. Officially, it was the *Craven 'A' Music Till Dawn Show*, reflecting a time when cigarette companies were major media sponsors. CKGM-AM was Montreal's first radio station to adopt the non-stop, 24-hour format. After midnight, it was strictly easy-listening music, a time when the idea was to play music designed to lull listeners to sleep. The radio job, CKGM management had told him, wouldn't interfere with his enrollment at Sir George Williams University. They needn't have worried. Morris had applied and was accepted as a mature student. But on registration day, he had trouble negotiating his way around the university's downtown campus, thus ending his attempt at post-secondary education within the span of one day.

Though CKGM-AM was playing the hit songs of the day, the station's DJs were soft-pedalling the music. The cult of the Top 40 radio DJ personality in Montreal rested solely with CFCF 600's Dave Boxer, but it wouldn't take long for CKGM to carve out its own Top 40 niche with Morris behind the mike as Buddy Gee.

In the U.S., many DJs did not use their given names on air, opting instead to anoint themselves with more memorable, radio-friendly tags and nicknames. J.P. "the Big Bopper" Richardson, Charlie Tuna (born Art Ferguson), Bruce Morrow, who threw the word "Cousin" between his given names, Sandy Beach (born Donald Pesola), and Wolfman Jack (born Robert Smith), among others, broke new ground. Some even used TV as a vehicle to enhance their radio profile. Top 40 DJs adopted a fast-talking, door-to-door salesmen idiom. This was the new radio world that Morris as Buddy Gee was thrust into – moving from the sleepy, slow tunes of the midnight to 6 a.m. shift to evening prime time, spinning and hyping 45-rpm singles aimed squarely at a hungry-for-hits adolescent demographic. He wasn't keen on the name (one given to him by committee) but it had a friendly quality to it.

With the *Buddy Gee Show*, CKGM-AM management took their cues from CFCF-AM, which had shaken up its programming a few months earlier by giving another well-travelled DJ, Dave Boxer, rock 'n' roll carte blanche with a Top 40 show also geared to the high school student demographic. Boxer's head start forced Morris to hit the ground running, as the new Top 40 competition. In no time flat, he found himself behind the mic right opposite Boxer competing for the teen audience. *The GM Affair* was history and, as far as his new audience was concerned – none of whom were up when he was soft-talking Montreal through the night – he was the other new guy in town. Morris turned up his volume, and for four hours every weekday, he became Buddy Gee – the "big boss with the hot sauce treating you right."

Though Morris had little preparation for his new role, he had done some homework listening to DJs like Cousin Brucie on WABC in New York and Sandy Beach on WKBW in Buffalo. He tried not to be an imitator, but it was the Top 40 style he needed to get a feel for. With an armful of 45s, a follow-if-you-will playlist, some brand new jingles, and a new persona, he was left more or less to his own devices.

It was a fast-paced format, with listener requests, sound effects (toilets flushing, doors slamming, cows mooing, cannons blasting,

CKGM-AM ran the Buddy Gee show up against Dave Boxer's every week day night. His style was more frenetic than Boxer's and they battled for listeners until 1968.
Courtesy Dan Kowal.

and machine guns firing, among his favourites), breaks for news, commercials and, of course, music. Top 40 DJs had taken to creating a language all their own, designed to be their signature, to set them apart from the competition. Morris' was "oobajaboo," a kind of primal exclamation he made up – something that came out of his years of improvisation-based yo-yo days.

The shift in pop/rock music styles from 1963 to 1964 could not have been more dramatic. Morris and dozens of other Top 40 DJs wandered into the beginning of the sweetest spot in rock music history. Seldom heard from again after 1964 were major 1950s recording artists like Connie Stevens, Bobby Vinton, Bobby Rydell, Bobby Darin, Perry Como and Brenda Lee. The Beatles were the new sheriffs in town and, by the end of 1964, there were no fewer than eight Beatles singles on that year's *Billboard* Top 100 hit list. That same 1964 *Billboard* Top 100 chart was flush with other British acts like Manfred Mann, Billy Kramer & the Dakotas, the Dave Clark Five, Peter & Gordon, Dusty Springfield, Gerry & the Pacemakers, and the Searchers. The face of U.S.-dominated Top 40 charts was changed forever.

On September 8, 1964, Morris found himself on stage at the Montreal Forum with Dave Boxer and French Top 40 station CJMS DJ Michel "Ya-Ba-Da-Ba-Dou" Desrochers for two sold-out Beatles concerts. Morris introduced two of the four opening acts, Jackie DeShannon and Bill Black's Combo, before the Beatles. He got two words out, "And now . . ." before all hell broke loose. The Beatles did a 35-minute set at both the afternoon and evening concerts. After the last note faded, they were off the stage in a flash and gone, leaving 16,000 weeping, screaming, and exhausted teenagers. In a strange bit of serendipity, in the audience that night was Morris' future wife Susan, who was 13 at the time. He would only discover this many years later when he noticed her in a Montreal museum poster promoting a Beatles retrospective featuring a photo of three young girls going nuts at that 1964 concert. Though the Beatles concert was a DJ's wet dream, the beat went on. There was no resting on your laurels as a Top 40 jock. There was always the competition to worry about. Getting that new single or that exclusive on the air, before the other guy did, was like the plot of a *Hunger Games* film.

Morris flew to Cleveland, ostensibly to vet a possible job offer. Instead, at a Monkees concert, Morris sweet-talked lead singer Davey Jones into relinquishing the sweaty shirt he wore on stage during the concert. Morris flew back to Montreal and used it as fodder for a Coca-Cola-sponsored contest. He also established a fruitful relationship with an Air Canada pilot who flew twice weekly to the U.K. and would bring back new singles by the Rolling Stones or the Beatles. Morris played the records on his show and thus garnered bragging rights as the one to play a new song first. The Dave Boxer/Buddy Gee rivalry was always about who could get which hot record on first.

When 1960s music turned to the so-called psychedelic phase, CKGM-AM sponsored the Jefferson Airplane and the Grateful Dead – both bands were part of the emerging San Francisco sound. They played a couple of songs as a kind of pre-concert promotion for the evening concert at the Forum. It was a free concert and thousands showed up to see Buddy Gee emcee and hear the sounds of Airplane lead vocalist Grace Slick ricochet off the buildings surrounding Place Ville Marie. It was a new high for Morris, but not so much for the Grateful Dead, who like the Beatles, would never come back to Montreal after the group was left high and dry at Place Ville Marie waiting for concert organizers to pick them up along with their equipment.

For the next four years, Buddy Gee and Dave Boxer were the go-to Top 40 DJs on English-language radio in Montreal, the talk of the town. There weren't many TV channels to choose from in Montreal in the 1960s, so the chatter in high school hallways was more about what new single you heard on CFCF or CKGM the night before, or which of your friends had managed to get through to the request line and win something in the seemingly endless array of contests.

It must have been especially disappointing and exhausting for Morris because, no matter how hard he tried to be fresh and ahead of the Top 40 rock curve, he always trailed Boxer in the ratings. The CKGM brain trust of the time had Morris plugged into the 4 to 9 p.m. time slot, while Boxer cranked it up weekly from 6:30 to 11 p.m. The logic might have been to get teens coming home from school to tune in to CKGM and leave it at 980 on the dial for the five hours Buddy Gee was on. Of course, there was some dial spinning happening, and

Boxer had a head start on Morris. Those two hours, 9 to 11 p.m., hampered Morris and CKGM in their attempt to make a dent in Boxer's listenership. A 15-year-old rock 'n' roll fan would not be going to bed at 9 p.m.

Morris had good pipes, as they say in the radio biz, and by 1968 he started freelancing on the side just before his stint as Buddy Gee ended at CKGM. He started his own production company, Listen Audio – a concept house for radio commercials that worked directly with advertising agencies and clients. He famously did some radio and TV spots for St. Hubert, the popular Quebec barbecue-chicken restaurant chain. Morris' St. Hubert commercials helped raise the chain's profile, as he adopted the on-camera guise of Texas RJ Rooster in a series of hilarious commercials in which his character deliberately fractured the French language with a super-Anglo accent. They were a cult hit. His Texas RJ Rooster persona was plastered on the side of Montreal buses. The commercials gave Morris more exposure, and more money, than his entire radio career.

He eventually sold Listen Audio, built a studio in his basement and dubbed it Great Northern Larynx, pumping out liner work for radio stations, becoming the voice for news intros, promotions and contests – and made a lot of money doing it. You can still hear his voice on Lotto 6/49 commercials as well as TV and film narrations.

At 71, Morris still lives in the city that made him Buddy Gee, his business now a part of the no-borders digital scene. There was no flaming out for this DJ – the man who came a long way at such a young age, travelled to so many cities, sat behind so many mics, survived the 1960s, and parlayed his talents and voice into a lucrative post-Top 40 DJ career. He is still the boss with the hot sauce, with just a little oobajaboo on the side.

CHAPTER TWO

Geoff Stirling
Founding Father of CKGM-AM and FM

A MAN OF MANY MISSIONS

Geoff Stirling was many things: journalist, newspaper publisher, author, politician, TV and radio station pioneer, visionary, eccentric and mystic. Moreover, he was a proud Newfoundlander. With his rugged good looks, charisma and a rogue-solid business savvy, he became one of the most successful and colourful businessmen to come out of Canada's 10th province.

By the time he hit his 30s, he owned newspapers, and radio and TV stations in Newfoundland. Then he added three more radio stations, in Quebec and Ontario. It was under Stirling's guidance and ownership that Montreal radio stations CKGM-AM and CKGM-FM evolved into two of the most successful enterprises in his media empire. It was the combination of his interest in Eastern mysticism and his willingness to take risks that gave birth to the experimental, groundbreaking sounds of CKGM-FM (later known as CHOM-FM) in 1969. Stirling's legendary benign but beatific leadership guided both of his Montreal stations through more than a decade of success, thus changing the fabric of rock radio in the city. It was a spiritual journey, much like the trips Stirling would take to India to hone his meditation skills. But there was also some money to be made.

Geoffrey William Stirling was born on March 22, 1921, to Edgar, a businessman who owned the popular Stirling's Restaurant on Water Street in downtown St. John's, and Ethel (Uphill) of Salisbury,

England. Ethel had a rather harsh introduction to Newfoundland: the ship she had sailed on from England, to visit her brother, ran aground. The passengers, like the seal hunters of the day, walked into St. John's harbour over ice floes. Although Ethel survived the dangerous walk to the shores of St. John's, she was killed in a car accident in 1945.

Stirling worked in his father's restaurant, frugally saving a thousand dollars which he used in 1946 as a start-up fund to purchase 60 tonnes of newsprint from the then defunct *Humber Herald*, owned by his friend Joey Smallwood. Stirling launched *The St. John's Sunday Herald* – a scrappy tabloid. The first edition (May 12, 1946) had "Hitler's Son Alive in Germany" as one of its front-page headlines. With World War II barely over, that headline would have grabbed readers by the throat. With Newfoundland preparing to join Confederation, Stirling used his newspaper as a platform to further his political agenda on the subject, maintaining that Newfoundland would be better off expanding its relationship with the U.S. He was pretty much a one-man operation at the *Sunday Herald*, writing everything except the newspaper's columns, printing it, selling ads, and helping to deliver it. He would even drop bundles of *Herald*s on the ice floes for the seal hunters, the same ice floes his mother had negotiated some 20 years earlier. There wasn't much advertising, but the *Herald* made up for it in circulation, eventually putting out 75,000 Sunday copies at its peak – a difficult task considering Newfoundland's transportation infrastructure at the time was rudimentary. The province wouldn't have a coast-to-coast highway until 1966.

Eventually renamed the *Newfoundland Herald* after becoming a daily, the newspaper celebrated its 65th anniversary two years before Stirling's death in 2013. In what turned out to be his last interview, Stirling shared his thoughts on the *Herald*'s history and mission. "You can see that we were pointing out things that weren't being pointed out," he said. (Those "things" turned out to be an eclectic news package of UFO sightings, crop circles, the mystery of the Island of Atlantis, Eastern mysticism – one of Stirling's lifelong interests – Stonehenge, the importance of buying gold, and the Shroud of Turin.) "This is the kind of thing we've always done at *The Herald*," he said. "You were heralding in news. It's up to you to not be afraid. Most people don't want to be shaken. They want things nice and simple."

Stirling had an abundance of charisma and matinee-idol good looks, too. Over six feet tall, he was a natural athlete. At Bishop Field College in St. John's (from which Joey Smallwood made an early exit), he set a record for the high jump, which lasted 31 years. After a year in pre-law at the University of Tampa, he became bored and that was the end of his formal education.

In 1950 Stirling teamed up with Don Jamieson to start radio station CJON. Jamieson had been active in the politics of Newfoundland's confederation with Canada and spent some time as an advisor to new premier Joey Smallwood. Stirling overlooked any differences in political views to strike a business deal if the climate was ripe. Five years later, CJON radio spawned CJON-TV, now NTV, "Canada's Superstation." Jamieson would eventually leave Newfoundland to become a federal MP and cabinet minister in the Trudeau-led Liberal government.

By the end of the 1960s, Stirling owned five Newfoundland TV stations. Less than a decade after founding CKGM-AM, in 1959, (and then CKGM-FM in 1963) in Montreal, he added CKWW-AM and CKWW-FM in Windsor and CKPM in Ottawa, and became one of the major independent media barons in Canada. With two FM stations in major Canadian markets, Stirling was at the vanguard of a revolution in radio – stereophonic sound.

Under the Maisonneuve Broadcasting Co. Ltd. banner, he got a license for an AM Montreal station and, in December 1959, he launched CKGM-AM. The new kid on the block became the competition for CFCF-AM (on the air at 600 on the AM dial since 1933) and CJAD-AM 800 (founded in 1945). Just to the right of CJAD on the dial, 980 CKGM broadcast 24 hours a day, something no other English-language station did. CKGM opened studios in the heart of downtown Montreal on Drummond St., under a skywalk that crossed above de Maisonneuve Blvd. The interior was straight out of a 1940s Hollywood film, with floor-to-ceiling glass-encased offices.

Stirling announced the launch of CKGM-AM in Montreal, circa 1959, with a full-page newspaper ad. The studios were located on Drummond Street. *Courtesy of Don Major.*

As one of a small number of women in the predominantly male world of radio, New Brunswick-born Joanne Rudy started out in the accounting department at CKGM and eventually became Stirling's trusted information envoy. She was the chief liaison between Stirling and his Montreal radio stations. He was always only a phone call away, whether he was in Arizona or at an ashram in India. In time, Rudy would become director of operations for both of Stirling's Montreal stations as well as station manager on the AM side of the business. Stirling was not exactly the hands-on owner type, but when he rolled into town – mostly unexpectedly – employees snapped to attention. "He had exceptional charisma and presence," Rudy says. "He could command a room. People tended to be in awe of him." Her loyalty to Stirling and his family remained intact, even after 1985 when he sold CKGM and CHOM to CHUM Ltd. of Toronto. When she finally retired in 2001, Rudy had logged more time than any other employee. Stirling's death in 2013 left her shaken.

Stirling liked to show up at CKGM without any fanfare. He made surprise phone calls through a special line, a tactic he used with both his TV and radio stations. Sometimes in the St. John's NTV studios a red light would turn on on the studio phone: his personal hotline through to NTV Mission Control. He could call at 2 a.m. or any other time he had some personal programming requests. It might be Stirling interviewing Joey Smallwood, Stirling's metaphysical ramblings on Eastern mysticism, highlights from animation film festivals, features starring the Stirling-created superhero Captain Atlantis (a.k.a. Captain Newfoundland) and Captain Canada. Sometimes it would be all-night tributes to Elvis, the Beatles or John F. Kennedy. All weird, all late-night- and early-morning-long.

One of Stirling's favourites was *Waiting for Fidel*, a 1974 NFB documentary filmed in Cuba starring Joey Smallwood, Geoff Stirling (the chief financier for the project), and NFB director Michael Rubbo. The three sometimes discordant Canadians, hoped to get an audience with Fidel Castro in Cuba. The film depicts a Cuba more than 20 years after the Castro revolution had taken hold. The discussions, especially those between Smallwood and Stirling about capitalism versus socialism, seemed to test the depth of their longtime friendship. NTV has rerun *Fidel* hundreds of times in the early morning hours, so much so that it has cult status. The scene where Stirling is philosophizing with Smallwood on a Cuban beach, while standing on his head, is priceless. When Stirling embraced Indian mysticism and Buddhist teachings in the 1960s, he was already well into his 40s. It seemed, however, that Stirling and the 1960s were made for each other.

Bob Gillies came to CKGM a little over a year after it was launched in 1959. It was his first gig as an AM jock, playing the popular hits of the day – a mixture of some beach music, early R&B, with a little Bobby Curtola and Paul Anka thrown in for some Canadian flavour. Gillies met Stirling on the radio-people party circuit in Montreal and they struck up an easy friendship. Even though Gillies was working for the competition (CFCF), he got a job offer from Don Wall, the station's GM at the time. Though it was pre-hippie days by about five years, Gillies thought Stirling qualified as a hippie ahead of his time. He was somewhere between a beatnik and a hippie, Gillies thought. Though Stirling was congenial with him,

Gillies was always aware of the possibility of that dreaded red light on the phone turning on in the announcer's booth, he was spared any direct Stirling intervention on his shows. Later, when Gillies worked with Ted Turner and CNN in Atlanta, he was reminded of the visionary characteristics that Stirling and Turner shared.

Stirling decided to pop into the CKGM studios late one night on one of his famous unannounced visits. Not every employee had encountered Stirling face to face, so he was something of a mystery to new employees. Such was the case when music director Bob Johnson, who had just started what would be a four-year stint at 'GM in 1964, was doing double duty on the all-night shift, spinning some mellow MOR music for the all-night crowd in Montreal. He and a few others were waiting for their order of St. Hubert barbecued chicken to be delivered. It was a freebie delivery, as St. Hubert was one of CKGM's sponsors. When there was a loud banging on the street-level door, they thought it was the St. Hubert delivery. Johnson went down, only to find a tall man in a sleek black suit – minus the chicken. "Who the hell are you?" Johnson asked. "I'm Geoff Stirling," was the reply. "I don't know you, go away," Johnson said. The man in the black suit then apparently went across the street to a pay phone and the boys in the control room got a call from station GM, Don Wall. "Let Mr. Stirling in," was the command. Humbled and somewhat fearful for his job, Johnson went to the door and let Stirling in, apologizing profusely. After finishing his shift, Johnson was called into Wall's office; Wall told him that he had done the right thing, and that Stirling wanted to meet him. Stirling gave Johnson a raise. Rewarding Johnson's vigilance may have been a result of a February 1963 incident, the first of three to visit the station, when a Quebec separatist group, the Réseau de résistance, which would later regroup as the Front de libération du Québec (FLQ), threw a Molotov cocktail into the lobby of CKGM. Fortunately, no one was injured.

His friends said that Stirling could see the future, and anticipate it, which was perhaps ideal for a speculator who crossed a natural spiritual bent with a sharp money-making mind. In the early 1970s, Stirling urged his fellow Newfoundlanders to buy gold. Intuition? The ability to see the future? Whatever it was, his advice to his fellow islanders turned out to be über-prescient. He would have, admittedly, a lot more money to invest in gold than most Newfoundlanders. Some who took his advice probably sent him a thank-you note. Gold, which was at $35 an ounce in 1970, peaked at $875 an ounce by 1980. Stirling, who was already a millionaire, made a bundle. His son, Scott, who now runs Stirling Enterprises, said in a 2004 *Globe and Mail* Report on Business interview that his father "sees things other people can't. He's not afraid to try something everyone else believes will fail."

What Stirling saw in CKGM-FM in the late 1960s was an opportunity to change the relentless easy-listening sound typical of the FM radio of the day. When, in 1969, former college radio DJ Doug Pringle pitched him a totally new kind of free-form FM radio, Stirling bought the idea. Soon, the change in format was the talk of the town. Rock albums were played in their entirety, shows eventually played jazz and folk music, and Pringle, besides his groundbreaking four-hour shift, had a two-hour spiritual program on Sunday night, which often ran longer at his whim. Stirling, who was heavily into meditation and Eastern religious practices, enjoyed the adventure. CKGM-FM/CHOM became his baby, his personal experiment. He called it tribal radio.

That same year, while staying in London with his son, Scott, he decided to contact John Lennon. The message he sent was simple: "I've heard your 'Come Together' [the lead track on the Beatles album, *Abbey Road*] so here I am." The next day Lennon and Yoko Ono invited Stirling and his son to the Beatles' Apple Studios for an interview/chat. They spent a couple of days with Lennon and Ono. Stirling then returned their hospitality: "Why don't you come to Montreal?" In May of 1969, Lennon and Ono would take Stirling up on that invitation with a seven-day "Bed-in for Peace" at the Queen Elizabeth Hotel. Thanks to Stirling's charm and Lennon's fame, Montreal's reputation as a happening city enjoyed prime time in the national and international spotlight.

Stirling's cozying up to John Lennon and Yoko Ono in London came just after the Beatles had travelled to India to study transcendental meditation (TM) with the giggling guru, Maharishi Mahesh

Yogi. Stirling's very own guru of choice was Swami Shyam, who had trained under the Maharishi. From time to time, Stirling went to India to attend Swami Shyam's ashram. He also brought the swami to Montreal, and his Westmount home's basement served as an ashram. It was pretty much an open invitation to dedicated meditators, and they didn't necessarily have to be Stirling's radio employees. Swami Shyam was an occasional guest on Doug Pringle's *Spiritual Hour* show in the fledgling years of CKGM-FM/CHOM. Stirling would also invite the swami to be a live-in guru at his Arizona home as well as at Big White in the Okanagan Valley in British Columbia. Meditation and Eastern spirituality were trending in the late 1960s and early 1970s. Thanks to his relationship with Stirling, Swami Shyam took in more converts right across the country. Stirling could afford his spiritual wanderings. Various assessments of his net worth come in around the $100-million mark. He could fly off to India, build a log home in Torbay, NL, or spend all the time he wanted at his Arizona ranch. He was a quietly generous man, not one to make a big splash with his wealth. It wasn't very Canadian – and certainly not the Newfoundland way – to be ostentatious.

With his FM experiment launched, Stirling turned his attention to the AM side of the business, which was languishing in the ratings after a decade on the air. He did a little housecleaning and poached Jim Sward, an up-and-coming sales manager from the No. 1 Top 40 station, CFOX, making him general manager of the station. Then he added programming prodigy John Mackey in the program director spot. Sward saw the writing on the walls of CFOX. It was a station in decline and it was time for him to make a switch and rebuild CKGM-AM into a force in the Montreal Top 40 market. Sward had the ideas, Stirling had the money. When Sward and Stirling discussed boosting CKGM's listenership, Stirling's directives were unequivocal: "The station is losing money. I don't want to lose this kind of money. You've got "x" number of dollars that I'll put behind it to turn it around. And, if it isn't turned around by the time the money runs out, you're gone."

Sward remembers Stirling's management style as being all about presence, charisma, and charm, backed up by a well-developed sense of entrepreneurial spirit. He had no trouble getting the employees' attention. When Stirling rolled into town on one of his infrequent and unscheduled visits, things got done to his satisfaction before he would leave town. Managers like Sward and Mackey were given a lot of freedom, as long as things were going well. His point person in Montreal, Joanne Rudy, received early-morning phone calls from Stirling and she passed on the information to management. If he felt he needed to be in Montreal, he was. At the height of the 1970 October Crisis involving the FLQ's kidnapping of British trade commissioner James Cross, and with the subsequent murder of Quebec Liberal cabinet minister Pierre Laporte, Montreal was like a city under siege. Stirling flew to Montreal and suspended the daily music operations of CKGM-AM and CHOM-FM, and went into full talk-radio format for two days. These were serious times and he didn't think that Top 40 music and alternative rock was the medicine listeners wanted. Stirling gave listeners a two-day forum to air out their frustrations.

About a year after Stirling gave Doug Pringle the green light to convert easy-listening CKGM-FM into a free-form/alternative rock station, Pringle got a personal visit from his CEO. CKGM-FM/CHOM had been given free rein by Stirling. This was his blank radio palette and he was anxious to see how things were progressing. At first CKGM-FM ran very few ads and was opposed to big, bad corporate sponsorship. This was part of the unwritten, but accepted hippie alternative radio code. No Coca-Cola ads. No Big Four car companies. They had a few local business ads, some poster and hippie paraphernalia shops and one of their favourite record stores, Phantasmagoria. When Stirling showed up that day, with all the staff present, he asked them: "Who wants to be fired?" Understandably, no hands went up. "Good," he said, "then let's see some ads. Time to make some money." The times, they were a-changin'.

Stirling was probably amused when, in 2011, he was at No. 15 on theindependent.ca website's Top-50 Most Influential Newfoundlanders of All Time, joining such names as actor/comedians Rick Mercer, Cathy Jones, and Mary Walsh. His buddy Joey Smallwood fared better at No. 4. But Stirling is in more Newfoundland

Halls of Fame than any of his fellow islanders. He was inducted into the Newfoundland Athletic Association's Hall of Fame, the Newfoundland and Labrador Business Hall of Fame, and the Royal St. John's Regatta Hall of Fame. In 2009, he received the Order of Newfoundland and Labrador. But perhaps the most gratifying award came in 2001 when he was inducted into the Canadian Association of Broadcasters Hall of Fame. From dropping bundles of *The Sunday Herald* on the ice floes all the way to multiple tributes to his many pursuits, Stirling probably found this satisfying on a number of spiritual levels. With his death in 2013, a new flock of tributes poured in. At the Order of Newfoundland and Labrador ceremony, John Crosbie, who made his own mark on Canada and the province, said that Stirling had "left deep footprints in the Newfoundland landscape." He left some deep footprints everywhere he went. Just ask anyone who had anything to do with him.

Stirling Communication International (SCI) in St. John's, NL, is now run by Geoff Stirling's son, Scott. SCI still owns OZ-FM, the *Newfoundland Herald* and NTV. It may not be the heyday of the 1960s and 1970s, but it is still the business that Geoff Stirling created, minus his stations in Montreal and Windsor, which were sold in the 1980s. It was the beginning of the end for entrepreneur-owned radio. It wouldn't be an exaggeration to say that Geoff Stirling occupies a special place in the pantheon of Canadian media pioneers.

Stirling directed his radio stations with a kind of benign business style, and despite his Eastern mysticism leanings, making money was at the core of his character.

[CHAPTER THREE]

The CKGM-AM Years
From the Campus Club to the "Great '98"

BOB GILLIES: FORERUNNER OF TOP 40 RADIO

Vancouver-born Bob Gillies is the classic renaissance radio man. More than just a voice behind a microphone, he is a man of many talents. Born at a time when the big bands ruled, it's doubtful he could have imagined himself two decades later hanging out with the members of some long-haired British rock band.

A child of the 1940s, he grew up as a big-band aficionado, listening to the likes of Artie Shaw and Tommy Dorsey. Listening to the radio in the early 1950s, Gillies knew all the words to the popular songs of the day, singing along with artists like Nat King Cole, Doris Day and the Mills Brothers. In his early teens he got a gig as the in-house pop singer on a 15-minute 1950s CBC show. However tempted he was, a full-time entertainment career was too risky an option. Instead, it was onto the serious business of pursuing a journalism degree at the University of British Columbia. But he had been bitten by the entertainment bug and went to work at the UBC student radio station where he had his own show. He faked his classical music knowledge and got a gig at Vancouver's CKWX playing classical music all night long on the show *Concert Under the Stars*.

One night, just before his midnight classical show was to begin, he came in to find Bill Ward, the host of CKWX's nightly one-hour rock 'n' roll experiment, *The Bill Ward Doghouse Show*, passed out on top of a record. Gillies gently pried Ward from atop the turntable and took over his show. Gillies scored some important improvisational points that night with the station's boss.

With his journalism diploma in hand, he got a job as a news reporter at CKGL in North Vancouver. He worked closely with talk-show hosts Pat Burns and Jack Webster, both of whom had strong on-air personalities in the acerbic, straight-shooting, talk-radio style. Gillies felt he needed out of the Vancouver market. In the early 1950s, the city of Vancouver proper was the third largest city in Canada, but the big radio markets were in Toronto and Montreal. Gillies was aiming for Toronto, but after sending out a number of audition tapes, it was CFCF radio in Montreal that he heard from first. His mandate at CFCF was as news reporter and interviewer. He interviewed many of the celebrities of the day, like actor Charlton Heston and band leader Xavier Cugat, who rolled into town. CFCF was hardly a hip station: it played mainly adult-oriented pop. Songs like "The Happy Organ" by Dave "Baby" Cortez and His Happy Organ, Burl Ives' "Lavender Blue," "Alvin's Harmonica" by Alvin and the Chipmunks, and Annette Funicello's "Tall Paul" were the white-heart 1950s-style pop music being played on most radio stations in Canada. Before Dave Boxer's 1964 Top 40-format foray, this was about as funky as CFCF got in between talk, news, weather, interviews, and sports.

Barely into his third year on the air at CFCF, Gillies ran into CKGM owner Geoff Stirling at a social event, and they struck up an easy friendship. Soon after, he received a call from Stirling's station manager, Don Wall, who lured him away with the promise of a hipper CKGM sound and more money. It was his first real stint as a full-time DJ, hosting *The Coca-Cola Campus Club Show*, with a playlist that was a lot more rock 'n' roll than CFCF's. No Chipmunks, but instead songs by artists like Paul Anka, Bobby Rydell, the Four Seasons and Chubby Checker – hot rock acts in the early 1960s. Top 40 radio still had a soft centre, but Gillies' *Campus Club* was out in front of a whole new younger listening demographic.

Though he was now a CKGM DJ, Gillies kept a connection with his old station, joining the CFCF-TV show *Like Young*, which had gone on the air in 1962, with hosts Jim McKenna, Diane Dickinson (and later June Mack), and had quickly found a young audience. *Like Young* was being careful not to be an obvious imitator of Dick Clark's popular ABC show, *American Bandstand*, which first came out of Philadelphia before moving to Los Angeles. *American Bandstand* was a huge hit, drawing some 20 million viewers at its height. Incredibly, given the limited lifespan of most TV shows, Clark's *Bandstand* would last 30 years, before wrapping up in 1987. A spot on *American Bandstand* was important for artists like Ike & Tina Turner, the Beach Boys, Stevie Wonder, Fats Domino, and Simon and Garfunkel, as well as others who would see spikes in their record sales after an appearance.

Like Young was no *American Bandstand*, but for a newly minted TV station, it attracted a surprisingly rabid teenage following in a short period of time. Unlike Clark's show, which was primarily a studio production, *Like Young* sent their hosts out into the community to meet teenagers on their own turf, such as pool parties at local swimming pools. In 1971, *Like Young* was picked up by Dick Clark and syndicated nationally, the only Canadian show of its kind to achieve this. Renowned rock and R&B acts which came to Montreal to play clubs and arenas would appear on the show – Ben E. King, Diana Ross, Tommy James and the Shondells, a nasty Frank Zappa, and an agitated Jerry Lee Lewis who, unhappy with the way the interview was going, took the mic right out of host Jim McKenna's hand and told him, "You don't know what you're doing." Then he threw the mic to the ground and left.

Like Young was also an important stop for local Montreal bands trying to make their mark. Guests included J.B. & the Playboys, the Haunted, the Rabble and, in its later years, artists like April Wine and Andy Kim. *Like Young* had a solid 12-year run on CFCF-TV, but Gillies was in an awkward position as both TV and radio personality at two competing stations. After one year as a teen-TV show host, he left to concentrate on his radio gig at CKGM.

The programming at CKGM was a mix of news, sports, talk radio, and music. Gillies called it a hodgepodge of music that had been part of the big-band era, beach music, a sprinkle of R&B, and the requisite Paul Anka-style, swooning rock 'n' roll. That hodgepodge was

Bob Gillies, whose radio career with CKGM started in 1963, was multi-talented; he was a DJ, co-host on CFCF-TVs popular teen dance show *Like Young*, singer, and scored many films in Hollywood after leaving radio in 1968.
Courtesy of Bob Gillies.

reflected everywhere on the *Billboard* charts for the first year Gillies was behind the mic at CKGM. The No. 1 hits of 1963 featured an array of artists whose rock 'n' roll credentials were dubious and diverse. Las Vegas crooner Steve Lawrence, Lesley Gore, Stevie Wonder, and the Singing Nun all had No. 1 hits that year. Gillies occasionally showed his distaste for some of the rock fluff on CKGM's early 1960s play-list. Much to the chagrin of his music director of the day, Gillies re-fused to play songs like "Hey Paula" by Paul & Paula, easily one of the corniest songs of 1963. He hated "Dominique" by the Singing Nun so much – a No. 1 hit on the charts that year – that he tossed the 45 out of the Drummond Street CKGM studio window. Then, to put the final nail in "Dominique's" coffin, he drove the CKGM Corvair (unsafe at any speed) over it.

Montreal was a good time for Gillies. He loved its vibrancy and nightlife. Coming from a much tamer and much more Protestant Vancouver, he succumbed to some of the temptations of the city's legendary laissez-faire attitude. He fed off the energy of CKGM-AM, a station that, after all, was barely four years on the air when he started. Married at 18, and the father of three children, he neverthe-less lived a kind of free-wheeling bachelor life. The allure of Mont-real's after-hours entertainment soon put a strain on his marriage. With much of his energy funnelled towards his new radio and TV shows, there was not much family time going on and, by the end of 1961, his wife returned to Calgary with the children. Two years later he was divorced.

There were always plenty of promotions and giveaways that were an integral part of the Top 40 radio format. People loved win-ning stuff and Gillies' *Coca-Cola Campus Club* shelled out free loot, mostly concert tickets and 45s. If listeners signed up to be members of Club 98, that increased their chances of winning one of 25 "Best Bet of the Week" 45s. And if they filled out the "Pick Tomorrow's Hits" form attached to CKGM's Top 30 hits chart, then the reward was a free LP. Hearing their names announced on the air meant bragging rights the next day, and winners became unpaid ambassa-dors for the station. All the jocks had something to give away, cour-tesy of the record companies and product sponsors. Of course, they took requests, the backbone of any Top 40 show where the DJ got to do a little lightweight flirting with teenage callers, then spin the request along with a dedication.

Gillies also worked his crooner side by singing and cutting re-cords with RCA. He admits they were a tad on the corny side and didn't get any airplay, but they nevertheless became part of the early 1960s jukebox circuit, and are now given new life on YouTube. He made occasional appearances singing at Montreal nightclubs.

Gillies was networking more than the average AM DJ of the day, even hooking up with the National Film Board of Canada dubbing French, Spanish and German films into English. He became the voice for major national clients like Belair cigarettes – king-sized menthols put out by Imperial Tobacco in Canada in 1960 – in an ad that ran in Canada and the U.S. He was not a trained music man, but he nevertheless scored commercial jingles, doing both the singing and the voice-over. All this would serve him well in his post-CKGM days. The extra work meant more money in the bank; a 1960s DJ did not make a whole lot of money.

In 1964, the arrival of the Beatles and their music changed everything. Gillies and CKGM dug right into the British Invasion. Their competition was CFCF's Dave Boxer and the two stations battled to see who would be first to get their hands on the latest single out of the U.K. CKGM enlisted the services of British ex-pat hustler Tim Hudson, whom Gillies dubbed Lord Tim. Hudson was somewhat vague about his history with his native country but intimated that he was somehow peripherally involved in the John Profumo scandal in Britain. (Profumo, British Secretary of State for War in the Harold MacMillan Conservative government in 1963, found himself knee-deep in scandal when his affair with would-be model Christine Keeler was revealed.)

Lord Tim said he was well-connected in the U.K. Gillies thought Hudson had a streak of the street hustler in him but was willing to gamble on his bravado. He had promised the station's management some hot-off-the-press British singles. Complete with bowler hat and umbrella, Lord Tim was given 15 minutes of fame on CKGM, mining his connections. He claimed to know the Beatles and the Rolling Stones, and he shared hot U.K. music gossip with CKGM listeners. He became Montreal's link to Carnaby Street, the happening music Mecca and fashion centre of London in the 1960s. His major coup was delivering a fresh acetate of the Beatles' new single "Ticket to Ride," lifted right out of the studio. No one wanted to know how

Lord Tim got it, but CKGM may well have been the first station in North America to play that song.

CKGM sent Lord Tim to England on music- and gossip-collecting missions. Because of Lord Tim's shady past, Gillies was never sure he would return. Every couple of weeks, Lord Tim loaded up on singles and interviews with up-and-coming groups and artists like Mick Jagger, Ringo Starr, the Zombies, and the Moody Blues. He delivered on both counts and his reports gave Gillies' show major credibility with the teen audience listening to his primetime 6 to 9 p.m. slot.

Lord Tim was a big Rolling Stones booster and, after the Beatles had played the Montreal Forum in September 1964, CKGM decided to bring the Stones to the Maurice Richard Arena on April 23, 1965. At that time, the Stones didn't have the same drawing power as the Beatles, so the 5,000-seat arena seemed like a good venue to test the waters. Gillies, with sidekick Lord Tim, went to the airport to greet the Stones. There wasn't nearly the frenzied mob scene that the Beatles' arrival had generated. After packing a few of the Stones into the backseat of the car, they headed to their downtown hotel.

It was a feverish crowd that gathered that night in a venue that was built for hockey games, not 5,000 fired-up Stones fans. Concerned about the safety of fans who had gathered near the stage, Gillies and CKGM asked Mick Jagger to cut the group's set short – the

CKGM and Bob Gillies promoted the Rolling Stones' first Montreal concert at the Maurice Richard Arena. The spelling of his name on the poster advertising the show gave Gillies honorary francophone status. *Courtesy of Ted Brennan.*

Stones played a set that was less than 30 minutes long. The Stones, like the Beatles and other groups making their early-career stage debuts, didn't have a particularly deep song catalogue to draw from. In the end, organizers were lucky to get everyone out without all hell breaking loose. Stones' crowds were always edgier than the Beatles'. This was further illustrated when the group came back to play the Forum in October of the same year and all hell did break loose.

CKGM was happy that their first big concert promotion effort didn't end in disaster. After the show, Gillies took a few of the Stones out to sample a taste of Montreal's famous nightlife. With drummer Charlie Watts, bassist Bill Wyman and a few "arranged dates" squeezed into the backseat of his car, Gillies suggested the Heidelberg, a German-style bar he frequented on Drummond Street. Wyman was apparently intrigued. This was not the usual post-concert decompression entertainment the Stones were used to. Nevertheless, Gillies, Watts, Wyman, and dates spent the rest of the night quaffing steins of German beer and listening to down-home oom-pah-pah classics. Wyman referenced that night at the Heidelberg in his 1997 autobiography, *Stone Alone*, where he pays tribute to Gillies' esoteric taste in bars.

"The Stones had gotten into a lot of trouble in England," Gillies says. "I think even the Archbishop of Canterbury denounced them. I've run into stars and musicians who were way worse than the Stones. They were very well-behaved, like perfect little English gentlemen." Gillies came away from that concert with a rare souvenir, one that is still in safe storage at his mother's home. In an early pre-printing run of the CKGM-sponsored poster for the Stones concert, an "i" had been left out of his name. He became, at least on some posters before the error was caught, an honorary Quebecer: Bob Gilles.

With some of the sheen coming off the British Invasion and his Top 40 radio career, Gillies decided that the U.S. was the new land of opportunity and more money. Plus, he was bored with AM radio, and his skills as singer and producer gave him some latitude. "Around the mid-1960s, [Top 40 radio] became more automated, and the show was all about pounding out the music, playing a jingle, then a commercial, then do it again. The DJ's personality was not featured anymore. That's when it got boring for me."

In 1966, with green card in hand, Gillies headed for L.A to do screen trailers and commercials. (Coincidentally, Lord Tim was headed in the same direction in 1966, using his street smarts to carve out jobs in radio, music management, film voice-over, and later as an artist.) Gillies' networking and varied entertainment capabilities got him a foot inside some important L.A. doors. Most other DJs would not have had the kind of transferable skills that Gillies had to make the jump smoothly from AM radio to the studios of L.A. He produced variety shows for Cher and Don Adams (of *Get Smart* fame) as well as game shows. For a time, he was hired by American International Pictures to promote films by legendary B-film producer, writer, and director Roger Corman. With an office in the Sunset Vine Tower – L.A.'s equivalent of New York City's Brill Building, the epi-centre for aspiring song writers and musicians – Gillies set about establishing himself in the burgeoning L.A. music scene. "It (the Sunset Vine Tower) was music heaven," he says. "Especially for the Canadian community who had come to town to seek fortune and fame." At his home on Wonderland Avenue in Laurel Canyon, he could call Joni Mitchell, Frank Zappa, and country singer Bobby Gentry as neighbours. One of the frequent visitors was struggling singer/song writer Charles Manson, who generally made a nuisance of himself at Vine Tower. "He was always hanging around," says Gillies. "No one took him seriously." It wasn't until after the Tate/La Bianca murders that Manson got the attention he so desperately sought. He and his "family's" crimes sent shockwaves throughout the Hollywood community. It was a turning point for the innocence of the 60s generation. People dug in, fences went up, and it was never the same again.

While in Atlanta for a two-week contract working on the famous Coke/Pepsi Challenge commercials, he was snapped up by Ted Turner – who was about to unveil CNN – to work on a comedy/variety show for one of Turner's stations, WTBS-TV. Now in his late 70s and still busy as a filmmaker and composer, Gillies' love of radio, TV, and music has not waned. Those days and nights in Montreal have left their mark on him, and he is still in touch with some of his *Like Young* and CKGM-AM pals. Somewhere out there in the ether of the Internet is a Bob Gillies Golden Oldie, "Summer in the Sand," a perfect singing metaphor for how he played the Top 40 game in Montreal, like being in Brian Wilson's bedroom, only without all the angst.

RALPH LOCKWOOD:
THE "BIRDMAN" RIFFS & ROCKS MONTREAL

The Montreal Alouettes football season is over, but the big game – the 1973 Grey Cup – is taking place just down the road in Toronto. For inveterate partiers who happen to be football fans, it's a great opportunity to drink, and maybe even watch the game. CKGM's morning man, Ralph Lockwood, is a big sports fan and Alouettes booster, so what better way to show support for Canadian football than to hook up with a few drinking buddies and make the six-hour drive southwest. Lockwood's plan is to finish his Saturday morning show, then hop into the car with his pals: former Alouettes linebacker Mike "Crescent Street" Widger (a nickname Lockwood gave Widger – a frequent flier at the bars on that downtown street) and CJAD's Ted Blackman, who never passed up an opportunity to party.

Alas, the plan was not written in stone as Widger and Blackman are impatient and leave Lockwood in Montreal: they don't want to lose valuable drinking time in the Toronto bars that have notoriously un-Montreal-like closing times. By the time they hit Toronto, they have some catching up to do with other Grey Cup revellers from across Canada. They get there in time for Friday night festivities. The game is played Sunday, so there's plenty of time for multiple pre-game warm-up beverages.

Lockwood has a show to do Saturday morning, after which he is supposed to head off to Toronto. A bit ticked off, he decides to have some on-air fun to make up for being left high and dry by Widger and Blackman.

Knowing that pre-Grey Cup celebrations are pretty alcohol-intensive, he gets his traffic reporter, Mary Anne Carpentier, to phone

61

the hotel where Widger is staying. Lockwood enjoys a certain cama- raderie with Montreal sports figures, and Widger has a reputation as a Crescent Street player; he played hard on and off the field. Lock- wood wants to see how his Friday night in Toronto went.

Reluctantly, Carpentier goes along with the gag, but she's a bit nervous. She knows how Lockwood likes to play. She gets through to the hotel reception desk; Lockwood has the whole thing going down live on the air.

"Hi, my name is Mary Anne Carpentier from CKGM and we have an important call for Mike Widger," she says. The reception- ist, impressed by the fact that it's the radio station calling, puts her through to Widger's room.

After fumbling with the phone a few times, a very sleepy and sexy woman's voice answers. At this point, Lockwood takes over the call.

"Hello?" says the sleepy, sexy voice. "Who is this?"

"It's Ralph Lockwood from CKGM calling. Is Mike Widger there?"

"Who?" replies the woman. Lockwood repeats the name. She looks over at her bedmate. "Is your name Mike?" Widger identi- fies himself to his bedmate, perhaps for the first time, and takes the phone from her.

"Mike, thanks for leaving me behind," says Lockwood.

"Ralph, what the hell are you calling now for?" says Widger, more than a little irritated. "It's early morning. Why are you call- ing me now?" Widger is trying to buy some time. He sounds pretty groggy, quite possibly hungover. At this point, Widger realizes he's on live morning radio.

"Because we thought it would be a lot of fun," Lockwood says.

"I'm gonna get you for this one, Ralph," says Widger, suddenly back in linebacker mode just before hanging up on Lockwood.

That story would be the talk of the town for weeks, even years, afterwards. In fact, by the time Widger surfaced from his Royal York hotel room, word about Lockwood's call had begun to circulate. Widger took the kidding in stride. He couldn't recall even talking to Lockwood.

Ralph Lockwood was a coal miner's son, born in the heart of the foothills of the Pocono Mountains in Hazleton, Pennsylvania, where coal was once king, fuelling the massive furnaces of Bethlehem Steel Corporation. Lockwood's grandfather worked the mines after immigrating from Italy. It wasn't uncommon for mining jobs to be passed on from father to son, but the Lockwood family coal mining legacy ended with post-war-born Ralph.

Lockwood's father would be the last of his family to make a living from coal mining in Hazleton, when coal became uneconomical to fuel steel plants. Lockwood saw the writing on the wall. After graduating from high school, he left for the Philadelphia Academy of Dramatic Arts. When money in the family got tight, he ended his brief tenure there and was at a loss for something to do, and he did what thousands of other young, wayward American males did when they turned 18: he enlisted.

The U.S. Air Force had more cachet to it, Lockwood thought, and in 1958 he found himself stationed in Turkey near the border with the former Soviet Union – about as far away from the Poconos and Hazleton as any of its young men had been. "This place was in the middle of nowhere," Lockwood says. "You just didn't think about phoning home or anything. You didn't talk to anybody from home unless it was a Red Cross emergency." There was a lot of downtime in the defence against creeping Communism, so Lockwood hooked up with some navy personnel to build a radio station for the troops. The navy guys put up a radio tower and soon they had their own *Good Morning, Turkey* gig going on, complete with a Top 40 format. Lockwood was one of the DJs, doing a Robin Williams-type show years before Vietnam became the focus of the next post-Cold War U.S. military endeavour.

Transferred to Frankfurt, Germany, Lockwood became a regular fixture at the Armed Forces Radio Network (AFRN) studios there, making connections with some of the AFRN men. He loved the radio vibe. Although he never had a show, nor was he directly involved in the day-to-day operation of the AFRN, he thought he had the chops to do what they did. "I figured, if I was good enough to be considered for the Armed Forces Radio Network, I might be able to make it on the outside," says Lockwood. "Besides, I was tired of the military life." After putting in his full four years of military service, he was States-bound with no particular game plan, just happy to be out of uniform.

In 1961 he was back in his hometown, with his military radio gigs as the only serviceable skill he had to offer any prospective employer. But there is a side door to the job behind the mic if you look in the right places. For Lockwood, the side door led to a behind-the-scenes job at WAZL-AM in Hazleton and, for a short while, he did some on-air work for them. His morning-man radio career took off when Richmond, Virginia, radio-station owner Lou Adelman created a brand new Top 40 station, WARM-AM, in Hazleton. WARM-AM was on only 12 hours a day, but the new Top 40 format created some excitement in the moderate-sized town. For the next two years, this is where Lockwood honed his morning man skills. Over the next seven years, he was the morning man on four different stations in the Pennsylvania area. He was young and travelling light: just load up the trunk and drive a few hours. He was single and happy to be doing what he loved without having to salute anyone.

While working at WHLO in Akron, Ohio, Lockwood heard from friend and radio biz colleague "Big Daddy" Bob Ancell, who would be responsible for helping Lockwood turn a whole new page in his radio career. In 1967 "Big Daddy" had made the move north to CFOX, then an up-and-coming Top 40 station. He knew Lockwood was unhappy in Akron and suggested he send him an audition tape, which he then passed on to station owner Gord Sinclair, Jr.

Sinclair was not that impressed with Lockwood doing impressions of W.C. Fields and using characters he'd invented. So he made another tape and toned it down a bit. "Just play some records, do a few jokes as part of the intro. Keep it simple," suggested Ancell. The toned-down version got him the gig. After looking up Montreal on a map, he packed his trunk once again for what would turn out to be a much longer stay than he had anticipated.

Lockwood knew he was not coming to CFOX as its morning man. Dean Hagopian had been the morning man for almost two years and management wasn't about to upset that apple cart for the new guy.

Ralph Lockwood was brought in to CFOX with a recommendation
from "Big Daddy" Bob Ancell in 1970.
Courtesy of Dan Kowal.

Lockwood was used to a freestyle approach to radio, but when he
settled into the 'FOX afternoon drive shift, he found he didn't have
time for the improvisation he loved to do. Born in 1940, Lockwood
grew up in an era of vaudeville-influenced radio and television, and it
was still a factor in 1950s television and radio. Steve Allen and Johnny
Carson were his heroes, both quick on their feet. "I looked at Allen
and Carson and said, 'That's what I want to do on radio.' And basically, that's what I tried to be. Like a Johnny Carson type of thing with
the Carson Players. Stand-up shtick. I did a lot of shtick."

   Doing the quickly paced afternoon drive, he had little time to
stretch out. Instead, he sprinkled some flippancy into his Top 40 song
intros. Depending on the time between the musical intro and the
vocals, he had to be quick, so it came out something like this: "Here's
the Beatles' 'Can't Buy Me Love'. . . unless you're down at the corner
of St. Lawrence and Ste. Catherine Street at night." (A reference to
Montreal's red-light district.) "It was goofy stuff, but it got people's
attention," he says. His goofiness got the attention of listeners and

eventually the attention of CFOX general manager Doug Ackhurst, who decided Lockwood would be ideal for the all-important morning time slot. Feathers were ruffled when Lockwood and Hagopian switched shifts, but Lockwood snuggled into the slot he was most comfortable in. He loved to wake people up.

Separated from his first wife, Lockwood had a new woman in his life, Lois, whom he'd met in New York. She would wait behind in Akron while he got settled in Montreal. A few months later, after his divorce was finalized, Lois joined him in Montreal, where they were soon married. It was a new beginning for both of them. What they knew about Quebec could have fit on the back of a matchbox. They were living in a primarily English-speaking part of the island. However, towns on the West Island like Dollard-des-Ormeaux presented a problem for Lockwood, who took to phonetically spelling out the names of things he couldn't pronounce. To help himself on air, he would write out, "Dollard des ORMO."

He immersed himself in the language as best he could, mocking his inadequacies with humour but making a genuine effort that French-speaking Quebecers would appreciate. He rolled his letters when trying to pronounce something difficult. While at CFOX, he had an opportunity to introduce the Beach Boys in concert and threw some of his fractured French into the intro. By now, Lockwood had piled up a significant number of bilingual francophone listeners eating up Top 40 English rock 'n' roll, so up on the stage that night as emcee, it was "*Bonsoir mesdames et messieurs à l'arène Paul Sauvé,* the Beach Boys," he said in his fractured, flat French. The crowd loved it. They knew he was from the U.S. and that he had made an effort to speak some French, even briefly. Just that small gesture probably generated more good word-of-mouth in the French community. It was worth its weight in gold – and new listeners.

That Montreal Beach Boys concert remains memorable to Lockwood due to an eerie backstage encounter. While waiting for his cue to introduce the band, he was given a hard time by one of the band's roadies. Or at least that's what Lockwood thought he was. He was being particularly aggressive, demanding to know what Lockwood was doing hanging around backstage. Someone who knew

Lockwood intervened before the incident escalated. The next time Lockwood saw that same face he had tangled with backstage was almost a year to the day after the Beach Boys August 1968 concert in Montreal. In August of 1969, while watching the news, he recognized the face of Charles Manson, a suspect in the murders of actress Sharon Tate and four others, as well as the murders of Leno and Rosemary LaBianca. Manson, an aspiring singer, had conned his way into the Beach Boys' entourage through his friendship with drummer Dennis Wilson. Manson's face was one Lockwood would never forget.

While some DJs were content to stay behind the mic, hop into their car and head home, Lockwood fed off the energy of meeting people and making new friends and listeners. He hit a Montreal still riding the high of Expo 67 and Canada's 100th birthday. By 1969, Montreal had a major league baseball team, the Expos. A sports guy with a particular liking for baseball, Lockwood was as happy as a beaver in a lumberyard to see pro baseball come to town. Many of the Expos players settled in the suburbs of Montreal's West Island, and it wasn't long before Lockwood got to know some of them.

Lockwood was star-struck. "Growing up as a kid, you follow sports," he says. "I never thought I'd be friends with major league baseball players." Lockwood had arrived at just the right time to ride the wave. The Expos struggled at first, as new teams will, but they had the backing of Montreal fans, who were patient, at first at least, thinking maybe one day they'd see a World Series in Montreal. So fond of the Expos was Lockwood that he did his entire morning show from Jarry Park for the Expos first home game on April 14, 1969. The CFOX broadcasting booth was dug in deep in the mud behind home plate. It was a chilly debut for the Expos at outdoor Jarry Park, and Lockwood was underdressed, wearing a sports coat and slacks. He was miserable that day, but he was part of history. The Expos won their first home game ever, beating the St. Louis Cardinals 8–7. The game was broadcast nationwide on CBC-TV. The living room was a much warmer place to be than the stands, where 29,000 and change stood that day, most of whom had on their winter/spring transition gear.

Lockwood and his wife didn't suffer from any serious culture shock. What he didn't know about Quebec politics didn't seem to bother him. Just months before the Montreal Expos were about to settle into town, the FLQ were ramping up their reign of terror. Though Quebec politics must surely have been the topic of conversations at the Hymus Tavern, which was conveniently located below the CFOX studios, Lockwood carried on, perhaps insulated by the fact that he was new to Quebec. "It didn't bother me," he says of the tumultuous Quebec politics. "You know, when you're young you don't think about that stuff. I didn't even know about the Parti Québécois. I had no idea."

Lockwood was more into the job and sports. His newly adopted Montreal Expos finished last in their division with a 55–110 record that year, with the New York Mets winning the World Series. Also a passionate Montreal Canadiens fan, he was disappointed by the team's dismal fifth-place finish in the 1969–70 hockey season. It was not a good year for Montreal, either politically or sports-wise. It was, however, a pretty good year for music. Songs like Marvin Gaye's "I Heard It Through the Grapevine," the Stones' "Honky Tonk Women," the Beatles' "Get Back" and "Come Together," and "Leaving on a Jet Plane" by Peter, Paul & Mary all topped the *Billboard* Top 100 charts. Then again, so did "Sugar, Sugar" by the Archies, the song that made its Montreal-born composer, Andy Kim, a millionaire.

After riding high as the No. 1 Top 40 English station, the end of 1970 would signal the beginning of a slide in CFOX's fortunes. Though it would happen slowly over the course of a year, it was apparent that CKGM-AM was chipping away at the station's listenership. Still, it came as a surprise when, in 1971, Sinclair, Jr. called Lockwood and news director Russ Griffiths into his office to say he had to let them go. "We weren't doing anything to piss off management," Lockwood says. "We were just minding our own business. I couldn't believe it. We were doing so well. Starting to make money. We were starting to knock off some of the stations downtown. I was completely shocked. It came right out of the blue." The timing was particularly bad for Lois, who was in the early months of a pregnancy.

Suddenly, Lockwood was at loose ends. He had some money to fall back on but, as the sole breadwinner and with Lois pregnant, he had to have somewhere to go. He still wasn't that well-connected in the radio biz. Fortunately, a buddy from Wilkes-Barre, Pennsylvania, was opening up a station in West Palm Beach – where the Montreal Expos' spring-training camp was located – and Lockwood grabbed that opportunity. "CFOX was a great time," he says. "I was always allowed to do what I wanted. I was palling around with the baseball and hockey players. I was sad to leave all that behind." Listeners were sorry to see him go, but Lois was thrilled. She wasn't as outgoing as her husband, and she hated the cold.

So it was down to WPOM ("The new 'POM' in Palm Beach" was their slogan), where Lockwood and Lois would enjoy the easy climate. It was way more subdued and laid-back in south Florida, a stark contrast to the four-season curve balls of Montreal weather. During winter, there were plenty of Canadian snowbirds in the area who recognized a familiar voice on WPOM, and for a couple of months when the Expos held spring-training camp, he could cozy up to some of his baseball player pals who were still with the team. Lois gave birth to a son, Ralphie, Jr. It was the good life, but Lockwood missed the hum of Montreal: its youth, its ambience, the sports and the camaraderie of his Crescent Street drinking buddies. After almost two years, the WPOM gig dried up and the Lockwood family returned to Montreal, where CKGM wanted Lockwood in the premier spot on radio.

The call came from Jim Sward, former CFOX sales manager and now CKGM general manager, who was about to revamp the station's entire format to Top 40. He wanted Lockwood as his morning man. At first, they offered him the same salary he had made at CFOX. Sward told him the morning show would be his; they wanted a personality. The deal looked dead in the water until program director John Mackey sweetened the offer. They offered two weeks of vacation in the south, paid for by CKGM, along with $2,000 in spending money and a few other perks that eventually swayed Lois and Lockwood. The deal was sealed on a relationship that would have a surprisingly long and successful tenure in radio years.

On October 2, 1972, Lockwood reintroduced himself to Montreal radio, this time with the full weight of 50,000 watts and an urban audience of millions. CKGM management had already laid the foundation for its full-out foray into the Top 40 format. By the time Lockwood returned to the Montreal airwaves, it was the new No. 1 radio station in Montreal. Lockwood was a pivotal part of Jim Sward's vision for the new CKGM, so it was a big deal when Lockwood returned to his adopted home. To loyal listeners, it was like their favourite uncle had come to stay for the week, the one who told jokes and gave you Snickers bars when mom wasn't looking.

Lockwood immediately told his audience how glad he was to be back. He rolled out some new and old characters like Professor Frydock, who did "reports" from the Blue Bonnets Racetrack, Montreal's harness-racing centre. Using his W.C. Fields voice, the Professor would make some race predictions, the kind no serious bettor would take. "Tonight, in the first race, it's Number One, Betty Blue... Speaking of Betty Blue..." said Lockwood, channelling W.C. Fields, and off he went into some risqué Betty Blue-inspired joke. Then there were his now-politically incorrect send-ups of effeminate characters Dorion Gray and Longueuil Leroux, a nod to two CKGM listening areas. Lockwood would do some pre-recording for his morning show when he wanted to have two characters in the same place at the same time. Using either Longueuil (pronounced "Long-gay") Leroux or Dorion Gray, he would throw the irascible Quebec-born pro wrestler "Mad Dog" Vachon in the mix with poor Dorion or Longueuil. The two characters were pretty much interchangeable, both with heavy-duty lisps. He'd set the scene for listeners: (There'd be a knock at the door.) "It's me, the Mad Dog," says Lockwood, in his best gruff Québécois accent. "What's dis guy doing here. I don't like dis guy Longueuil Leroux."

"Oh, Mad Dog, leave me alone, you bully," says Leroux/Lockwood.

"I'm gonna take this wastebasket and beat you with it," replies Mad Dog. There's a lot of on-air noise indicating some kind of struggle going on. (Lockwood's banging on the studio wastebasket.) Meanwhile, Longueuil Leroux is saying, "Oooo, more." It was cheesy, sweaty, locker-room humour, but for his legion of listeners it was a tonic as they dragged their weary asses out of bed at 6:30 in the morning.

Lockwood calls it "crazy stuff." He worked like most stand-up comics: throw 20 jokes out to the audience and hope 12 of them stick. Only one other DJ at CKGM could pull that off: Marc "Mais Oui" Denis during his late night show. Listeners loved Lockwood's shtick and would try their hand at repeating a Lockwood routine around the office water cooler. It was aimed squarely at a young, male demographic. Female listeners had trouble getting it. They weren't sure who "Mad Dog" Vachon was. Lockwood's two gay characters would be socially unacceptable on today's radio, but those were different times. Lockwood never called the characters gay. Nevertheless, he does remember getting a call from a McGill University student, who was part of a fledgling gay student association at the time. He told Lockwood that he liked his gay characters Leroux and Dorion, but he was gay and he didn't talk like them. So occasionally, he had to assure recipients of his shtick that it was all in fun. His humour never had any hard edges to it. Lockwood's famous catchphrase – "How's your bird?" – was a regular rhetorical question he threw out to listeners. Just those three words had a shelf life of several years. If someone spotted Lockwood on the street, in a bar or at an event, they would invariably ask him, "How's your bird?" On air he even took to asking the question in his phonetic Greek and Italian, another attempt to reach out to his diverse audience. When he was in the Greek or Italian parts of Montreal he would hear back, "How's your bird?" in those languages. It was the birth of his nickname, "The Birdman."

If it was a cold day, he advised Montrealers to "put on their Côtes-des-Neiges," a play on words using a major Montreal thoroughfare for his bilingual pun. For listeners in their cars, he would riff on French street names advising drivers to "Take the Pie-IX cut-off [a street name pronounced 'pee noof'] and cut off your pee noof." Though the joke was crude, he knew his morning fans weren't expecting refined humour. He beat out most morning show announcers in that time slot, so whatever stuck to the wall was what he was going to go with.

Lockwood probably had the highest visual profile of any DJ in Montreal. Unlike some other DJs who were more comfortable indoors and behind the mic, Lockwood was a major schmoozer outside of CKGM studios. He had advertising contracts with the Bar-B-Barn, a chicken and rib restaurant in Montreal, Dorion Suits and Cheers, a bar. Montrealers had no trouble matching the face with the voice.

Lockwood was one of the few CKGM DJs who worked with an operator/producer, freeing him up to put his full energy into just performing. Behind the controls of the Lockwood morning show was former CFOX and CJAD operator, Bruce Morel. "On the morning show you're like a traffic cop," says Morel, who now calls Nova Scotia home and has been heavily involved in the healthy east coast music scene for years. "You're guiding the programming content."

Morel, dubbed "Crazy" Bruce by Lockwood, became a part of the morning show's cast of characters. "The chemistry I had with Ralph was fantastic," he recalls. "We really clicked and I could anticipate him. He was the wild, bucking pony and I maintained the overall flow of the show. Ralph wasn't someone who pretended to enjoy what he was doing; he really liked what he was doing."

When Lockwood's brother-in-law rolled into town for a visit, they went for a stroll down Ste. Catherine Street. It seemed like every second person called out, "Hey, Ralph, how's your bird?" Or, "Hey, Birdman, good show today." Or "Bonjour Ralphie, I enjoy your show." Across the street a Hare Krishna guy playing his tambourine yelled out, "Hey, Ralphie, how ya doin'?" His brother-in-law was impressed. "Do you know everybody in this city?" It was just another day for the Birdman, who said hello to everyone, even the guy who was looking for some spare change.

For radio, Lockwood's tenure at CKGM was unusually long. The only other morning radio man who logged more time behind the morning mic in English radio was CJAD's George Balcan, with 23 years at the same station (1975–1998.) The 10 years Lockwood spent at 'GM, from 1972 to 1981, might have been cut short had former CKGM general manager Jim Sward had his way. At the top of his game in 1978, he got an offer from Sward, who had moved

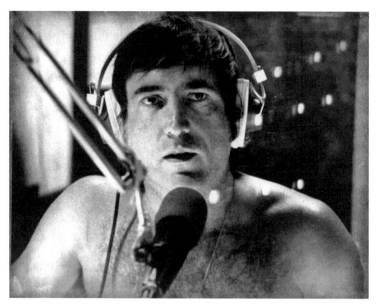

Lockwood was at his best shirtless behind the mic. He generated a lot of heat and kept the studio temperature down low.
Photo by Michael Dugas, 1977, Montreal Gazette.

to Toronto to become president and general manager of Rogers Broadcasting. Sward wanted Lockwood for Top 40 mega station CFTR, which in 1978 was about to unseat rival CHUM-AM as the No. 1 Top 40 radio station in Toronto. Lockwood had good ratings in Montreal, but CFTR was pulling in a million listeners during peak hours. Sward had a sweet deal for Lockwood, including paying off the mortgage on the Cape Cod home he had just bought and Toronto Maple Leafs season tickets. Sward knew about Lockwood's sports-hound predilections.

Then CKGM got wind of the possible Toronto deal and Lockwood was suddenly in the midst of a bidding war. He hired an agent (something no other DJ had dared to do) named Charles "Cookie" Lazarus, a Montreal lawyer who represented some Montreal Expos and Canadiens players. Lazarus handled all of the negotiations, playing both sides for Lockwood's services. CKGM did not want to lose him. John Mackey had taken over from Sward after the latter's departure, and he knew Lockwood well enough to realize both his value and his attachment to Montreal. He punched all the right buttons with his counter offer. "I took Cookie in with me to all the meetings," says Lockwood. "We sat down and for the first time in my life I realized why athletes have agents. It was unbelievable. Cookie took care of everything and I came out with more than I went in with." So, with the pot sweetened, Lockwood remained a CKGM morning man. It's a decision he still wonders about to this day. "Maybe I should have taken the job," he says. "But I loved Montreal. Toronto seemed too buttoned-down at the time."

Three years later, however, he would take a risk – one that did not involve leaving Montreal. He got calls from two other Montreal stations interested in his services, CJAD and CFCF. At first glance, Lockwood thought neither station was suited to his freestyle approach to radio, but the CFCF offer had one important perk: TV. CFCF wanted him to do an afternoon drive radio show plus a morning TV show. The dough for each show would add some significant cash to his CKGM yearly salary. The whole offer appealed to his vanity, which was what put CFCF's offer over the top. Lockwood was in Cape Cod when Lazarus phoned him from Montreal. "I think you should take the television deal. It's a step up." Lockwood didn't have to think too long. " 'What the hell?' is what I told Cookie," says Lockwood. "I flew first class into Boston, then to Montreal. I hadn't even met the guys I was going to work with. I came into the airport and all the guys at customs were glad I was coming back to Montreal." It was goodbye CKGM and a move uptown to CFCF's Park Extension studios.

CFCF eased Lockwood in front of the cameras with a summer show called *Hi Noon*. He was mostly out and about Montreal doing man-on-the-street and celebrity interviews with some musical acts thrown in. It was mostly a live half-hour show, so it was a test of Lockwood's ability to think on his feet. He was nervous at first, but his good people skills got him through some early rough edges. However, all was not well with the afternoon radio gig. After filming his show, it would be a quick dash back to the studio to start his 3 to 6 p.m. shift. He was used to being the morning man; the afternoon thing was not working out. There was no room for him to stretch out within the confines of a tightly packaged, straight-ahead format. It was less of Ralphie on the air than he was used to. He quickly grew to hate it and took the problem to CFCF management.

CFCF was good about it and swallowed the money he was contracted to earn for his radio work, and left their original financial deal intact. The *Hi Noon* show morphed into a weekly half-hour in-studio show: *The Ralph Lockwood Show*. The set featured his name all dolled up Vegas-style in big, bold, lit-up letters behind him. Again, it was mostly local talent he brought in, including a very young Céline Dion who made a guest appearance and lip-synched her way into viewers' hearts. The show did well for its mid-morning time slot, garnering a local following of women, his new demographic.

At roughly the four-year mark of *The Ralph Lockwood Show*, CFCF pulled the plug, citing new budgetary constraints as the reason. It was a good run. Lockwood didn't have much time to feel sorry for himself as CKGM came calling again. CKGM missed Lockwood. Ratings had taken a tumble since sister FM station CHOM had outperformed CKGM in 1979. Many Top 40 AM stations across North American were suffering from declining ratings due to the incursion of FM album-oriented rock. Lockwood returned in 1985 to a station now owned by CHUM Limited, a Toronto-based company with massive TV and radio holdings. However, he was hardly coming back to the same station he left. Most of the familiar faces from just a few years earlier were gone. The year after he went back on the air at 'GM, the station changed its format to "Lite Rock, Less Talk," and shortly thereafter to "Favourites of Yesterday and Today."

Less talk, more rock hardly seemed like a format tailor-made for Lockwood. However, the new station owners made a big deal about his return, with billboards around town featuring Lockwood's face amongst a couple and their baby in bed. After a few months back, he began to wonder where all the fun had gone. "It was all this yuppie stuff," he says. "Ties, and sweaters draped over the shoulders. Just an entirely different approach to radio. I really tried hard to adjust to it." Instead of doing shtick, he'd talk about last night's TV shows and riff on that a bit. Like the B.B. King song, the thrill was gone, and by

75

1988 he had had enough. His contract up and ratings down, he was once again at loose ends. Only now, he was headed into his late 40s; he was no longer a young man just freshly out of the military.

The next year was a dark time for Lockwood and his family. Whereas in the last decade his reputation had attracted bidding wars, now he could barely get people in the radio biz to return his calls. When they did, the conversation went something like this: "We can't hire you; you're too good." Or, "You'll get too big and we'll lose you. You'll end up going to Toronto." This is what he heard from program directors and station managers across Canada. "I had a whole year I couldn't buy a cup of coffee," says Lockwood. "I called all across Canada. Guys who used to work with me, guys who were getting my coffee." Though he wasn't hurting financially, he felt a bit like a one-hit wonder. After about a year, he decided to return to a station in York, Pennsylvania. He was back on home turf, but not on his own terms. Between a rock and a hard place, the decision was easy: he needed to work.

Lockwood was back to the basics, playing records and doing shtick and doing remotes around town, which in other bigger markets had gone the way of the dinosaur. On cruise control and in an unstable market where stations had abandoned the Top 40 format for all-news or talk radio, by 1999 Lockwood ended his York radio stint doing talk radio. For a guy who was studiously apolitical on air, he was pretty much out of his element. He was just hanging on now and before the new millennium broke, he semi-retired from radio, taking on the odd remote gig here and there, but for all intents and purposes, it was over as he hit 60.

Back in his home state, Lockwood kicked back to enjoy retirement. But tragedy interrupted his laid-back time when Lois, his lifelong love, was diagnosed with cancer. When she died in 2008, he was devastated and heartbroken. He and Lois had been together since 1966 and she had stuck by him, a steadying influence in a business that had more than its share of distractions and temptations.

On his own since Lois' death, he now does some part-time promotional work, just to get out and meet people. He's ventured back to Montreal a few times since he left in 1988, touring some of his old haunts, but he realizes those heady days of his star Top 40 DJ status are but memories in a yearbook. Now 74, he has come to terms with his single life. He still gets calls from the old crowd in Montreal, like former Canadiens player and general manager Bob Gainey and former CKGM DJ Marc Denis. "I could still go back to Montreal and get a free meal at the Bar-B-Barn," says Lockwood. There aren't too many from Lockwood's halcyon radio days left in Montreal. But if he did decide to come back for a visit, he'd find his old Bar-B-Barn owner and pal Manny Barnoff still around. He'd probably give Lockwood his regular table. "Over here, Ralphie. Good to see you again. This one's on me."

STEVE "THE MOVER" SHANNON: FROM PUMPING GAS TO PUMPING OUT THE HITS

In the middle of the night, Steve Shannon lets himself in through the side door at the CFOX studios in suburban Pointe-Claire. Though he no longer works there, he's still got a key. He knows the building is empty, with the midnight to 6 a.m. time slot running on pre-programmed music and ads, and no DJ. It's 1972 and less than a year earlier CFOX was in its prime, the No. 1 Top 40 AM radio station in Montreal. But now, its fortunes are fading fast. As a result, for at least six hours a day a shelled-out version of its former self on automatic pilot is rolling out a stream of "golden oldies." This is pre-*Network*-the-movie time, but Shannon is about to pull a Peter Finch. He's mad as hell and he isn't going to take it anymore. He goes upstairs to the studio (he could find his way in the dark, having spent almost three years making that same walk, first as all-round, go-to guy, then behind the mic as one of the 1470 CFOX-AM Good Guys), he pushes a few buttons, takes the station off auto-pilot, and takes command of the ship. CFOX is saving money with pre-programmed, fully automated music. This is Shannon's last stand; he's doing it for free. He sits behind the mic, takes control of the sound board and begins his first and only dry-land pirate-radio gig. He boards the station and has his way with it until he runs out of rage. He pulls no punches,

77

telling whoever is listening what a sad ending it is for a once-vibrant station, now reduced at night to a robo-DJ spinning the hits of yesteryear. He's there for a couple of hours until he runs out of gas. Then, he puts the station back on auto-pilot and leaves. Anyone who was up late that night and tuned into 1470 on the AM would have caught a DJ laying it all out, interrupted only by the tunes he wanted to play. It was one for the books. Strangely, no one called security. By that time, apparently not even management was listening. It was a kind of bloodless radio coup d'état. Shannon found the whole experience therapeutic. He was headed downtown anyway.

Shannon was hardly a natural-born rebel. He had come into radio at the bottom and worked his way up to become one of Montreal's finest Top 40 jocks. His strong work ethic was inherited from his father, a French-Canadian carpenter by trade, stationed in England after World War II with the Royal Canadian Engineers where he had met and married his British wife. It was culture shock when his father decided to return to Quebec in 1964, his wife, daughter, and 16-year-old son Steve in tow.

Shannon was born Steve Castonguay, a British-born teen – now on the West Island of Montreal – with a mid-Atlantic accent and a French surname that made him slightly self-conscious. "Having a bit of an English accent was a plus during the British music invasion," says Shannon. "But I was trying to fit in and didn't want to put on a British accent. Besides, my accent was from the wrong side of the tracks."

With the British equivalent of a high school leaving certificate, and accustomed to getting his hands dirty, he got a job managing two gas stations. He also became the proud owner of a Canadian essential, a tow truck. Between the two gas stations and the tow-truck business, Shannon was making good money in his adopted land. He was always flush, as gas and towing were up there on the list of basic Canadian needs, just behind Kraft Dinner and beer.

When you pulled into a gas station in those days someone came out to do the pumping for you, check your oil, maybe even throw in a windshield cleaning. There were repeat customers, two of whom worked at local radio station CFOX – DJ "Big Daddy" Bob Ancell and Bill Lowell. These guys knew a radio voice when they heard one. Shannon's dulcet baritone spoke to them through the car window. The "Fill 'er up, check your oil?" and ensuing chit-chat must have impressed them. This guy was a Murray Westgate in waiting. Ancell and Lowell "discovered" Shannon, encouraging him to come over to the station and talk to owner Gord Sinclair, Jr. The notion of working at a radio station had all the romance of the movie business to a 19-year-old with an oily rag hanging out of his back pocket. He was intrigued.

Much to his parents' dismay, Shannon quit his gas station and tow-truck business to get into radio. He said goodbye to his $150-per-week job for a $47-per-week gig as CFOX's gofer boy. It was hardly instant stardom, as Shannon had to pay his dues for at least a couple of years, doing pretty much anything the station asked of him. He'd set up the equipment for weekend sock hops and remote broadcasts, and in the process he became familiar with the turntables, tape machines, microphones and cartridge decks. He drove the CFOX 1470 mobile, occasionally got to do traffic reports and even some news stories. He was getting a complete education in radio multi-tasking, occasionally even dressing up as Charlie Fox, the station's mascot. "I wasn't kissing ass or anything, but management noticed how hard I worked. I never said no to a job they asked me to do. I think I made an impression," Shannon says.

His multiple duties, including those forays out in the CFOX mobile, as a kind of on-the-move news/traffic reporter, often could be the fodder for some golden live radio moments. CFOX had a designated traffic reporter, Stu MacIsaac, who sometimes reached out to Shannon for on-the-spot traffic updates. CFOX was low budget; there was no traffic helicopter like at the other stations. One morning, new CFOX morning man Ralph Lockwood went to MacIsaac for a regular traffic report and there was the dreaded dead air. Apparently, Stu had slept in. So Shannon hopped in the mobile and headed out into traffic to fill in. Things were going relatively smoothly, as Shannon moved about the city and called in his reports on the car's CB radio. At some point, possibly trying to give a report and drive at the same time, Shannon became part of the morning rush-hour news.

The news guy gave him the cue to finish up the on-the-hour news, reporting a little fender-bender on the Decarie Expressway. "How many cars are involved?" asked newsman Gord Logan. "Three," said Shannon. "A black Fiat, a Chevrolet, and the CFOX news cruiser."

When not attending to his flex-time job, Shannon was tuning up his would-be DJ skills, making tapes of himself and playing them back to see how they sounded. He had other DJs listen to them and give him feedback. He had no illusions at the time, not confident enough to think he was Top 40 DJ material. Eventually, the opportunities came – at first as a fill-in when one of the regular jocks was sick or away. "There were many days, whenever someone was sick, I would be called in to do an all-night show after working the whole day. Then I'd start my daily duties all over. So, there were days when I worked all day, all night, then all day again. I had youth on my side, so I could pull it off." For each show Shannon did, he got paid an extra $15 to add to his $47 take-home pay.

His gruelling schedule did have its perks. To further augment his meagre pay, Shannon would both set up and emcee Saturday night dance concerts at the Bonaventure Curling Club. There was always a live band, sometimes local, sometimes an up-and-coming performer from out of town to promote a hit record. One Saturday night it was Irish rocker Van Morrison riding the success of his Top 40 hit single "Brown-Eyed Girl." Morrison and his band were tuning up while Shannon was at the mic as emcee trying to give away some prizes. Shannon asked Morrison to hold it down until he had finished. Morrison, a short, quick-tempered artist with a feisty personality, was not pleased. A very public argument ensued, with Shannon throwing the first punch, which fortunately did not hit its intended mark, Morrison's face. The dust quickly settled on that little power struggle with only two bruised egos to report. What could have ended badly resolved itself years later when Morrison, now a much bigger star, was appearing at Place des Arts. Shannon asked promoter Donald K. Donald if he could go backstage after the show. There, Shannon approached Morrison and asked him if he remembered their little fracas, admitting he had been totally out of line. "Oh, you're that fuckin' announcer who was gonna beat the shit out of me," Morrison said. "I'm Irish; if I don't pick a fight every week, nothing's normal in my life. It's all water under the bridge." They both toasted their Irish-British reconciliation with a couple of backstage pints.

Soon, Shannon's dog days of being the in-house, all-round handyman were expanding. Having passed his apprenticeship with flying colours, he was on his way to having a role of his very own behind the mic on weekends at CFOX. He was a fresh voice and he went about it with great relish. He was just happy to be where he was, and it sounded that way on air. A robust six-foot-two with a full head of red hair, Shannon leaned into the mic with gusto, laughing naturally with a Santa-like heartiness. He was enjoying himself, so he felt there was no reason not to share that with his listeners. "I wasn't at all nervous," he says. "I didn't take myself all that seriously. I knew some guys in radio who really wanted it badly, whatever 'it' was. My attitude was, 'I'll give it my best shot. I'll try and have as much fun as possible and, if it doesn't work out, I can always go back into the towing business or maybe open my own gas station.'"

His deep-from-the-belly baritone laugh would become part of his on-air persona. Top 40 DJs liked to have at least one signature word or expression that would make them stand out in the crowd. Shannon had his laugh. Sometimes between records, that's all he'd do. No intro. No time-check. No temperature check. "Some people told me they liked listening because it sounded like I was having a gas. I took my cue from DJs like Dean Hagopian and 'Big Daddy' Bob Ancell. Those guys sounded like they were having fun."

There were different kinds of fun for Top 40 jocks, especially for those working the last or the all-night shift. The later the hour, the weirder it got. There was always that lifeline between DJ and listener, the 24-hour request line. It was always busy, but after the kids got home from school and after the homework was finished, the request line fairly hummed. After midnight the wheat was separated from the chaff. The calls got a little edgier. There could be some telephone flirting, more often than not, girls doing a little late-night fantasiz-ing. It was always a roll of the dice for the tempted Top 40 DJ. Phone flirting was a lot safer than actually trying to hook up with a nice voice.

One very cold winter night, Shannon altogether forgot himself on air. Montreal's infamous winter weather can change on a dime. Regular temperature checks were part of any radio station's programming, whether Top 40 or middle of the road. Announcers wouldn't go more than five minutes without mentioning the temperature and time. The CFOX studios had a thermometer that jocks could look at for up-to-date temps. It was hovering around minus four when Shannon checked it that night, something he normally did every hour. On this night he had forgotten to do his hourly check and, when he finally took a gander at the 'FOX thermometer, he was surprised to see a dramatic drop in temperature. "I was on the air and I thought I could do anything at this point," Shannon recalls. "So, I began with the weather forecast, '. . . clear with some snow flurries and . . . wait a minute folks. I don't have an updated temperature, so let me just look out the window here and see.'" The temp had dropped 30 degrees in about three hours. "Do you know what the temperature is, folks?" he asked his listeners. "It's minus 34. Holy fuck, that's cold!"

Realizing what he just said, he figured he would be back pumping gas by morning. "People are phoning in, they can't believe what they just heard," Shannon recalls. Days go by, and not a word from management. He figured he's weathered that mistake. But a few weeks later, in the CFOX hallways, he ran into owner Gord Sinclair. They had a pleasant encounter about Shannon's progress on the night shift. Then Sinclair asked Shannon to step into his office. Shannon got that sinking stomach feeling, the one students get when called into the principal's office. "Well, you're doing a pretty good job," Sinclair told him. "You're getting the hang of it and that's good." The conversation seemed to be over and Shannon heaved a sigh of relief. They shook hands and, before Shannon could clear the office door, Sinclair said, "You'd better put a coat on, it's fucking cold out there." He was now wagging his finger in Shannon's direction. "Not on my radio station," he said. The swearing incident was a mistake Shannon would never repeat, not unintentionally, anyway.

From the middle of 1970 and into the next year Shannon was a very busy DJ, logging some serious radio time and lots of mileage on his car. From his weekend show at CFOX he would drive to

Quebec City to work days at CFOM, then back again. Then he was offered a job in Winnipeg at CFRW by former CFOX DJ Charles P. Rodney Chandler, the recently installed program director. Shannon had wanted a regular shift and got the prime afternoon drive slot.

This was the way radio DJs rolled: take the opportunity and go. However, the destination was not always what you would like to call home. For Shannon, Winnipeg turned out to be a town he wanted out of shortly after arriving, just as winter was setting in for its long, six-month stay. It was a Friday, a few months into his Winnipeg gig, when he called CFOX Program Director Doug Ackhurst to ask about any openings. He missed CFOX, but he missed his girlfriend back in Montreal even more.

Ackhurst told him that the all-night weekend slot was open but with one caveat: he had to be in Montreal for the Sunday midnight shift. He finished his Friday drive show at 6 p.m., told the station he quit, hopped in his 1966 Buick Wildcat, and drove non-stop to Montreal in time to hit the air back on the 'FOX at midnight, Sunday. The 2,760 kilometres (1,715 miles in those days), numerous bladder breaks due to over-consumption of coffee, maybe a short nap or two, the wind behind him, his distaste for Winnipeg, and the anticipation of the warm embrace of his girlfriend all helped stoke him for some hard-ass driving. At midnight, he was back behind the mic at CFOX, the seat kept warm by the weekend six-to-midnight jock.

Shannon would make a number of lateral moves during his radio career, but his next move away from CFOX would be a step up. By the early 1970s, the 'FOX's Top 40 fortunes were fading and everyone at the station knew it. There will always be a soft spot in Steven Shannon's heart for the CFOX Good Guys and their heady days as Top 40 number one in Montreal. But with the emergence of CKGM, suddenly there was competition, and Shannon believes that management panicked when they changed the format from Top 40 to golden oldies. "I learned from some amazing people there [at CFOX] – announcers, radio programmers, and others. I was like a vacuum when I started there, sucking up information, because it was just a whole new world compared to anything I was dealing with before. It was a great training ground."

Shannon had done his boot-camp radio at the 'FOX and was battle-ready. CKGM had come to Shannon's door with offers many times, but he demurred, his loyalty to his first station unshakeable. After his rebel one-night stand with CFOX on oldies auto-pilot and fading fast, he decided to cut ties and sign with CKGM. There was, however, one snag. Before he could work at CKGM, 'FOX owner Gord Sinclair reminded Shannon of the six-month non-compete clause in his contract. So instead of downtown Montreal, Shannon headed to Hamilton and Top 40 station CHAM for a kind of radio purgatory that lasted for about four months, before Sinclair relented and freed him up to return to Montreal. He was about as fond of Hamilton as he had been of Winnipeg.

By then the CKGM team of general manager Jim Sward and program director John Mackey had recruited other CFOX alumni. Shannon joined former 'FOX colleagues Ralph Lockwood and Jim Patton in the "Great '98" lineup. Shannon recognized Sward and Mackey as king-makers and, by offering Shannon a place with CKGM, they showed their faith in his abilities – that and three times the money he was making at CFOX sweetened the deal. He walked into a more elaborate and professional radio station set-up; more front-office employees, more production studios, a bigger record library, a bigger newsroom, and a good on-air studio all combined to send Shannon into a short-lived bout of culture shock. "Holy shit," Shannon said to himself after taking a look around. "This is like big-time radio. I guess I should start to take this seriously."

Although he would come and go from CKGM four times in the next 18 years, Shannon had found a home, and he would not be making any more 48-hour marathon drives for a job. He arrived just at the right time, as CKGM would occupy the No. 1 spot in Top 40 radio for a decade. It was a magical time for Shannon at CKGM, ultimately his favourite period of his long radio career, right alongside the soft spot he will always have for CFOX. Jim Sward remembers that when a show was rocking and rolling for Shannon, he was one of the best Top 40 jocks in the business. Shannon's move to CKGM could not have been better timed. By the end of 1970, after about six months in a Top 40 format, CKGM had taken over the No. 1 spot from CFOX.

Steve Shannon, circa 1985, on location for CKGM at Disney World
in Orlando, Florida.
Courtesy of Steve Shannon.

Although Shannon was now behind the mic at an up and coming Top 40 radio station, the next few decades were filled with instability and personal turmoil. He bounced around several radio stations, his marriage in a steady decline, along with an increasing personal debt and a burgeoning drug habit. He eventually had to declare personal bankruptcy,

Shannon took stock of where he was and decided it was a bad place. He got away from radio and did some soul searching. He eventually cleaned up his act and dug himself out of a major financial hole. "Those troubled years. I got back on my feet and put my life back together." He went back to Montreal and CKGM for a final fling in 1988 when the Great '98 was in its declining years, mired in the doldrums of constantly changing formats. In 1988 it was Favourites of Yesterday and Today, heavy on the Bette Midler and Lionel Ritchie sound. GMs and programmers thought listeners had outgrown rock 'n' roll. Shannon hated it, so he left and opened up a radio school. Then he left for western Canada, taking on odd jobs in radio, driving a forklift, and working in a steel factory.

In Vancouver in 1995, his personal rehabilitation hit a high note when he fell in love with an actress and professional hairdresser. They spent a good part of the next nine healthy, happy years together. In 2004, she was diagnosed with terminal cancer. He was devastated. "She was the love of my life, a kind of rebirth for me," says Shannon. "She was very independent and career-oriented. She was the most perfect woman in the world."

He could easily have packed it in at this point in his life, maybe wallow in the mire. Instead, he bought an RV and toured rural British Columbia, looking for a small town that needed a radio station. If he was going to do this again, he would be his own boss. Finally, in 2009 he settled on Barriere, a recently incorporated forestry town about 60 kilometres from Kamloops in the North Thompson River Valley. He scouted a location, parked his RV, and set about introducing himself around town. There was a lot of paperwork and many hoops to jump through. But by January 2014, the Bear, 93.4 FM, in Barriere went on the air, with Shannon as morning man. After close to 40 years in and around the radio biz, this was his first foray into the most important slot in any radio station's day. The whole town was listening.

Shannon serves as CEO, janitor, programmer, ad man, salesman, GM, and DJ for the Bear. If anyone needs him, they can find him out back in his RV. Shannon is back to basics. "It all started with the 'FOX and now it's the Bear," he says, the radio animal metaphor too obvious not to mention.

Now reconciled with his three sons, he's finally found a home. "I couldn't be happier. I'm working my tail off, but I've never forgotten my days at CKGM. Right now, most of the people working at the station are volunteers, but I find myself giving them the same advice Jim Sward and John Mackey gave me. I hope I can build a team to make this station work, just like they did."

Jim Patton: The Multi-tasking Radio Guy
From DJ to Eye in the Sky

Jim Patton could have been a preacher man. Post-puberty, he was blessed with made-for-preaching pipes and, after many forced weekday confirmation sessions with the minister, it seems the "Reverend Patton" was ready for prime time. He could rouse a United Church Sunday morning crowd so much they'd dig deeper into their pockets when the collection plate came by. Okay, maybe on just one beatific Sunday at the Montreal West United Church, where he and his parents were regular worshippers. Whether he volunteered or not is uncertain, but one Sunday he was called upon to do a Bible reading in front of the congregation. He nailed it. On that day, on the way out of the church for the usual post-service handshakes, the minister gripped the patriarch of the Patton family and pronounced his son to be minister material. This might have been a revelation for the minister and for his father, but Jim Patton's own reaction to this possibility was on a very different spiritual plane. "Fuck it," he said, quietly enough so that not even God could hear. "I'm going into radio."

Here was a guy who loved radio and who had been weaned on Montreal Top 40 DJs like Dean Hagopian, Dave Boxer, and George Morris. With his homemade Heathkit radio, he tuned in to some of the top U.S. DJs, like WABC's Cousin Brucie and Charlie Greer, as well as Joey Reynolds from WKBW in Buffalo. As a teen, Patton practiced reading the newspaper out loud on the can while pretending to be a news announcer. "It was in my blood," says Patton. "It's a calling, I think. It's all I wanted to do from my mid-teens. I was desperate to become a radio announcer."

No doubt influenced by his teacher father, Patton took an academic approach to prepare for a possible radio career. He began by taking correspondence courses through the National Institute of Broadcasting (NIB), a Winnipeg-based company that sold boxes of albums with step-by-step instructions on how to do commercials, write newscasts, and speak on air. Each lesson required him to make a short tape and then take a written test, both of which he would then send to the Winnipeg office for evaluation. So, off he went to buy himself a cheap Japanese tape recorder and begin his lessons. There were about 40 lessons and tests in the $300 NIB package, a fair amount of money for the mid-1960s, which Patton was able to afford thanks to his parents. Holed up in his parents' Montreal West home and working diligently, Patton completed the program and passed all the tests. He was a new NIB graduate. Now what? CFCF Radio's Keith Randall, who had sold Patton on the idea of the NIB courses, offered to help him make a professional demo tape to send out to radio stations.

At the CFCF studios he sat before the solid-state microphones of a radio station and not the puny mic of his portable Japanese tape machine. "I was nervous as hell because I'd never been in a professional studio before. Suddenly, I'm in the studio behind these big Neumann and Sennheiser microphones, and huge reel-to-reels in the next studio. It was most impressive and frightening," Patton recalls.

He read a few commercials and some news stories; the end product was a tight, five-minute, ready-for-distribution audition tape. Randall made several copies, handed Patton a suggested list of radio stations he should send his tape to, and sent him on his way. Patton proceeded to send his demo to radio stations big and small across the country, and waited to see what might turn up. Eventually, he got a bite from a station in Thunder Bay, Ontario. After looking up Thunder Bay on a map, he was pumped and ready to go. The day before he was set to leave, the station reneged on its offer; they'd found someone else. Patton was crushed. "I should have known right then that radio was going to be a terrible disappointment," he says sardonically. At 65, he can look back at his radio career through the tainted lenses of experience. But at 17, he was bound and determined to get started in the "biz."

A short time after that first disappointment, his connection with Keith Randall turned up again with information about a job at a station in St. Jerome, in the Laurentians. CKJL-AM played to a fairly small, mostly French-speaking demographic. But on weekends, when the English-speaking cottage crowd came up, the station's owner thought some English programming would be good for business. Enter Jim Patton as the new weekend guy at CKJL. This was small-time radio, but for a fresh NIB graduate, it was big enough.

Patton, who didn't have a driver's licence yet, took the bus from Montreal, travelling the same road as all the retreating cottagers heading up to their country homes. He worked some odd on-air hours – one hour on, then two off – all weekend until Sunday night, when he hopped back onto the bus for home.

But he soon realized that the weekend gig was more like a trip in the Twilight Zone. The radio station was in the basement of a sketchy motel, and as the new weekend guy, he was put up in a cell-like room in the motel, barely able to squeeze his six-foot-two frame onto the cheap motel mattress. The CKJL record library was not hall-of-fame deep, so after his first weekend of playing whatever was lying around the station, he took to bringing his own collection of 45s.

More interesting than the job was the night scene in the bar up-stairs, where he would recycle some of his wages alongside the other radio station employees who had nothing better to do. The bar had a lonely, desperate feel to it. With a clock that ran backwards and some of his meagre earnings going back to the station owner (since the latter also owned the motel and bar), Patton began to wonder what he had gotten himself into. After one month he decided to pack up his 45s and not come back. The station manager begged him to stay, as it was hard to find English-speaking announcers will-ing to stay in a postage-stamp-sized room all weekend and entertain the weekend cottage crowd with their own records. This was now the second consecutive disappointment in Patton's young DJ career, but he remained undeterred.

His next move was less rural than CKJL, if suburban Oakville, Ontario, in the late 1960s could qualify as such. At the time, Oakville was a growing community, fuelled by a major Ford Motors plant. CHWO had an opening for a news announcer and Patton was off to one of Ontario's versions of the Motor City. He was, as it turned out, a terrible newsman. Hated doing it. Hated writing it. Only 19, when he wasn't working he was holed up in a tiny apartment (shades of the St. Jerome weekend accommodation), a lonely walk to and from the radio station. He decided to persevere, doing a job he didn't want to do. Isolated and unhappy, he endured another humbling experience. In the process he decided to exercise his devious, rebellious side, seeking ways to test the patience of management. On Sunday afternoons, CHWO played religious programs paid for by different churches in the area for those too lazy or indifferent to show up for Sunday service. Behind the controls one Sunday, driven by a kind of subversive fervour, Patton cued up a tape from a local Japanese church and let it roll – backwards. Within a half-hour, the phone lines lit up, with Japanese-speaking listeners wondering just what the hell was going on. Patton's backwards religious Japanese sermon caper was his last at CHWO.

"One thing I'll say about radio," says Patton, "it does train you to be fired. You get fired and you move to the next job. You quit in anger. You have a fight with the program director. You walk out. It happens. I've heard people talk about how traumatic, how life-changing, being fired is. I say, 'Are you kidding? Get another job.'"

And that's exactly what he did. Patton's next stop was at CKOC Hamilton, his first Top 40 rock jock job. Hamilton was a big steel town in those days – the heartland of the tough but honest blue-collar worker – dominated by huge smokestacks that belonged to the biggest employers in town, Stelco and Dofasco Steel. Patton's all-night shift gave him some flexibility to play the music he wanted – some album cuts mixed in with some Top 40 hits, but with solid blue-collar credentials. The format also called for some country music to be thrown into the mix. Patton had some firm ideas of what a good Top 40 station should be. Alas, that didn't include country music. For his part, the program director at CKOC had some pretty weird standards for rock music. A bit of a lightweight, he instructed his DJs that if they played the Beatles' "Hey Jude," they had to fade it out when it got to the Paul McCartney screaming part because it was too loud. It was just the kind of attitude to irk the Top 40 sensitivities of a purist rock jock like Jim Patton. "Shit, the McCartney screaming in 'Hey Jude' is the best part of the whole song," he says.

Being close enough to Windsor, Patton checked out the sounds coming from CKLW "the Big 8" – a very hot radio station in the late 1960s, whose legendary status would only grow. The station was almost more American than Canadian, since the bulk of its listener-ship came from the millions across the river in Detroit. With 50,000 watts at night, its signal reached as far as the western portion of Michigan and parts of New York in the other direction. Like many North American stations, in 1967 CKLW was in transition from an easy-listening format to the Top 40 format. It immediately caught fire, incorporating the Motown sound into its programming to bring in more Detroit listeners. Patton loved its tight, Bill Drake-like format. CKLW was a Mecca for Top 40 DJs. That's the kind of station he wanted to be on. Eventually, he'd get his chance.

Running afoul of the CKOC program director, Patton found himself out of a job once again, but one that at least had come close to what he really wanted. So, he combed the Stelco steel dust out of his hair and headed back home, his ego once again a bit battered. "CKOC was a good education for me," he recalls. "It was a good introduction to the business of Top 40 radio. It was after that job that I realized that if I was going to work in this business, I'd have to develop a bullet-proof ego." By his own admission, Patton had no shortage of ego. He may have been overestimating his talents at that time, the result of naive, youthful bravado, but when he got the boot from CKOC, he took stock of the situation: "It didn't matter if the fuckin' guy fired me. I thought, 'Screw you, man. I'm better than that.'"

Back home, he spent a couple of months smoking weed with his old Montreal West buddies, registered for university, and plotted his next move. Everybody deserves a break after getting fired, but going back to live with his parents was motivation enough to get to the task at hand and build on whatever radio career momentum he had. A tip from CFOX program director and DJ Charles P. Rodney Chandler put Patton back behind the mic as the weekend night jock at the No. 1 Top 40 station in Montreal, the perfect shift for a guy who was now also a full-time university student.

Suddenly, his busy schedule got even busier. He got yet another call from his good buddy Keith Randall at CFCF, who was now flogging National Institute of Broadcasting courses, and he knew Patton was back in town. He recruited Patton as an NIB salesman, offering him $50 for every course he sold. The courses were an easy sell for Patton; he would just say, "Hey, I took the course and look at me!" CFOX was the only English-language Top 40 radio station in Montreal, and it was riding high when Patton joined it in 1970. DJs like Dean Hagopian, Charles P. Rodney Chandler, Roger Scott, and "Big Daddy" Bob Ancell had laid the foundations by the time Patton arrived. By that time, CFOX had enjoyed No. 1 status in Top 40 radio in Montreal for five years, despite its West Island location and a weak signal that wavered into downtown Montreal. But that would change later that year, when CFOX sales manager Jim Sward would meet with CKGM owner Geoff Stirling. Stirling offered Sward the general manager position, mandating him to overhaul the station and make it a Top 40 contender. Sward, in turn, would recruit Patton and Steve Shannon to CKGM (and later Ralph Lockwood).

Gone was Jim Patton's CFOX nickname, "PT" (public transport) Patton. He was finally where a Top 40 DJ could lay it all out, with all of CKGM's 50,000 watts behind him. The call from Sward was a big boost for Patton's ego; he and Shannon were the only two CFOX DJs to get the offer, before Lockwood also defected.

When CKGM began its Top 40 empire-building mission, Patton was allotted the 10 a.m. to 2 p.m. shift, then the 8 p.m. to midnight, followed by the 6 to 10 p.m. shift, before settling into the plum 3 to 6 p.m. afternoon drive show. With this last move, Patton was in heaven. He didn't have to give up school, scheduling his classes around his shift. Meanwhile, his show reached an average audience of about 600,000, more than at any time in his career so far. Other than the morning show, the drive-home shift was the most important in a radio station's programming. Radio stations put their best announcers in those two pivotal time slots. When CKGM came in with its first BBM (Bureau of Broadcast Measurement) ratings book in late 1970, its numbers were huge. Its Top 40 experiment had caught fire – at the expense of CFOX, which never recovered.

There was cause for celebration at CKGM, and some took the ratings jump to lobby for more money. Patton and fellow announcer Michael W. Morgan were two of the more aggressive jocks looking to get a share of the new fortunes. "[Morgan and I] thought we had

Jim Patton in the CKGM studios. He started his professional radio career at 17 in Hamilton. Two years later, he was back home when CKGM was taking over the Top 40 English rock radio business.
Courtesy of Rachel Irwin.

taken the station that was nowhere and turned it into this huge machine, and that we deserved tons of money," says Patton. "I'm sure it happens in other businesses. And they [management] said, 'No, we can't do that.' But what we forgot was that the company [Maisonneuve Broadcasting Ltd.] had been losing money for years. In retrospect, I can say I was young and egotistical. I thought I was worth way more money than I probably was." CKGM eventually fired Morgan, though it's still not clear if his aggressive "share the wealth" tactics were the reason. It was a teachable moment for Patton, who got his raises when management decided the time was right.

After a significant amount of time and some mellowing, Patton has come to terms with the money and the Top 40 biz. But when he was in the thick of things in his early 20s, there was always a sense of restlessness about him. He wanted more, and the possibility of more would come from the legendary CKLW "the Big 8" in Windsor.

While CKGM was rolling along, gaining momentum in Montreal in the early 1970s, Patton got an offer to work at CKLW. The station flew him down and gave him the royal tour. A week or so later he got a call from influential program director, U.S.-born Paul Drew, who had made a name for himself in the CKLW makeover from easy listening to Top 40. This was a big deal. Drew told him they liked what he did and offered him what amounted to a part-time gig, maybe two or three days a week for the same money that he was making at CKGM for five days' work. Tempting, yes, but Patton told them no deal. "It was at that point that I knew I was done," he says. "I was done with [Top 40] radio. I just didn't want to do it anymore, not rock radio anyway." The disappointments had caught up with him. Contemplating yet another move, he remembered the basement radio, the attempted newscaster venture, the rejection in Hamilton, the money in Montreal; it had all worn him down. Like the proverbial business executive who had reached a kind of ceiling and would never see the prime corner office, Patton had peaked at close to number one, but not quite.

Patton moved in different circles compared to other DJs who might not have much to fall back on if their radio career foundered. Often, DJs found themselves hopping from station to station until they burned out or ran out of options. In contrast, Patton was pursuing a university degree, and he had a steady relationship and friends outside of the radio business. He also had something no one could take from him – his pipes and a natural ability to retool and sell himself.

With his Association of Canadian Television and Radio Artists (ACTRA) membership card in hand, Patton lent his voice to various commercials for clients like Delta Airlines (the Wings of Man), the Bay, and London Drugs. Most proudly, he was the voice of Molson's in Quebec, owner of his beloved Montreal Canadiens. He made good money. Walk into the studio, start to read, and the meter started at $120.

Though he never returned to Top 40 radio, Patton's radio days in Montreal and beyond were far from over. His next stint was a weekend job at CFCF, often coming in hungover after some heavy partying. Weekend morning shows at CFCF consisted of heavy doses of middle-of-the-road music. To amuse himself, Patton would sometimes test the boundaries of management's tolerance. He once introduced a song by New Zealand singer John Rowles called "Cheryl Moana Marie" as "Share My Marijuana Marie." Someone from management heard this and upbraided him. But apparently, it was not an indictable radio offence. From CFCF he moved on to CFCF's FM station, CFQR. There he spent nights supervising reel after reel of more MOR music, coming in every 15 minutes or so just to let listeners know there was someone there. Out of sheer boredom, combined with an innate subversive streak, Patton came on the air late one night at CFQR with a story about a new discovery: air toilets that didn't need to be flushed. When management got wind of that talk, they put him back on their AM side.

Patton's final salute to CFCF came when he knew he would be moving on to CJAD. In those days CFCF had a shortwave station, CFCX, whose broadcast signal could be picked up presumably worldwide. One night, during a lull in his shift at CFCF, Patton took a CFCX radio station ID cartridge which simply said, "You're listening to CFCX shortwave Montreal" into the production studio and did some creative splicing. He replaced the word "shortwave" with a huge, abdominally, Patton-air-powered belch. Then he went back to the announcer's booth and carefully put the cartridge back in its proper place, thinking that it wouldn't be long before someone discovered the chicanery. Months later, he was listening to his old CFOX pal Gord Sinclair, Jr., now the morning man at CFCF. Sinclair was abuzz about this weird CFCX station ID cartridge, and how embarrassing it was, and how they just discovered it. Sinclair was reluctant to play it at first, perhaps not wanting to offend his half-asleep mature morning-show audience, but for some edgy morning fun (the CJAD kind of edgy), he played it anyway. And there it was, in all its glory, the shortwave belch-by-Patton. "I thought, YES!" says Patton. "That is the highlight of my entire radio career. The greatest thing I've ever done. If I managed to piss off a few people, then all the better." You can take the boy out of high school, but not the high school out of the boy. This was Patton's radio wedgie.

While he was still at CFCF, Patton had shown his versatility by going along with the traffic helicopter reporter, Lee Murray, on regular afternoon aerial excursions. In the process, he learned the art of traffic reporting, and soon took over from Murray. He would reprise this role when he got the job at CJAD, patrolling the skies for the morning and afternoon drive shows. There are a lot of bridges leading off and onto the island of Montreal – names Patton had to be familiar with from about 2,000 feet. Every street name and every major highway and number had to be filed away in his head from an overhead perspective. Fortunately, Montreal's traffic woes were the same almost every day; the same streets, the same bridges and the same escape routes were fodder every day of the week for the traffic 'copter reporter. Patton, the pro that he was, never missed a beat. His reports had to be concise and accurate, delivered every eight minutes, with the occasional 'copter landing in a cemetery so he could relieve his bladder. He lost count of the number of times he said "Traffic is bumper to bumper." He counted his blessings that he was above it all, that his drive home, after a two-hour aerial gig, would be a lot less bumper to bumper after rush hour. The money was decent and he had his mornings and evenings to himself.

Partly driven by the annoying complexities of Quebec politics, partly by the challenge of new opportunities and the search for a more temperate climate, Patton and his wife Felicity – now a freelance lifestyle writer who had worked in the CKGM record library before she and Patton married in 1972 – decided to flee Montreal for the West Coast. In the process, they joined the huge demographic of Anglos who left Quebec post-1976 for either Toronto or Vancouver. Although Patton had no set game plan for this geographical change, he did eventually accept an offer to join his old CKGM colleague and friend Michael Morgan, whose company was producing specialty reports for segments to be sold on syndicated radio stations in North America. Patton produced and voiced "Celebrity Sports Report" and the "One-Minute Segments" for nine years.

At age 65, with the first government retirement pension cheque already cashed, Patton is comfortably settled in White Rock, just a stone's throw from the Pacific. With their two sons, Brett and Christopher, both working elsewhere in Canada, Jim and Felicity are now respectable empty-nesters. His moving days behind him, Patton is one bona fide, mellowed-out West Coaster who has a chuckle every time he tees up the ball on the golf course in November, while what's left of his old Montreal West posse lines up to get their winter tires installed.

Marc "Mais Oui" Denis: La Connection Française

It's 1974, and Marc Denis has Supertramp's first big hit single "Bloody Well Right" loaded and ready to go. The song has a 51-second piano intro before the first guitar chord comes crashing in, and another 45 seconds before Roger Hodgson unleashes his vocal, "Right, right, you're bloody well right." Denis is spinning his intro in his head – in two languages. Top 40 jocks love to hit the vocal. With this song, Denis gets to really stretch his linguistic DJ skills. He pushes the cart button and begins his patter, moving smoothly and seamlessly between both of Canada's official languages – like playing road hockey in Ste. Foy and Dollard-des-Ormeaux at the same time.

"Mais Oui remind you that, up for grabs, ce soir, right here and only here, les merveilleux super hot T-shirts jaunes CKGM I Love You Montréal je t'aime! Stand by for your cue to call at any moment to show me some L-O-V-E . . . and win! Until that magic moment, sous la pluie, on this rainy night in centre-ville, drive carefully, c'est super . . . tremp [sic] . . . RIGHT! RIGHT! You're bloody well right," says Denis. Then Hodgson's vocals come in with his own, "Right, right, you're bloody well right . . ."

In his intro, he has included two plays on words, one with his own on-air nickname, the other with the word "trempé," the French word for wet. He's plugged CKGM's bilingually printed yellow T-shirt giveaway – a salute to Montreal with a big heart on the front – and he's given a quick weather reference along with a caution to

97

drive carefully, "sous la pluie." It's an art Denis perfected over the years. It's what got him the job at 'GM. His bilingual DJ shtick is a breath of fresh air on Montreal's Top 40 landscape, a fresh-air front that would help expand CKGM's listenership among francophones and ultimately have competing Montreal French-language radio stations crying foul.

Radio in Montreal was a kind of metaphor for the so-called Two Solitudes, the historical gap between the English- and French-speaking citizens of Quebec. For French-speaking radio announcers, English has always been a difficult language to ignore. The British Invasion – the musical one – hit Montreal's French-language radio stations pretty much the same way it hit English ones; teens, French or English, wanted to hear the Beatles. The Beatles could be "Les Beatles," but "I Wanna Hold Your Hand" or "Twist and Shout" were off limits to any possible translation.

Behind the mic at CKGM in the 1970s, Marc Denis would become the epitome of Montreal's linguistic adaptability and tolerance when it came to popular music. He grew up living in both languages from his birth in Hull (present-day Gatineau), to Quebec City, and then to the definitively anglophone West Island of Montreal. In his teens, Denis was spinning his dial from Dave Boxer at CFCF to Roger Scott at CFOX, and then to AM French-language powerhouse CJMS and Top 40 DJ Michel Desrochers. Denis remembers the fine line that made him both French and English, depending on where he was. "Because of his job, my father was always being transferred around," Denis says. "When we were living in Quebec City, I was the only one in my neighbourhood who spoke English, so I was 'l'anglais.' Then, on the West Island, I was 'the Frenchie.' Playing road hockey in the Quebec City suburb of Ste. Foy, and the West Island, I was not only developing an ear for both languages, but also living biculturally."

Denis was absorbing both cultures via both TV and radio. The West Island was home to Top 40 radio station CFOX, where Denis tuned in to the smooth, British-accented, Top 40 stylings of Roger Scott and the frenetic American-inspired rat-a-tat-tat of Charles P.

Rodney Chandler. Then he'd spin the dial to CFCF 600 and check out Dave Boxer; then over to 1280 CJMS and Desrochers' Top 40 show. It was a cocktail of two languages with basically the same music to make it go down smoothly, and Denis was taking it all in.

He took his love of radio to his post-secondary school, Collège Bourget, where he helped resurrect the school's radio station, rebooting it from the ground up. Then he lent his expertise to nearby Collège Querbes to get its campus radio station going. He did the same thing once again while attending the bilingual University of Ottawa by putting that school's Radio Campus 670 AM back on the air. In his third year of a political science degree at the U. of Ottawa, Denis spotted an ad in a local paper from CJRC in the Outaouais region, just across the river from Ottawa, for a weekend news announcer. It was the perfect job for a student who loved radio a lot more than political science. "So that's where it started," Denis says. "I remember every news item at CJRC was interrupted by this little sound effect, and you had to be sharp and not forget to play it between news items. I felt a bit like a real DJ and, secretly, during my time there as the news announcer, I was looking at the jocks on the other side of the glass in the studio thinking, 'I'd love to be doing what they're doing.'"

And so, like hundreds of other aspiring radio announcers, Denis put together a demo tape with his best impression of a Top 40 DJ – in two languages – and began the process of flogging it to local radio stations. He put the personal touch to his job search by actually taking his demo tape over to the program director of CKCH-AM in Hull. "I bugged that program director so much, I'm surprised he didn't have me kicked out of the station," Denis says. Wearing the program director down with his persistence, he got the job. "Sure, kid. The weekend all-night show is yours," he was told. "Now get the hell out of here." And just like that, he was on the other side of the glass.

CKCH in Hull was all-French programming. But for a while Denis had a blast on the all-night show where he had more flexibility to practice some of his bilingual DJ routines. It wasn't long before yet another opening came up at CKCH, this time as the weekday evening jock. Towards the end of his studies in political science, Denis

99

Marc "Mais Oui" Denis, a nickname given to him by fellow CKGM
DJ Steve Shannon, was the cornerstone of the station's bilingual years, as
part of "La Connection Française."
Courtesy of Marc Denis.

had some free time for his first five-day-a-week radio gig. CKCH
was, at the time, a formatting experiment for owner station CKAC
in Montreal, with a mix of music from past and present; a pop music
combo of new hits – Top 40 songs – mixed in with oldies. The eclectic
format gave Denis a chance to hone his skills for the sophisticated
bilingual Hull/Ottawa listenership that appreciated his special blend
of linguistic patter.

Setting his sights on a bigger audience and market, Denis took
his B.A. in political science and moved back to the big city after an
offer from powerhouse CJMS to do a weekend gig. In the back of his
mind he thought this opportunity could lead to a better shift; maybe
he could be the next CJMS superstar DJ like Michel Desrochers.
The CJMS gig, didn't last long, however, as Denis could see that he
would never realize his dream of doing bilingual radio there. In the
meantime, a new station, CHOM-FM, had become the forerunner
of bilingual radio in Montreal. The station had been extremely successful making inroads with francophone listeners, employing native

francophone DJs right alongside anglophone ones. Why couldn't this approach fly on AM radio, Denis wondered?

In the spring of 1974, Denis took this question, his pitch, and his profile to management at Maisonneuve Broadcasting, which owned both CHOM-FM and CKGM-AM. He was happy to just get an interview with CKGM program director Tom McLean. On McLean's desk was an intimidating pile of audition tapes, evidence of the passage of other Top 40 DJs' dreams. As Denis looked at that pile, his heart sank. But Denis had something unique to offer and, instead of hearing the expected, "Don't call us, we'll call you," Denis heard McLean ask, "When can you start?" Faking aplomb, Denis said he would have to give CJMS two weeks' notice. He was trying to be cool, as if he got job offers like this every week. He was back to the all-night shift, but this time on the No. 1 English Top 40 station in Montreal.

Denis didn't exactly get carte blanche from McLean. CKGM was, in fact, testing the waters with a bilingual Top 40 DJ. On the all-night show, he was allowed three bilingual intros per hour. The all-night shift was where many DJs often improvised and experimented with different bits. Denis decided to add some bilingual comedy to his show. Taking his cue from CFOX DJ Dean Hagopian, famous for his retinue of on-air characters, Denis created the character of Ernie, the CKGM janitor, who would drop in at about 3 a.m. for his mid-morning break. Ernie was patterned after the stereotypical Montreal blue-collar guy. His girlfriend Mona would check up on Ernie "on the job." Denis would sometimes have a three-way, back and forth, speaking in his own voice, as well as in Ernie's and Mona's – two alter egos that kept Denis company in the early-morning hours. Ernie always had a joke to tell, and listeners could tell it was Ernie time when Denis ran vacuum-cleaner sound effects. He and Ernie shared a mid-morning snack and a joke. Mona had the hots for Ernie. She didn't say much, but cooed a lot when she was around Ernie. Ernie was a hit with Denis' loyal followers, and when Denis was given the weekend swing shift (6 p.m. to 12 a.m.), he had Ernie and Mona get married on live radio, adding in the voice of the minister. It was a glorious event, but really it was Denis' way of delicately and respectfully getting rid of the Ernie and Mona characters that wouldn't play as well on the evening shift (though he brought the two back one last time when Ernie and Mona returned from their honeymoon.)

Meanwhile, PD Tom McLean was happy about the way Denis' bilingual show was working out – so much so that he decided to expand the bilingual CKGM experiment by bringing in two other DJs to the mix: Marc Carpentier (retagged Scott to avoid confusion between the two Marcs) and Rob Christie. McLean knew that almost half of CKGM's listeners were either bilingual or unilingual French. It seemed like a solid business decision to test the linguistic waters even more. CKGM's 1976 lineup from 6 p.m. to 6 a.m. the next morning – half its entire programming day – was henceforth given over to a triumvirate of DJs doing their job in both English and French.

Denis was a big hockey fan and, at the time, the NHL's Buffalo Sabres had a high-scoring line comprised of three Quebecers – René Robert, Gilles Perreault, and Richard Martin. They were nicknamed the French Connection in the press, inspired by the popular 1971 detective film/thriller starring Gene Hackman. Denis threw out an idea to CKGM's management: why not take a little poetic license and name the three Quebec-born DJs after the Sabres' star line, but in French? So, with back-to-back-to-back shifts, Denis, Carpentier, and Christie became the Connection Française. Like the spectacular car-chase scene in the film, the boys were about to embark on the ride of their lives at Top 40 speed.

La Connection Française was off and running the same year that athletes from all over the world were running around a barely finished track at the Olympic Stadium in Montreal. In an unprecedented ad campaign, the faces of CKGM's Connection Française were plastered on the sides and backs of Montreal buses. With the exception of high-profile CKGM jock Ralph Lockwood, other CKGM jocks toiled in anonymity, just disembodied voices. Many were happy to keep it that way. Meanwhile, the Connection Française had a kind of celebrity status not usually given to Top 40 rock jocks. They were rollin' through all parts of the city – east, west, north and south – their three faces looking at Montreal, with Denis front and centre, complete with wide-brimmed cowboy hat and a classic 1970s moustache. CKGM marketed T-shirts with their faces emblazoned on the front, selling or giving them away as contest prizes. CKGM was pulling out all the Top 40 radio-circus marketing tools they could think of. The station was riding an Olympic-year high, all the while growing a bigger audience, and making minor celebrities out of the Connection Française.

The 1976 fall rating numbers were very good, with CKGM hovering around the 800,000-listener mark. "It was an exciting year," Denis recalls. "Montreal was on the map of the world and CKGM was on top of its game. We reached our peak. For an English station in a predominantly French-speaking market, those ratings were big. Really big. Almost twice what CHOM had. That was CKGM in the mid-1970s."

Denis had had a big year, too. In addition to being the senior member of the Connection Française, he had been the in-house announcer for the Olympic gymnastics events held at the Montreal Forum, where Romania's 14-year-old Nadia Comaneci had become the first Olympic gymnast to ever score perfect 10s.

Despite the intrusion of disco music on the Top 40, 1976 was a pretty good year for music, too. Top 40 AM radio was now including some album cuts as part of its playlist, as record companies cut down on releasing prime album cuts on 45s. There were still singles, of course; 1960s artists like the Beach Boys, Diana Ross, the Four Seasons, Paul Anka, and even 1950s Brit heartthrob Cliff Richard bounced back with hits that year. Albums like the Eagles' *Hotel California,* Stevie Wonder's *Songs in the Key of Life,* and Peter Frampton's *Frampton Comes Alive* would become classics. "Disco was part of it [the 1970s]," concedes Denis. "And we embraced it. People wanted to hear Abba, the Bee Gees, KC and the Sunshine Band, and Donna Summer. Even Rod Stewart went 'disco.' But the 1970s were great for music. There were great albums that produced plenty of Top 40 hits."

Because CKGM was now a major contender in the market, record companies gave them the first shot at albums just released, much like at CFOX early on when getting a fresh pressing of a new single gave you bragging rights – and more listeners. In the prime time slot, 8 p.m. to midnight, Denis would take three or four cuts from the just-released Fleetwood Mac album *Rumours* and promote a cut every 15 minutes to keep listeners hooked at 980 on the AM dial. Phone in and win; it was the essence of the spirit of Top 40 radio.

Denis got his "Mais Oui" nickname courtesy of fellow CKGM DJ Steve Shannon when they co-hosted the *Top 98* of 1974. Shannon had reached the end of his half of the *Top 98*, and started promoting Denis coming up next as "my friend, mon ami, Marc, mais oui, Denis." Shannon repeated it a few times (Top 40 DJs all had a little inner Dr. Seuss) before Denis came on, and by that time he had grown fond of the name. Marc "Mais Oui" Denis it was. He liked it so much, he's kept it well beyond his CKGM years. It's his brand. He still gets called "Mais Oui" more than four decades after the Connection Française's heyday.

Unfortunately, the Connection Française brand wasn't as lucky. When Scott Carpentier decided to leave CKGM, the continuity was broken. It was a noble experiment that lasted almost a year and a half, an eternity in radio time. Rob Christie was moved to the 2 to 6 p.m. afternoon drive show, where he continued to do some of his show bilingually, but he cut back on his use of French. Denis, still on the 10 a.m. to 1 p.m. slot, soldiered on, but there would be more obstructions ahead for CKGM's bilingual Top 40 radio foray.

CKGM owner Geoff Stirling had been given a certain amount of leeway from the Canadian Radio and Television Commission (CRTC) with CHOM-FM in its early years, allowing the station to do bilingual radio on a trial basis in the early 1970s. At first, the CRTC was willing to let it ride, to see how it would play out. Stirling and Maisonneuve Broadcasting did not have a French-language radio license, nor were they a community-oriented station that was licensed to speak several languages on air. For a period of time, none of the other French-language radio stations in Montreal seemed to care. But with CHOM testing the boundaries and getting traction with both French and English listeners, and with CKGM joining in with the Connection Française, a significant number of French radio stations began to get bent out of shape. CKGM was stealing their listeners; it was, after all, an English station. Stations like CJMS, CKAC and CKAM, CKOI-FM and CKMF-FM registered their complaints, and eventually the CRTC told Maisonneuve Broadcasting that its licenses would not be renewed if its stations continued to use more than a minimal amount of French.

CKGM, for its part, was merely throwing in a healthy dose of both languages tilted towards English; its playlist consisted of only English Top 40 songs. CHOM, on the other hand, was speaking French *and* playing Québécois musical artists. At CRTC hearings, Stirling dug in his heels and for years a kind of linguistic radio war roiled quietly behind the scenes. Both CHOM and Denis continued using French. Stirling told Denis, "Ignore them [the French radio stations and the CRTC]. Keep doing what you're doing. I love it." This was all about ratings. But with the federal government involved, when push came to shove, someone had to give. The battle between the CRTC and CKGM/CHOM went back and forth until the beginning of 1980, when the CRTC finally ruled definitively that no more than five percent of programming at English stations could be in French.

Even after the CRTC put its foot down, Denis was defiant. He did his bilingual show until September 1980. Up to his final show, Denis kept up the bilingual craft he had so diligently perfected during his seven years at CKGM. "I was still speaking quite a bit of French, actually. I knew that I wasn't supposed to," says Denis. "The station knew I wasn't supposed to, but they looked the other way. I was doing it, but I felt strange about it."

At least there was some humour, even if it was dark, after the despair of the CRTC ruling that year, as the first Quebec referendum on independence was set for May 20. Quebec split along two lines: *Oui* or *Non*. In the runup to the vote, tensions were running high. But a Montreal *Gazette* entertainment columnist was able to see a lighter side when he suggested that with the referendum coming up, CKGM might have to force DJ Marc Denis to lose his "Mais Oui" moniker. Not likely, but for a few weeks prior to the May 20 vote, Denis took to calling himself, Marc "Maybe" Denis. Listeners got it and appreciated his deft political touch.

1976 had been a golden year, as CKGM became the No. 3 radio station in Montreal, closing in on 780,000 listeners. Only French giants CJMS and CKAC were ahead of them. But by 1979, all that changed when sister station CHOM-FM overtook them. Denis, as well as all the AM staff, was despondent. Although they still had healthy numbers – 559,000 listeners – CHOM came in with 648,000 for the end of the 1979 and beginning of 1980 ratings book.

"Psychologically, you're still pretty strong," says Denis. "But you know you've just been passed by your little brother." The staff ratings party of 1979, which included both stations, was somewhat subdued. "I remember that ratings party at the hotel with everybody from CKGM sitting over here, and we were all in shock, wondering what the hell had happened," Denis recalls. "Then, there were the CHOM people sitting over there, some of them being cocky because they finally won their street cred; others were sheepishly proud. When I look back on it now, I realize that the erosion of AM radio was happening all over North America." That year would mark the beginning of a gradual ratings slide for CKGM, exacerbated by the 1981 departure of popular morning man Ralph Lockwood.

Denis was barely past his mid-20s in 1980 when he wrapped up his CKGM career. Looking back, it was a time when things were cookin'. Ratings were on the upswing, success was in the air, and it smelled good. Moreover, perhaps more than any other jock, Denis had created something: a smooth-talking Top 40 persona in two languages that entertained and, along with the other two members of the Connection Française, changed the demographics of CKGM while making a little history in the process. It had lasted barely a year and a half. As bilingual as Montreal likes to think it is, no radio station since has done what the Connection Française did. Denis broke new ground. "I owe everything to CKGM and the platform that I received, and what I was able to do with it," he says. "It set me for life. It's strange to say, even after I left CKGM, I was at the right place at the right time with young adults growing up. Whether they were French or English or allophone, when I moved onto other radio stations people would say to me, 'I used to listen to you when I was growing up.' That bilingual gig put me out there, allowed me to show what I could do. And once CKGM was history for me, I was able to do so many other things."

Before semi-retiring in 2009, Denis worked at eight different radio stations in Montreal and Toronto, completing the circle back to Montreal at CINW (formerly CFCF 600), then CIQC, before it switched frequencies to 940 AM in 1999. There, Denis was back spinning the hits he had helped break into the Top 40 back in the 1970s. His facility with English and French continued to be an asset with TV work as host of Télé-Québec's Muscular Dystrophy Telethon, other gigs on TVA, a spot on CFCF-TV as the resident gadgets and technology guy, and playing Monsieur/Mister Quaker State in French- and English-language advertising campaigns. Anyone on an Air Canada flight between 1989 and 2001 may remember hearing Denis' dulcet tones as host of an inflight program called "Coffee, Tea, or Pop."

More recently, Denis has become chief creator and curator of the bilingual online archives for his beloved CKGM with his CKGM Super 1970s tribute page as well as a smaller-scale tribute to CFOX. He keeps CKGM announcers, management, and support staff up to date with an annual newsletter. In 2009, to celebrate the 50th anniversary of CKGM-AM's on-air debut, he organized a grand reunion soirée in Montreal, bringing ex-CKGM people together for a night of entertainment and shared memories.

Robert G. Hall Takes One for the Team: CKGM-AM 980 DJ and Program Director, 1976–1980

Robert Hall is on Highway 401 headed east to Montreal from his home in Minneapolis. His girlfriend and his dog Freckles are travelling with him in his brand new Saab. He was working at Minneapolis' U-100, a pioneering FM station, until former colleague Chuck Morgan, now in Montreal with CKGM, gave him a call saying the station had a midday slot open. With at least one familiar face in an unfamiliar city, Hall decided to take a chance. So he packed Freckles and his girlfriend into the Saab and headed for a new job in a city and country he knew little about. It was a shot behind the mic at a No. 1 Top 40 radio station, and that's all he needed to know. They drove straight through to Montreal, a 20-hour drive when conditions are right. Hall remembers being treated to a spectacular northern lights display late that November 1976 night on a lonely stretch of the 401. It was a good omen, he thought.

Hall was still in high school in 1967 and looking for a part-time job when he wandered into the studios of WSNY in Schenectady, N.Y., and landed a job as the station's summer student gofer. Then he worked in production, before landing some DJ duties. He was a clean-cut, all-American-looking guy with a passion for Top 40 radio, and the station's management thought he was a good investment.

The next year, his senior at Burnt Hills Ballston Lake High School, he worked part-time at WTRY in Albany – coincidentally at the same 980 frequency as CKGM. He did the weekend news and occasionally filled in weekday mornings for the station's traffic helicopter reporter. He was the talk of the campus when the 'copter would land on the high school football field to drop him off in time for classes. But the CKGM offer was just too good to turn down, despite all the variables and stress that come with packing up and moving to another country. His buddy Chuck Morgan told him he was coming to the hottest Top 40 radio station in town. He and the station were on the move.

Hall was arriving in Montreal just a month before the ratings showed CKGM peaking at over three-quarters of a million listeners. The station was in a celebratory mood. Morgan's sales pitch to Hall, however, may have failed to include any information on Quebec's socio-political climate. Montreal was in the midst of a post-Olympic hangover, and Hall arrived the same month as the Parti Québécois victory in the provincial election, mostly on the promise of separating the province of Quebec from the rest of Canada. The city was on edge, especially its English-speaking population. Hall had other concerns, but he had unwittingly walked into a tumultuous time in both politics and radio.

He was in Montreal to be a Top 40 DJ, a job that was decidedly apolitical. Behind the mic, all exterior noise was shut out; if you wanted a dose of politics, you didn't tune into CKGM. Hall was a steady performer, a comfortable Top 40 format man. His accountability and reliability paid off when, after a couple of years behind the mic, he replaced Reg Johns as program director. He took a long walk before he decided to take the position, but ultimately he was a team player, putting CKGM ahead of any gut feelings that told him the job might be, in his words, a "suicide run."

"It was a bad time to get your first command, with no true leadership experience," he says. For his first management role in radio, Hall was facing some erosion of listenership and general station morale. When he took over as program director in the spring of 1979, he recalls, "The station's ratings were in a nosedive after Reg John's approach stalled. No fault of his [John's] because AM was dying, even with CRTC Canadian-content crutches. Ralph [Lockwood] was getting stale, [VP and GM] John Mackey was pitting CHOM against CKGM. The sales staff were dispirited and angry as ratings plummeted, and a huge part of our English audience got up and left town, because of the political situation."

Between 1976 and 1979, when Hall was program director, a steady stream of English-speaking Quebecers left for other parts of Canada. Exact numbers are difficult to pin down, but observers need not have looked further than the cultural microcosm that was CKGM to see that the talent was headed west to Toronto or Vancouver.

Hall admits to making his share of mistakes as the new PD, including when he brought in Quebec radio personality Roch Denis to try and revive the halcyon days of bilingual radio, when the Connection Française had lit up the ratings. It turned out to be bad timing: in 1980 the CRTC put the brakes on both CKGM and CHOM's attempts at presenting themselves as bilingual radio stations. Roch Denis was a failed experiment that Hall had to let go of, and now both CKGM and CHOM reverted to being predominantly unilingual stations, further eroding their francophone listenership. CKGM suffered the most in terms of ratings, but the CRTC edict was not the only factor undermining CKGM's efforts at bilingual Top 40 AM radio. There was disco, too. CKGM was off balance trying to please the rock purists while, at the same time, trying to satiate Montreal's growing appetite for disco music. Add to that the countdown to the May 20, 1980, Quebec referendum on sovereignty, and Hall was about to find out just how off balance one of CKGM's loyal listeners was. But it had nothing to do with disco.

Patrick Di Falco was not a well man. Just 16 days before the Quebec referendum on independence was to take place, he reached his breaking point. The prospect of Quebec separating from Canada was just too much for him. Breaking into his father's gun collection, he selected a Browning 9-mm pistol and headed down to CKGM, his favourite radio station. It was his first day out after being released from a mental hospital. On the drive there, he took pot shots at cars from the window of his vehicle. It was a miracle that no one was hit.

When he showed up at the Greene Avenue CKGM outer offices, his behaviour set off alarm bells with staff. The receptionist called into the studio where Hall and music director Roch Denis were auditioning an album. (To this day, Hall remembers it was the Rupert Holmes album *Partners in Crime*.) Hall decided to call the police, before going to the front-office area where Di Falco was pacing back and forth. He was muttering something about wanting to get then-prime minister Pierre Trudeau and Quebec premier René Lévesque together on CKGM to resolve the whole independence and referendum issue on air. Hall saw the look on Di Falco's face and steered him away from the front-office area and into his office. He talked to Di Falco and tried to calm him down. He then sat down behind his desk and looked up in time to see Di Falco's gun aimed straight at him. "I saw the flash of the muzzle right in front of those mad-dog eyes," he says. "I felt the bullet whiz right through my hair." The bullet lodged in the wall just inches above Hall's head.

Inexplicably – and fortunately for Hall – Di Falco only fired once. Hall managed to assuage him by telling him he would let him on the air. With a gun pointed at his back, Hall moved the drama outside his office towards the announcer's booth where they encountered two police officers with their weapons drawn – both of whom turned out to be rookies. Hall dove out of the way, as both the policemen and Di Falco exchanged gunfire. Despite the close quarters, neither the police nor Di Falco turned out to be particularly good shots. After several shots the two rookies in blue managed to overwhelm Di Falco, before pounding him to the floor. Reinforcements soon arrived and he was handcuffed and taken away.

Months later, off balance, suffering from what would later be known as post-traumatic stress disorder, Hall testified at Di Falco's trial. Hall had come face to face with the man who had almost killed him. "He had the craziest eyes I have ever seen on a human being," Hall says. (For a couple of years after Hall left CKGM, he kept a gun nearby when he slept.)

Di Falco's lawyer tried to deflect the seriousness of the crime by citing the beating that his client had been given by the two policemen. Di Falco was ordered to undergo a 30-day psychiatric evaluation and after a trial was acquitted on all charges. Whether he spent time in a psychiatric facility is impossible to know; after so many years, all court records have been expunged. Hall never felt safe at CKGM again.

After two more anxious years at CKGM, he left in 1982 to take up a job launching the Satellite Music Network in the U.S., at that time in its very early days of development. It was a massive success, growing to 3,000 stations and 10 national formats, before being sold to ABC, where Hall eventually became senior vice-president of programming. He retired after helping to resurrect national network radio – a somewhat double-edged experience for him, since network radio now dominates in the U.S. market, squeezing out local programming.

"My memories of Montreal are bittersweet," he says – an understatement given that his tenure as PD was more like front-line military duty. "The mistakes I made in Montreal were invaluable. They prepared me for much greater things. But I was sad to see the Camelot that was CKGM turn to dust."

CHAPTER FOUR

CKGM's Top 40 Masterminds

JIM SWARD: THE MAN WITH THE MIDAS TOUCH

When the phone rings late at night, it's never good news. There was plenty of tension already in the air on October 10, 1970. Just five days after British trade commissioner James Cross was kidnapped from his Westmount home by four Front de libération du Québec (FLQ) terrorists, Quebec Deputy Premier and Minister of Labour Pierre Laporte was similarly abducted at gunpoint while playing football with his nephew on the front lawn of his home in Montreal's South Shore.

That same night, with Quebec on high alert, a young Jim Sward, barely a year on the job to resuscitate radio station CKGM-AM's fortunes as its new general manager, was awakened by a late-night phone call. The panicked employee on the other end of the line breathlessly told Sward that several men had broken into the station's Westmount studios on Greene Avenue. They had beaten up a security guard, shut down the AM broadcast and were now occupying the station's FM studios, effectively taking over programming.

Reports from the employee were understandably sketchy. He thought maybe there were 12 guys. They were drunk. One had a gun, he thought. Sward turned on his radio, that was always tuned to 980 AM, only to hear silence. Switching to 97.7 CKGM-FM, instead of music or the voice of the night DJ, it was the ranting of a very agitated man, apparently the spokesperson for the group. Sward's French was elementary, but he recognized anger when he heard it.

Then the phone rang again; this time it was the police, with their version of events. On the heels of the Laporte kidnapping earlier that day, the authorities were not in an accommodating mood;

brute force was the course of action. By the time Sward arrived at the radio station, there was significant police presence in front of the building. He could feel the tension, as he sought out the commanding officer for an update on the situation.

For all the 1970 success that CKGM and rookie GM Jim Sward were enjoying, the dynamics of the emerging Quebec separatist movement proved to be a serious reality check for the station. That separatist fervour had arrived at their Greene Avenue front door, and then inside. It was the beginning of the October Crisis and English newspapers, radio stations, and other institutions were feeling vulnerable.

The group took over the CKGM-FM mic and spouted separatist rhetoric. In an attempt to avoid violence, Sward formulated a plan with the police. He would go into the building and turn on his office light within 10 minutes. If the light did not go on, the police could do what they thought was right. He even put his instructions in writing at the insistence of the police. He knew he was giving the police carte blanche to take whatever means they thought were necessary.

He did not receive a warm welcome after getting off the elevator. Some members of the group roughed him up a bit, but he persevered with calm. "I said to them, 'Look outside. And here's what's gonna happen. There's gonna be a lot of people hurt and maybe killed, and the only way it won't happen is if you sit down and talk to me and we can come to some kind of an arrangement.'" The men (no one was counting heads, but Sward recalls there were three women in the group), were still running on adrenaline and revolutionary fervour, but the reality of the consequences of their actions forced them into a more conciliatory mindset. After seeing the heavily armed welcoming party on the street below, they agreed to talk to Sward.

Sward took them to his office, turned on the light and sat down to play mediator. He told them that all but three of the group would leave the building and surrender to police. Three could stay on the air as long as they wanted. Those three stayed another four hours on the airwaves before running out of rhetoric and Led Zeppelin records to play. At 5 a.m., they decided they'd had enough and they too surrendered to police.

In the wake of this incident, the CKGM building was put under 24-hour surveillance, and in the days immediately following Sward was driven to work by a private security firm. Staff were reassured about their safety with added main-floor security. Management chose to say nothing about the event on the air the next morning and the story was never reported in any Montreal newspaper, TV or radio station. Somehow, the story did appear in the *New York Times*. An uneasy normal returned to both CKGM-AM and FM, but neither station said anything more about what had happened. Sward was thankful that a potentially dangerous situation hadn't gone south. He had shown the breadth and depth of his managerial mojo.

As the family of a sergeant-major in the Canadian military, Jim Sward, his four siblings, and mother were used to moving around. Sward didn't know it at the time, but this would prove to be good training ground for his eventual career in radio, which involved moving from place to place. The oldest of five, Sward attended 11 schools on 11 different military bases in Canada, from kindergarten to grade 12. Into his teens, the only environment Sward was used to was the banal white and green of Canada's various military bases.

Being the son of a military man is one step removed from actually being in the military. At 15, when he joined the militia, it seemed as if Sward was headed in that direction. He became a certified sharpshooter three years later, with standing orders to report to government-designated "orange areas" in Canada. In the event of a nuclear attack, he would presumably be part of a post-apocalyptic chaos cleanup. Sward, a registered marksman with his FNC 17.62-millimetre rifle, was on his own kind of high alert, ready to do his duty.

He was good with a gun, but Sward was not that enthusiastic about the possibility of a military career. He had a strong streak of the rebel in him – a rebel with a cause, as it turned out. In grade 12 at General Panet High School on the Canadian Armed Forces Base in Petawawa, Ontario, he was president of the student council. He led a minor student rebellion over the school administration's plans to enforce a new student uniform policy. It was 1962, and the cultural climate of the time did not encompass 17-year-olds' flighty behaviour over school uniforms. As it turned out, he had more than a few followers who left school to demonstrate outside. The principal was not amused. Neither was his father, a man for whom the uniform had been an important symbol all his adult life. It was his mother who fielded the call from the school administration advising her that her son would not be welcomed back next year. Sward took a major hit for his cause, and suddenly found himself academically adrift with no chance to earn a high school diploma. He would need his grade 13 diploma if he were to have any post-secondary educational options. With no other nearby high schools, Sward packed his bags for Ottawa. His army brat life was over.

His plan was to complete grade 12 at Laurentian High in Ottawa by taking night classes and working the day shift to support his new-found independence. He got a job selling shoes and for a while managed to combine the academic and work life without falling asleep in class. Coming home alone each night to his $100-a-month one-room apartment was a definite change of pace for a young man used to the constant activity of a large family.

One day, former Canadian Football League Ottawa Rough Riders player Bruno Bitkowski came in to buy a pair of shoes. Retired from the game, Bitkowski was the sales manager of radio station CKOY (formerly CKOC, Ottawa's first privately run radio station). He bought a pair of shoes, handed Sward his business card and told him to give him a call. A few days later, Sward made the call, and bid adieu to his shoe-sales career to become CKOY's copy boy, fetching commercial copy after the CKOY salesmen had sold an account with local businesses.

For a kid growing up on military bases, life was pretty predictable. But some events have an indelible impact on the impressionable mind of a young boy. For Sward, it was the occasional visits of his uncle, his mother's favourite brother. He would roll up in the summer to their home on the base in his all-gold Pontiac Parisienne convertible, a monster of a car typical of the Detroit auto industry's 1950s halcyon design days. To complete the picture, his uncle always had a beautiful girl beside him in the front seat, her blonde, lacquered hair sitting high on her head, protected from the wind by a white chiffon scarf. His uncle was a radio man at CFCF in Montreal and the business, from an outsider's perspective at least, had been good to him. The biggest car Sward had ever seen was the base commander's Chevrolet Biscayne. His uncle indulged his young nephew by spinning yarns about "civilian" life, a life Sward was unfamiliar with. The more he heard, the more he realized he wanted a life on what army regulars called "civvy street." Better if it came with all the trappings that his uncle had. A young radio wannabe was born, and CKOY was his first step towards the Pontiac Parisienne – and maybe the blonde to go with.

At 18, Sward was in the radio biz, even if it was as a humble copy boy. The first casualty of his new job was his education. He had rent to pay and food to buy, and the new job at CKOY just got in the way of his attempt to get his high school graduation diploma. Bitkowski had become something of a mentor to Sward, but his sudden death brought in a new sales manager at CKOY – one who had a much different style of management to which Sward took an immediate dislike. He was convinced he could do a better job than the new sales manager. After a few months with the new boss, in a moment of pique, Sward quit. He packed up his brand-new used car and headed east for New Brunswick, where he had heard there were some radio job opportunities. Lying about his age, he talked his way into a job as sales manager at CHSJ-AM in Saint John, New Brunswick.

The station was owned by K.C. Irving of the powerhouse family that had extensive business interests in the province, including newspapers, radio and TV stations, forestry, oil, and agriculture. Sward had the occasional tête-à-tête with K.C. Irving himself, which were more pep talks and quick job evaluations than anything else. Irving did not know that his new sales guy was not yet 21. Once, Sward was at the Admiral Beatty Hotel in downtown Saint John with one of the station's biggest clients, the Kent Department Store. When they ordered drinks, the waiter asked Sward for ID. In an instant his age charade was up: he was asked to leave. It was an embarrass-

116

ing moment, but fortunately not dramatic enough to put the Kent Department Store sponsorship deal in any jeopardy. Nevertheless, CHSJ and Sward would part company two years later, by which time Sward could at least have had one final beer at the Admiral Beatty – legally!

By 1967, Sward realized that Saint John was not the market he wanted to settle in for too long. So he took his experience at CHSJ, packed his bags, and headed for Montreal to take up a similar position at CFOX, which had by then become the No. 1 Top 40 radio station in the city.

Sward knew this kind of radio had enormous sales potential. He had it all figured out: "The youth market, 18–34, had commercial viability, so that if you could get enough of them, young listeners, preferably with some disposable income, you could get advertisers. If you got enough of them, you could sell cars. When you think back to the beginning of time – the very beginning of time – was there any sweeter spot to be born in than between 1946–1952? There's no generation before or since that has had that same kind of momentum, influence, and power."

Sward was passionate, but he must have been a bit disappointed as he pulled into the CFOX parking lot for his first day of work in early 1968. CFOX studios were in a nondescript two-storey building in suburban Montreal. At first, he wondered if he'd wandered into another backwater radio station. Despite its location, CFOX's rank in the Top 40 radio market was undeniable, and soon Sward knew he was in the right place, smack in the middle of that sweet spot in radio history.

After a few years, his initial love affair with CFOX waned. It was a rock station alright, but everybody who worked there lived on the West Island: from owner Gord Sinclair, Jr., to many of the on-air personalities and front-office staff. "It [CFOX] was West Island-focused, and it wasn't a sort of big-city rock station that was involved in big-city events like concerts," he says. "The only real exposure they had to big-city events in those days was through concert promoter Donald K. Donald [a.k.a. Donald Tarlton] Productions." Still, under Sward's guidance, the CFOX sales and promotions department knew how to rouse their young listeners. Sward had a job to do and he was not going to sulk and whine about that over which he had no control. He went about selling airtime that allowed CFOX to hire good people. "We did very well and I was able to bring in more money, and that freed up money to hire good Top 40 radio people," says Sward. That money brought in DJs like Ralph Lockwood from WHLO in Akron, Ohio; Charles P. Rodney Chandler from CJCH in Halifax; and British ex-pat Roger Scott from WPTR in Albany, N.Y. Adding those three into the mix of DJs like Dean Hagopian and "Big Daddy" Bob Ancell, who were a part of CFOX's 1965 Top 40 conversion, gave the station a winning lineup. Sward did what he did best at that time: he brought big clients like Pepsi into the CFOX fold. These were the guys who paid the bills.

Looking back on his time at CFOX, Sward acknowledges that there was some great talent on staff. The professionalism of the station's owner, Gord Sinclair, Jr., was unquestioned. Alas, when Sward left CFOX for CKGM in 1970, Sinclair was not pleased. "I wanted to give my two-week notice, but Sinclair wasn't interested. He just kicked my ass out of there. I lost a few friends that day. While I appreciated that he had given me a break as a very young guy coming into sales, by the same token I had a dream, an idea [of what could be done at CKGM]. And if I didn't go, I would kick my own ass forever." Sinclair was losing a top-grade sales manager, but he couldn't have been prepared for how Sward's move would impact the station he owned.

Sward had received a call from CKGM owner Geoff Stirling, who had heard through the tight English-language radio market grapevine that Sward had made a significant impact in his two years as CFOX's sales manager. It wasn't as if Sward was shopping himself around, but if Geoff Stirling called, you answered. He met with Stirling at the swanky Ritz-Carlton Hotel, where he was serendipitously part of a historic conversation that the CEO had arranged with a young university radio DJ, Doug Pringle. Sward sat quietly as Pringle pitched Stirling the idea of transforming CKGM-FM into an alternative rock station. It wasn't exactly the job interview he was expecting and, by the time the meeting wrapped up around midnight, he still hadn't gotten any firm job offer. He knew one thing, however: Stirling was an impressive man. Sward could feel it, even though this was only his first encounter with him. "The second most charismatic man I ever met was Billy Graham," Sward recalls. "The first was Geoff Stirling."

The next day Stirling popped over to Sward's house for a follow-up conversation. "I want you to come in and run it," Stirling told Sward. "You weren't freaked out about last night's conversation or where we want to go or what I want to do, so come in and run this thing." Sward had aced the job "interview" without having to present his CV or do some serious self-promotion. He signed with Stirling, but with one important caveat on the table.

"Stirling told me he had a certain amount of money in the bank set aside for his two Montreal stations' makeover. And then he told me, 'Jim, that's the money you have to fix [CKGM-AM], and when that money runs out and you haven't fixed it, you're out of a job.'" Both stations had been hemorrhaging money for years. Sward knew he did not have an infinite amount of time to work with and, if he went over budget or didn't produce results, the gig was over. "It was a very dangerous job to take," Sward recalls. "But my theory was, I was 24 years old and I didn't have a lot to lose. I was getting a chance to do something that few other people would ever have a chance at."

By the time Sward got to CKGM-AM, it had gone through a number of mixed formats: easy listening, white-bread pop music interspersed with some solid rock 'n' roll shows in the evening, and talk radio. In the mid-1960s, CKGM had brought in the acerbic Pat Burns from CJOR in Vancouver to fire up afternoon listeners. Burns took to the airwaves as a radical element of the growing separatist movement in Quebec had begun to carry out random acts of terrorism, including bombings and bank robberies, to finance their operations. Burns was not shy about trumpeting his views on English-language rights and his disdain for the separatist movement in the province. Apparently a nice enough guy off air, it was his hard-line English-rights stance that got him into hot water. The station received bomb threats, and management was already anxious as a result of a Molotov cocktail incident in 1963 at their Drummond

119

Street studios. Burns was even denounced by Union Nationale Premier Daniel Johnson, Sr. In the end, it was mostly the sponsors' exasperation that led to Burns being asked to leave town. So it seemed to Sward that CKGM had been a radio station that couldn't make up its mind about what it wanted to be. Stirling told him to simply fix it and make the station a Top 40 contender.

With a fresh mandate in hand, Sward set out to put CKGM on a new course in the Montreal Top 40 English-language market, and in the process he aimed squarely at usurping the top spot of the only other English-language Top 40 station, CFOX. Sward began to assemble his resources for a January 1, 1970, Top 40 rock format change. He didn't have to clean house completely, at least not at first. He kept announcers Robert Bell and J.P. Finnegan, who'd been around during the talk show period.

On his first day, Sward gathered the employees together for a casual chat. He outlined what he wanted to do with CKGM. He was not a big, desk-thumping, inspirational speech kind of guy. He outlined his mission and then went looking for the best management talent he could afford. He brought in John Mackey from CJME in Regina and appointed Tim Pratt, from among the salespeople, as manager. Next, a consulting engineer was brought in to boost the signal, kick up the overall sound, and put equalizers into the lines, thus improving the mid-range sound of the station. When the DJs were on, they had everything at their fingertips: songs, jingles and commercials all loaded up. Hit the button and it all flowed like a Smokey Robinson song. "There was no dead air," Sward recalled. "It was Phil 'Wall of Sound' Spector all the way."

Without any big-name advertisers on board, the re-imagined CKGM at first began churning out the hits almost ad-free, saturating the Top 40 airwaves with 50,000 watts of unadulterated rock 'n' roll. When going to advertisers hat in hand, radio station sales staff had to come armed with good BBM ratings to make their pitch. A mail strike in the spring of 1970 prevented Sward from doing that, which meant he had to keep stretching the monthly budget constrictions Stirling had dictated. Finally, in early December of that year, they had the BBM book they needed. CKGM had put a heavy dent in CFOX's listenership. That was a month that sent Gord Sinclair into some serious reflection about the future of CFOX as the No. 1 Top 40 radio station. It was then, too, that Sinclair realized his former sales manager meant business. Sward eventually lured two current CFOX DJs, the big-voiced Steve Shannon and swing-shift powerhouse Jim Patton, to CKGM. The icing on the Sward-baked cake came when he brought back popular morning man Ralph Lockwood from his brief exile in West Palm Beach, Florida, at WPOM.

If Sinclair had been aggrieved by Sward's lack of loyalty – and he definitely was – he was even more so when he saw three of his DJs go to the rival station. Money was a big part of their decision: Lockwood was offered twice what he was making at CFOX. The radio biz is fairly cutthroat and there's not much wiggle room for English radio stations in a largely French-speaking milieu. With a new trimmed and focused programming format, CKGM went right after CFOX. It was nothing personal, but Sward, along with his right-hand man and newly hired program director John Mackey, took a certain delight in demolishing the station that had owned the No. 1 Top 40 spot for the last five years. In the course of one calendar year (from January to December 1970), after Sward took the general manager's position, CKGM had overtaken CFOX. After one year of cranking out the hits, Sward knew the momentum was unstoppable: "We were acting like a big-city radio station in one of the most wonderful cities in the world," said Sward. "And we were winning."

Sward and PD John Mackey worked some magic over the time they spent steering CKGM towards major contender territory in the 1970s. Sward considers Mackey one of the finest radio programmers he's ever worked with. Brilliant, even. He credits Mackey with being the architect of CKGM's programming success during its 1970s renaissance. The market in Montreal was carefully researched (CKGM had 40-percent francophone listeners at its peak in the 1970s, proving that music transcends language.) The bottom line was simple: never let the listener down.

The team of Sward and Mackey were on a roll with the up-front part of the station's makeover. But the behind-the-scenes people like sales manager Tim Pratt, front-office co-ordinator Joanne Rudy and accountant Len Joseph also had a hand in the transformation. They all came together for biweekly meetings called by Sward. He didn't like surprises. Issues got resolved.

Those were some very heady times for a 25-year-old general manager at the helm of a transitioning Top 40 radio station. "It was really exciting for me," Sward recalled. "It was the first time in my career that I had the management controls of a full radio station. I've always had a passion for radio and I had a whole bunch of ideas, so it was thrilling to see it work so well."

Back at CFOX, the DJs that Sward recruited to CKGM could see the writing on the wall. Lockwood, Shannon, and Patton all understood that downtown was where the action was. They could smell an up-and-coming station. It was a shot at the big time. Lockwood, who had a top-rated morning show on CFOX was lured away by Sward in 1972 and immediately installed in the morning drive slot, the most important slot in radio. With his light, breezy patter and a stable of on-air characters, Lockwood was a great morning schmoozer, and his ratings soon took off. Sward looked at this as good economics: if you've got a powerful morning personality, in spite of all the day-long dial hopping that goes on, the next morning the dial is back on 980 CKGM.

The craft of programming, the same craft that would take Sward eventually to the top tiers of Canadian communication companies, was not necessarily based on trying to get listeners to tune in, but rather on keeping them from tuning out. Sward would do the same at CFTR in Toronto when he was hired in 1979 to take on the long-time No. 1 Top 40 station, CHUM-AM. Listeners only had to wait out a 90-second newscast, then it was back to music, probably something from the station's Top 10. "We were trying to say to the listener, 'Don't touch that dial. It's gonna be OK,'" Sward recalls.

Sward put some fine talent behind the mic at CKGM during his years there. Holdovers Robert Bell and J.P. Finnegan were joined by the likes of Ron Able, Michael W. Morgan, Lee Smith, Tom McLean, and Jim Patton. There would always be comings and goings, as it is with most Top 40 radio stations. Other talent included Dave

Marsden, Lee Murray, Mark Edwards, Mike Williams, Bob Charles, Dan O'Neil, Gary Bell, Dave Cannon, Chuck Morgan, Ron Legge, and Donny Burns.. In the mid-1970s, Marc Denis, Scott Carpentier, and Rob Christie would become the Connection Française. Ralph Lockwood would prove to be the most durable and most popular CKGM jock ever.

With CKGM's tight format, Sward knew what a jock was going to play and say at any time of the day. "The announcer's mandate was to stick to the [Drake] format," he says. "At the same time, you wanted them to project an enthusiasm, a momentum, and a charisma that would let the listener know they were having fun. You want listeners to say, 'He's pounding out the music for me and my favourite song is just around the corner.'"

Some of those songs being "pounded out" were by new Canadian rock artists. In 1971, the government got involved in the content of commercial and government-supported radio. The CRTC decided that the Canadian recording industry needed some help. To support Canadian musical artists, they instituted a 30-percent Canadian-content rule on radio stations, famously referred to as the CanCon rules. General managers like Jim Sward had some decisions to make.

But where the hell would they find enough Canadian content to fill almost a third of their music playlist? To address this problem, Sward set up the Maple Leaf Group, a kind of consortium of AM radio programmers from across Canada who would consult with each other, to share the names of acts and songs in their respective cities they thought had the moxie to qualify as CanCon. Out of this came names like the Five Man Electrical Band (Ottawa), Chilliwack (British Columbia), Lighthouse (Toronto), the Stampeders (Calgary), Anne Murray (New Brunswick), the Guess Who (Winnipeg), Joni Mitchell (Saskatchewan), Neil Young (Manitoba), Gordon Lightfoot (Ontario), and the Bells (Montreal). At first, there were slim pickin's. Some listeners must have wanted to shoot their radios if they heard Murray's "Snowbird" one more time.

As far as Sward's Maple Leaf Group was concerned, this was a regulation that was not going away, so they aimed to make the

CKGM general manager Jim Sward (left, beside George Balcan, Donald Tarlton, Gord Sinclair, Walter Machny, and the *Gazette*'s Ian Macdonald with back to camera) represented CKGM (Geoff Stirling also made an appearance) at the Canadian Radio and Television Commission (CRTC) Canadian content hearings in Montreal, 1971. *Courtesy of the Montreal Gazette.*

best of it. "When we [the Maple Leaf Group] consulted each week, we came up with two or three songs we thought would work. It was easy with the Guess Who and 'American Woman,' but not so easy to agree on a folk song like Murray McLauchlan's 'Farmer's Song,'" he says. (Sward was not all that keen on the song. But it was a good decision for the Maple Leaf Group, as "Farmer's Song" went to No. 6 on the Canadian charts and won a 1974 Juno Award for Best Folk Single and Best Country Single, and a nod to McLauchlan as Best Songwriter.)

As a result of the CRTC CanCon regulations, Canadian artists had a symbiotic relationship with Top 40 radio stations. And CKGM, as an emerging powerhouse on the scene, had much to do with promoting and playing Canadian talent. The local concert promoters had a key role to play as well. April Wine, a Halifax-based group that moved to Montreal in 1970, is a prime example of a Canadian group that greatly benefitted from CanCon. GM Sward, with PD John Mackey, worked hand in hand with Montreal concert promoter Donald Tarlton.

By 1970, Tarlton had formed Aquarius Records (with Terry Flood, Bob Lemm and the Lazare brothers, Dan and Jack) and signed April Wine to the label. Tarlton introduced April Wine to CKGM and soon cuts from their album were on the station's playlist. Of course, April Wine was a damned good band. Their first single "Fast Train" got some airplay. Then their follow-up single "You Could Have Been a Lady" topped out at No. 5 on the Canadian charts and made the U.S. Billboard Top 30 for 11 weeks. Everybody benefitted from April Wine's success: DKD Productions promoted their concerts on CKGM, and the station reaped the advertising dollars that came in with it. April Wine songs caught on in every major Top 40 city across the country, including secondary markets where DKD Productions worked with other local promoters to have the band come to their town.

Sward was happy to play the game: "April Wine would be getting concert offers from Sudbury or offers to be the opening act for big rock groups coming into Toronto. The purpose was to put wheels under some of these very talented groups so we could see an output coming in from them."

By 1976 CKGM was a well-oiled machine, celebrating Montreal's Olympic year in fine fashion, with listenership topping 779,800, the highest since its 1959 beginnings, and heavily bolstered by a significant francophone contingent. They should have received an Olympic medal. That was their zenith; they'd never have those kinds of numbers again. In 1974 Sward had brought in announcer Marc Denis who formed the Connection Française with Scott Carpentier and Rob Christie: Sward scheduled them into back-to-back-to-back time slots.

By 1977, Sward felt he had pretty much achieved what he wanted with CKGM. His Midas Touch reputation had got around the tightly knit Canadian radio managerial circuit. He was in a league of his own, having successfully built a No. 1 Top 40 AM station from the ground up. There was only one other market bigger than Montreal's. Sward got another Stirling-like call, this time from Toronto radio station CFTR owner Ted Rogers, son of radio industry pioneer Ted Rogers, Sr.

Sward's nation/station-building days were not over. There was one more mission: to knock off the juggernaut Top 40 radio station in Toronto, CHUM 1050. CHUM was an institution in Toronto: it had adopted a Top 40 U.S.-style format as early as 1957, ahead of any station in Canada. Their opening song appropriately was "All Shook Up" by Elvis, the King himself. DJs like Al Boliska and Jay Nelson had star status, putting CHUM in the driver's seat as the *primo* Top 40 radio station in the city.

CFTR had started out in 1962 as CHFI-AM at 1540 on the AM dial before appropriating the 680 kHz from Windsor station CHLO. (The TR of CFTR was a tribute to radio pioneer Ted Rogers, Sr.) In 1973, CFTR bumped its wattage up to 50,000 and decided to go after CHUM. In 1978, just about one year after Sward arrived, CFTR took over the No. 1 spot. CHUM was seriously bruised after being top dog for almost 21 years, but it hung onto its Top 40 format for another eight years. CFTR also dropped its Top 40 format in 1993, but the "Rock 'n' Roll War" between CHUM and CFTR made for great entertainment while it lasted. Sward put the outcome of that war succinctly: "We beat their [CHUM's] ass; we shoved them out of the business."

Just as he had done when he left CFOX, Sward was not averse to poaching talent from CKGM to strengthen CFTR's run to the top. Initially, he thought he had talked Lockwood into coming to CFTR, but that deal fell through when Lockwood got cold feet. When all was said and done, he had lured DJ Tom McLean, CHOM program director Leslie Sole, and Peggy Colson-Weir to CFTR. The attempt to take Lockwood away from CKGM alienated more than a few people at CKGM: Lockwood was their one true guaranteed ratings ticket. For Sward, it was all about ratings, part of the business end of radio.

An even bigger accomplishment for Sward in Toronto was converting CFTR's sister FM station, CHFI, from easy-listening instrumental to soft rock, and making it the top FM station in Toronto. More importantly, under his direction, within about five years, revenue went from $1 million to $20 million. In 1989, after 11 years as president and general manager of Rogers Broadcasting, Sward decided to leave. His legacy was two stations ranked No. 1 – not bad for a former shoe salesman from Petawawa.

After Rogers, Sward took over as president of Cantel, then moved on to become president and CEO of Global TV, before retiring in 2000. "After splits, Global shares went from about one to 22 dollars during my time there," Sward says. "I worked for share options, so I retired after Global. All this was half luck (right place at the right time) and half hard work." That luck and hard work allowed him to join the Freedom 55 Club one year early.

During his career, Sward was active in the affairs of the broadcasting industry, including serving as chair of the Radio Board, then chair of the Television Board and, finally, chair of the Board of Directors. In 1989, he received special recognition for his work with the Canadian Academy of Recording Arts and Sciences. This award was partly in recognition for his role in helping to create FACTOR, the Foundation to Assist Canadian Talent on Records. In 1990, he was presented with the Edward S. Rogers and Velma Rogers Graham Award. He was inducted into the Canadian Association of Broadcasters Hall of Fame in 2001. His good friend Geoff Stirling, another CAB Hall of Famer, congratulated him in writing, "You gave me seven years of freedom from business worries [at CKGM]."

Since retirement, Sward and Gail, his wife of 47 years, have joined the legions of Canadian snowbirds who flee the cold. From his west Florida home, Sward takes out his 22-foot boat to fish for snook and redfish in the Gulf of Mexico. When the frost lifts, he's back to either his Haliburton cottage retreat or his home north of Toronto, where he entertains his son, daughter, and two teenage grandchildren.

JOHN MACKEY: THE IDEA MAN

John Mackey was a natural at sales and promotion. While working as a copywriter and music director in the mid-60s at CKWW, the Geoff Stirling-owned station in Windsor, Mackey and the sales team took on a challenge from an ad agency hired by Coca-Cola to promote a new soft drink. The agency had offered the opportunity to several small-to-medium-sized radio stations in southern Ontario to come up with the best idea.

As a junior member of the CKWW sales and promotion staff, Mackey thought this was an ideal opportunity to make his mark in the radio biz. He decided to put some serious sexy spin on a brand new drink. Mackey sold the station on the idea of putting up a platform on a billboard at a major intersection in downtown Windsor with a bikini-clad girl waving as people walked and drove by. Below the billboard a couple of hired souls gave out samples of the new soft drink, and it wasn't long before a crowd gathered. The combination of a girl in a bikini and free soft-drink samples was just too much to pass up. The Coke ad agency was very impressed, and Mackey's idea was copied in several other markets. The station's management took notice, as did its owner, who asked Mackey out to drinks with CKWW's managers. As he often did, Stirling held court at the bar table and talked about his Montreal station CKGM. He had a phone brought to the table and dialled a special number which hooked him up with CKGM's live programming. Stirling shared the phone with the others at the table. Mackey was impressed with Stirling's ideas and brilliance. It was 1966 and Mackey was just starting out, but he allowed himself the thought of one day working in Montreal radio. His time would come. But first, after Windsor, he was headed in the opposite direction to the considerably cooler and bikini-unfriendly confines of CFQC in Saskatoon, then CJME in Regina.

Mackey grew up in Mimico, which today is merely a geographic area in southwest Toronto after being absorbed by the Greater Toronto Area amalgamation in 1998. Mimico was a collection of 1930s and 1940s cottages built near the shores of Lake Ontario when Mackey was born in 1941. It was already in decline as residents moved to larger, more modern accommodations outside the town. Mackey's mother married twice. Her first husband died when Mackey was only two years old. Her second husband was a Lake Ontario fisherman who moved his new family around a handful of fishing villages like Port d'Or, Fort Erie, Wheatly, and Kings. They were not a happy family. When he turned 17, Mackey took a $17-a-week job as a dental technician in Leamington just to get out of the house. He had not finished high school, but he was tired of the combative family climate.

His future, however, was not in teeth. He multi-tasked as a sports writer for the *Leamington Post*, worked as a PA announcer for the local junior hockey team, then went on to write advertising copy for the local radio station, CJFP, where he wound up as sports director. Now hauling in 40 bucks a week, he was on a roll. Before heading for CKWW in Windsor, he worked about six months covering the city hall beat in Chatham, just 80 kilometres east of Windsor. Mackey was doing a kind of southwestern Ontario radio and newspaper circuit not far from his fisherman stepfather's life, but his subsequent move to Saskatchewan would take him well out of his comfort zone.

He had trouble adjusting to the brutal winters of Saskatoon and Regina, but as program director at CJME, he was growing the foundation of his radio business knowledge. "It was a great experience," Mackey says kindly of the two cities whose average winter temperatures put them in the top five coldest cities in Canada. That cocktail encounter in Windsor with Stirling came back to him during his second dark winter in Saskatchewan. He called CKGM station manager Don Wall, whom he had met with Stirling in Windsor that day, who had told Mackey that if he ever wanted to work in Montreal he should give him a call, which in business parlance is the equivalent of "Let's do lunch," a rarely followed up, casual kiss-off. But Wall was an honourable man and offered Mackey a job writing commercials for the sales team. The copywriting job wasn't exactly what Mackey had in mind. So there was another stop in Vancouver before he got a call in 1970 from new CKGM general manager Jim Sward, who offered him the program director job as the station prepared to crack the Top 40 market in Montreal.

Mackey had covered the radio business from the bottom up; he was, in his own words, an "up-and-comer." But after his stint in Regina, Mackey had almost given up. The travelling, the different cities, and the failure to settle in had been hard on his marriage. By the time he hit Montreal in 1970, Mackey's wife had returned to her hometown of Windsor. Mackey was on his own again, but this time would be radically different from his dental technician days in Leamington. He was about to become a major player in turning CKGM into a rock 'n' roll force at 980 on the AM dial in Montreal – a bumpy, but exhilarating ride to the top of the ratings.

As program director, Mackey worked closely with new CKGM general manager Jim Sward. With Sward's sales experience and Mackey's programming background, the two made an effective team. They set their sights on challenging CFOX, which had a five-year head start in the Top 40 market but didn't have access to a significant number of urban listeners. CKGM, however, didn't have what Mackey thought was an extensive enough collection of Top 40 records. However, he knew just where to go to beef up the record library. Hopping into one of the CKGM news cruisers one day, he drove to Detroit to do some cross-border shopping. (Growing up and working near the massive Michigan market, he could pick up stations like WABC in New York, WLS in Chicago and WKRK in Detroit.) In Detroit record stores were miles ahead of anything that Montreal had to offer at the time. With a fistful of CKGM dollars in hand, he bought over 600 singles – heavy on the Motown sound – turned around, and drove back to Montreal.

Montreal was a natural fit for R&B music, but it had taken a long time for Canada to catch on to the Motown Sound compared to the U.S. Tamla Records which broke new ground for a niche, mostly black, audience in 1959 when founder Berry Gordy, Jr., got it going with an $800 investment. A year later, Gordy renamed it the Motown Record Corporation, a blend of motor and town, symbolizing the essence of Detroit. Headquarters for Motown Records had "Hitsville, U.S.A." written on the front, and over the years that's exactly what they produced: 79 Billboard Top 10 hits between 1960 and 1969. Amongst Mackey's 600 records bought in Detroit was a collection of those hits, which would constitute the solid-gold portion of CKGM's Top 40 programming, rotated in and out of the lineup. The Motown sound never seemed to go stale and Montreal embraced it. Black artists were no strangers to Montreal: James Brown, Wilson Pickett, and even Duke Ellington had played the Esquire Show Bar, a club that regularly featured black artists. Rockhead's Paradise, sometimes referred to as the "Harlem of the North," was another club that featured mostly black jazz musicians. Mackey used the Motown sound as a promotional tool, running all-Motown weekends, where the first three records of every hour were R&B hits – and Motown Mondays. Those 600 singles became the backbone for the station's Top 40 success.

The Motown promotion was prompted by the success of another Mackey idea: the all-Beatles weekend, which was a huge ratings boost for the station. At first, CKGM was doing all of this with barely any major advertising contracts. DJs were playing four songs in a row with no commercial interruption. Although this was not great for the profit margin, the listeners loved it and word on the street had it that there was a new player in town. Because the station's 50,000 watts covered a lot of Montreal territory, CKGM attracted a significantly large young francophone demographic. Its signal reached east, west, north, and south of the island of Montreal, a major factor in its success and CFOX's eventual failure.

Mackey was good at promoting CKGM, growing its profile in a very short period of time. Building on its "CKGM, the Rock of Montreal" image, the station's promotional brain trust devised a contest which involved listeners trying to guess the contents of a black six-foot-by-six-foot plywood box planted on *Man and His World*, the former Expo 67 site. DJs would give out clues, mostly sly and deliberately vague. Then, a lucky listener (never the first caller – many listeners had radio stations on speed dial) would call and take a shot at guessing the black box's contents. It is a testimony to the times that no one took a chainsaw to the box to circumvent the contest parameters. In fact, there wasn't anything inside. Eventually, someone figured it out and won a $10,000 diamond ring – the "rock" – courtesy of the Rock of Montreal.

Then there was the promotional campaign designed to change the way Montrealers answered their phones. Listeners were asked to mail in their name and phone number so that they could get a call from a 'GM jock. If they answered, "I listen to CKGM," then they were $1,000 richer. Many answered with a "Hello," so the station was in no danger of going broke. "Such simplicity," says Mackey of the campaign. "But the point was we were embedding the call letters of the station into the minds of people."

There was a certain dark humour to another promotion Mackey hatched. Everyone in town knew CKGM stole its traffic reports from CFCF and CJAD, both of which could afford traffic helicopters. For some reason Mackey decided to rub that in a bit by running a billboard campaign that read: "98 CKGM: The Only Station Using Two Traffic Helicopters." The word "using" was key to CKGM's claim: they weren't saying the helicopters were theirs. CJAD's program director, Ted Blackman, took offence and placed a rebuttal ad in the *Gazette*. "Congratulations to CKGM, Montreal's No. 1 Teen Radio Station from CJAD, Montreal's No. 1 English Radio Station," the ad said on more than just one page of the newspaper. Mackey remembers that CJAD's ad was interpreted by some as a bad case of sour grapes. CJAD (and Blackman) later decided it was a bad move and called Mackey to apologize. "I told him there was no need to officially apologize [in a public way]," says Mackey. "I told him he'd done enough for us already." There was no bikini-clad woman on the billboard, but Mackey had managed to make a splash anyway.

The atmosphere at CKGM in the 1970s was buoyant after DJs and staff began to believe that the station's foray into the Top 40 market was not an ill-conceived notion. The success was palpable and quantifiable. Everybody was young; everybody was having a good time. Not everyone took the business as seriously as Mackey, though.

At its ratings zenith in the 1970s, a good part of CKGM's success could be credited to morning man Ralph Lockwood, whose free-wheeling style sometimes ran up against Mackey's idea of how a DJ should operate. Although Lockwood delivered the all-important morning-slot ratings and became the premier recognizable face of the station, Mackey felt Lockwood was not a team player. With his comic bits and character voices, Lockwood was not a strict follower of the tight Bill Drake-like Top 40 format that put music above personality. Lockwood *was* CKGM for almost 10 years after coming from CFOX in 1972, Mackey admits. But his casual attitude didn't jibe with Mackey's program director mission. "He was great," Mackey says. "But he could have been so much more. I told him, 'Ralph, you do the same thing every day. You need to prepare more, get some new bits, some new voices.' He was a lot of fun, but it seemed to me his radio show was secondary to his social life."

To make his point, Mackey even went so far as to post a sign outside the CKGM elevators, declaring the area a "danger zone" between 10 and 10:15 a.m., when presumably anyone coming off or waiting for the elevator could be run over by Lockwood leaving the CKGM building. Whatever Lockwood's faults in Mackey's eyes, no one could argue with the results: "When he [Lockwood] did a bit that was maybe too long, what are you gonna do when you're falling out of your chair laughing?" After all, while other CKGM jocks came and went, Lockwood enjoyed the longest tenure of any Top 40 DJ at the station.

Before Lockwood came on as morning man, CKGM had Donny Burns at the helm. Burns had a made-for-Top 40 radio voice, one that would have him doing 'GM's Donald K. Donald concert-promotion commercials. Burns was a one-take natural. His reputation, and his voice, would make him some major money in the profitable national radio commercial business. Mackey had called Burns in Halifax, where he was doing the afternoon drive show. It would be a step up for Burns to come to Montreal and do the morning gig. "He was a real jock with a great voice," Mackey says. "When he introduced a song, he could pull you right out of your chair to listen."

After Lockwood's arrival, Mackey moved Burns to the afternoon shift, not exactly a demotion but Mackey thought he lacked the personality to attract a bigger morning audience. Like Lockwood, Burns also had bad habits when he was CKGM's morning man. Mackey sometimes ran into Burns at a bar on Crescent Street late at night, when he knew his morning man had to get up at 5 a.m. This distressed the tightly wound program director. Mackey was concerned that Burns wasn't taking his job seriously enough and took a fatherly interest in one of his top DJs. "I told him, 'Donny, you've got your priorities mixed up.'" Burns, however, loved the life and cachet of being a Top 40 DJ in his prime. Mackey just wanted to see his DJs improve. Some were whacky and untameable, like Jeff

Newfield, who Mackey had brought in from CFRW in Winnipeg to work weekends. Renamed Bob Charles at CKGM, Mackey took a chance with Newfield, who had a frenetic, unpredictable on- and off-air personality. Newfield/Charles had a talent for mimicry. On one of his weekend CKGM shows, he pretended to be interviewing Ringo Starr in studio, only just slightly changing the first name to Dingo. His imitation of Starr was so convincing that hundreds of young, gullible listeners thought it was the real thing. They came downtown to CKGM's Greene Avenue studios in Westmount to catch a glimpse of Ringo himself. There were so many people on the street that Mackey got a call from the building custodian who feared the crowd was going to crush the windows of nearby storefronts, and CKGM's. Mackey got on the studio hotline and told Charles all hell was breaking out in front of the station. Charles was enjoying the reaction, but he was instructed to say on air that Ringo (Dingo) had been taken out the back door. The crowd was disappointed and quickly dispersed.

The next day Mackey got a distressed call from the Westmount police chief admonishing the station for pulling off the Ringo stunt. Ever the manager, Mackey told Charles it would have been better to do the bit with the fake Ringo over the phone. "I was trying to be mad with him," Mackey says. "But he was being creative." No one got hurt and hundreds of disappointed Ringo fanatics told all their friends. It was more free, word-of-mouth advertising, and Mackey loved it.

Charles was just beginning, as it turned out. He moved on to do some of his best work at Q107 in Toronto as Scruff Connors, actually dressing for the role by growing a beard and wearing grubby clothes. When in Toronto, Mackey occasionally met up with Connors, still attracted by his off-the-wall approach to life. It was easier when Mackey didn't have to be the boss. "He did some really crazy things. I think they [Q107] were sued at least three times for stuff he did on the air. For a brief time, that diamond in the rough was part of our [CKGM's] mix," Mackey proudly says.

Mackey had helped launch CKGM as the No. 1 Top 40 station in Montreal. Owner Geoff Stirling rewarded him by moving him to his two Windsor stations, CKWW and CJOM-FM, as general manager and vice-president. In 1974 he came back to Montreal as GM and VP of CFCF-AM 600 and its FM outlet CJQR, bringing in long-time CJAD morning man George Balcan, a move that proved ill-fated for both Mackey and Balcan. In 1978, he was back as GM and VP of both CKGM and CHOM-FM. He had helped coach CKGM to some major wins. By the end of 1976, ratings put them near the top, including all French-language AM stations, with almost 780,000 listeners.

With the AM side on auto-pilot, Mackey turned his attention to CHOM and brought in new sales manager Phil Parker, and Rob Braide as program director. Together they set about transforming CHOM from a loose, alternative FM radio format to AOR (album-oriented rock) programming. It was more or less the equivalent of the AM focus of "all the hits, all the time" only with selected prime album cuts on the menu. The CHOM purists, nurtured on the free-style approach since 1969, were bent out of shape. CHOM was going corporate, selling out to The Man. Just the transformation of CHOM made news, the kind of free advertising close to Mackey's heart. CHOM was Geoff Stirling's baby and Mackey was aware that if he dropped the ball, his job was on the line. He dared to rebrand CHOM as "Rock 98" CHOM-FM, dangerously close to AM-style labelling.

AOR took most of the control out of the hands of the individual DJ and put it into the hands of the program director and general manager. CHOM's unfettered format days were over. Results from the CHOM about-face soon came in. For Mackey, who, after all, was responsible for both CKGM and CHOM, the ratings for December 1979 brought him mixed emotions. CHOM had surpassed its sister AM station by a considerable number of listeners – 648,000 to 559,000 respectively. On the one hand, he could be proud of his CHOM gamble, but at the same time he was overseeing the decline of CKGM-AM – and Top 40 radio in general. The station would never be No. 1 again.

Geoff Stirling had faith in Mackey, and Mackey returned the favour by doing a stellar job of turning both of Stirling's Montreal radio stations into major league operations. But in the fall of 1981 or 1982 (Mackey is not sure), he flew to meet Stirling in Arizona where they had a heart-to-heart conversation about Mackey's future with Maisonneuve Broadcasting. Whatever it was that was bothering Mackey (he won't say what), he and Stirling had reached a professional impasse. Mackey resigned. "We reached a point where it was just time to shake hands and say goodbye," Mackey says. He didn't know it at the time, but his resignation was the beginning of the slow fade-out of his career in radio.

He took a break, did some cross-country skiing at his cottage in the Laurentians, and caught some sun and surf in Hawaii and Mexico. He was feeling a little off balance. He nonetheless jumped back into the game with CJBK in London, Ontario, followed by stops at stations in Ottawa, Toronto, Thunder Bay, and finally Vancouver. The 1980s were tough for Mackey, as he battled anxiety and depression. After the trailblazing days in Montreal, a kind of malaise just seemed to envelop him. It was getting more and more difficult to get up for the job. After a year in radio in Vancouver, he told the manager he just couldn't do it anymore. It was 1990 and the last year he would work in radio.

He retreated to familiar territory in southern Ontario, coming full circle and settling in a small village not unlike some of the villages he once lived in with his fisherman stepfather, mother, and siblings. When Geoff Stirling died in late 2013, memories of his CKGM and CHOM days came flooding back. He missed Stirling. "He was a mentor to me. I saw him as a visionary," he says. "It took me weeks to get over his death. I thought that even though we hadn't seen each other in 27 years, I really felt I'd lost my best friend. If he hadn't hired me for CKGM, my career might have been nothing."

[CHAPTER FIVE]

News, Weather, Traffic, and Sports, Top 40-style

Top 40 radio provided listeners with bare-bones news: generally 90 seconds twice hourly, except in the prime morning and evening time slots. If it wasn't for the fact that there were regulations stating they had to have a newscast, management probably wouldn't have bothered. Still, the dynamics of Montreal (and the province of Quebec) provided plenty of news fodder, even for stations whose newscasts came in highlight-package format.

The boys in the newsroom – and it was, for the most part, a male-dominated business – took their jobs seriously. With limited resources and severe time constraints, they did the best they could. Sometimes their news made the news and, just days before the Quebec election of 1976, the CKGM newsroom hit the equivalent of gold.

The election campaign sent the whole province, and country, into a collective hand-wringing and general anxiety. The newly formed Parti Québécois (PQ) had garnered only six seats in the previous election in 1973. Now, three years later, it was gaining traction with the general electorate. CKGM news director Gerry Dixon decided to take the pre-election pulse of Quebecers with a phone survey, asking a cross-section of voters if they thought the PQ might win the election. The survey found substantial support for the PQ. The majority of those polled thought the PQ would actually win the election, a revelation that the *Journal de Montréal* placed on its front page. It was rare for the French press to pick up an English-language story from other sources, especially a Top 40 radio station not known for its investigative reporting.

The CKGM poll predicted a PQ win, something that seemed unlikely, given the ground they had to make up. The Robert Bourassa-led Liberals went into the 1976 election with a 102-seat majority. When all votes were counted that November 15, the PQ came away with a stunning 71 seats; the Liberal Party won a paltry 23.

The political angst from that election is still being felt today, but for the boys in the CKGM newsroom, it was their *Washington Post*-Watergate moment. There would always be plenty of political fodder to report on, as the country held its breath for four years in the runup to the 1980 Quebec independence referendum. It was an exciting time to be in the news business.

GERRY DIXON: CFOX AND CKGM
NEWS ANNOUNCER/NEWS DIRECTOR

Gerry Dixon was an unlikely newsman. He started off as an aspiring rock musician with the Soul Magicians. Backed by a young Donald K. Donald, the group toured Quebec and Ontario in search of the proverbial big break. That finally came to an end when the guitar player, who owned all the equipment the band was using, decided to get married. With his rock star dream broken, Dixon did a little soul searching and decided radio would be his next move. His bilingualism got him through the front door at CFOX in 1972, first as the overnight DJ, then in the news department, though the 'FOX's fortunes were on the decline. A couple of years later, it wasn't a difficult decision to jump ship to CKGM, a station whose fortunes were headed in the opposite direction. The new job meant more money and more listeners. Under the tutelage of news director Lee Marshall, he learned the ropes of Top 40 radio news, and then took over when Marshall moved on.

The news day at CKGM began at 4 a.m., with the first newscast at 5:30 a.m. The morning man was in place at 6 a.m., but it wouldn't be until about 7 or 8 a.m. that a detailed newscast came on. Between 10 a.m. and 4 p.m., the CKGM news team ran 90-second updates. It was more like snapshot news, topped off with weather and sports.

In those days of teletype machines, which were fed mostly by the Canadian Press, there would be some "rip and read" stories hot off the teletype machine, though some rewriting was required to fit the Top 40 news format. "In those days, we deliberately said this was a 90-second news update," says Dixon. "We were saying to listeners, 'Hang on, don't change that dial, the music will be back in no time.'" There were CRTC guidelines requiring AM stations to run a certain number of minutes of news per hour and the updates fulfilled the regulatory body's guidelines. Occasionally, the news would run long, which led to arguments between the newscaster and the more aggressive DJs who were anxious to get back to their show. But with morale-pumping moments of glory like the 1976 election story, the CKGM news team took heart from the fact that they could compete – at least for credibility – with CJAD and CFCF, who devoted much more time to their newscasts.

It was a little disheartening, nevertheless, for the reporters at CKGM who had to contend with the resources and credibility of stations like CJAD and CFCF who, at news conferences, were always front and centre with their questions. These and other similar stations had their man at city hall, and even a dedicated reporter who covered Quebec City politics. "We were sort of like second-class citizens," says Dixon. For the 1976 election-night coverage, the very election for which 'GM had boldly foretold the results in their phone survey, the CKGM news team was in the studio taking results from local TV stations. The music kept rolling. There would be no continuous coverage at CKGM. "No budget for it," says Dixon. The morning after, CKGM news hyped the fact that they had correctly forecast the results. Their election newscast the next morning started with, "As predicted by CKGM News . . ." The Top 40 radio biz provided only a few bragging-rights opportunities for newsmen.

Despite the fact that he knew CKGM's news was secondary to the music, that didn't stop Dixon from doggedly pursuing news stories with a vigour true newshounds have embedded in their genes. The mid-1970s was a vibrant time in Montreal, filled with colourful characters like Premier René Lévesque, labour leader Louis Laberge, Prime Minister Pierre Trudeau, Mayor Jean Drapeau and prominent lawyer and future prime minister Brian Mulroney. The Cliche Commission was looking into corruption in Quebec's construction industry. Dixon interviewed them all. His facility in French opened doors for him that other 'GM reporters couldn't get through. That those in-depth interviews were ultimately edited down to 15-second sound clips is a discredit to Dixon's dedication.

Dixon came the closest to being part of the story when he and fellow CKGM newsman Alain Montpetit joined a police chase in the streets of Montreal. The police were hot on the trail of twice-escaped convict and murderer Richard Blass, who had attained mythical bad-guy status in Quebec. Dixon and Montpetit, in the CKGM news cruiser, followed the police who were pursuing Blass through the streets of Montreal at speeds of 60 mph. "I remember almost crapping my pants because it was very dangerous," says Dixon. "And here we are doing live reports on air. Nobody else had the story except for CKAC, who had a police monitor. We were monitoring them." Blass was dangerous. In October 1975, he and an accomplice walked into a Montreal bar and shot dead two men who had testified against him. Three months later, Blass went back to the same bar and murdered 13 people, ostensibly witnesses who had been there to see him kill the two men. Dixon and Montpetit gave up their pursuit, but not the police, who eventually caught up with Blass in a cottage in the Laurentian Mountains north of Montreal. In a Wild West kind of finish, Blass was shot 23 times by police. Led by Dixon, CKGM news was right in the thick of a major story and once more, the 'GM news team had a scoop.

Sometimes, the stories struck close to home and heart. A six-year-old girl had been reported missing, and police were on high alert searching for the girl. When the girl's body was found three days later, Dixon was one of the first reporters on the scene. It was not pretty. The girl's uncle had raped and murdered her. When Dixon phoned the story in, he was given time to present the story with the passion and respect it deserved. Dixon became emotional live on radio, a rarity for newsmen who strived to be impartial and detached. The story had struck a chord with the father of two young daughters. "As one of the first reporters on the scene, I was interviewed by other radio stations," says Dixon. "I took it upon myself to blast people who didn't take care of their kids. I was speaking as a father, not a reporter. I remember that one like it was yesterday."

Dixon is proud of his time as news director at CKGM. The CKGM news department never had any pretensions about what they were, compared to other more news-oriented AM stations. Everyone he worked with was professional and many went on to other careers in news, both in radio and TV. After CKGM, Dixon moved to CFCF. He received recognition in 1978 from a grateful federal government for his role as a hastily conscripted hostage negotiator at the Archambault Federal Prison, where some inmates took 19 people hostage and Dixon was instrumental in successfully ending a dangerous situation. "It's not something I would do again," says Dixon. "It was pretty tense. I never knew if I was going to get out of there alive."

Dixon has made more than a few job moves since his days in radio, finally retiring after two stints at CFCF-TV. "We were just a bunch of young guys trying the best to do our jobs," says Dixon, now 65, of his time at CKGM. "Anytime there was a news story, we were on top of it. We made every story count, with the limited amount of time we had. Then the music came back on."

RICHARD MAXWELL: CKGM NEWS ANNOUNCER

Richard Maxwell and Jeff Ansell both worked under the steady hand of Dixon when they first broke into radio at CKGM. Today, almost 40 years later, they are a team at Jeff Ansell and Associates, a Toronto-based communications consulting company established by Ansell in 1995. Ansell and Maxwell had stayed in touch over the years, despite the fact that Maxwell's tenure at CKGM lasted a brief 10 months in late 1976 and early 1977. A few years after leaving CKGM, they were together again in the newsroom of powerhouse Top 40 radio station CHUM-AM in Toronto. There's a certain symbiotic trajectory to their journey in the radio biz, so it was a natural fit when Maxwell partnered up with his old 'GM newsroom colleague.

Maxwell was barely out of high school in Ottawa when he went to work in the newsroom at CFGO. Just before the PQ election of 1976, he got a call from Dixon asking if he was interested in a job at CKGM. He could hardly contain himself as he drove to Montreal in record time. "He offered me $13,000," says Maxwell. In a somewhat foolhardy moment, Maxwell turned the offer down. "I held out for $13,500." The day he started at 'GM, René Lévesque was the premier-elect of Quebec. This would be his first day of French immersion. "I was living at this great apartment complex in downtown Montreal. I'm all of 18. The place had a sunken living room. I'm working at CKGM. It was the greatest," says Maxwell. CKGM had a sound that set his diaphragm afire. "It was the compression and reverb," he remembers. "With headphones on, you'd speak into the mic and it would sound like the voice of God was coming across the air. Jeff and I were so young. We couldn't believe they'd even let us on the air." In no time flat, he was immersed in the post-election politics of a PQ election victory. He must have been pinching himself when he had an après-news conference with René Lévesque. Vancouver-born Maxwell had a rudimentary high school French-language background, but he spoke to Lévesque in English. Lévesque may have taken a hard line on the French language in Quebec, but he was very comfortable, and eloquent, in both languages. They both smoked and chatted casually as Lévesque's guard was down for this essentially off-the-record conversation. "He was nice to me," says Maxwell. "I grew up in Ottawa, where Lévesque was vilified in the English press. He was the guy who wanted to break up Canada. Maybe it was because I was so young and he was just putting up with me, but I didn't see him as anything but a nice man." It was a moment in time that wouldn't make it to air, not even as a 15-second Top 40 news clip, but that encounter remains one of his more profound radio memories.

For news guys on the road covering an event live in the 1970s and 1980s, communication with the newsroom was a technological chore. The engineers at CKGM had put together something akin to a portable phone, an apparatus Maxwell says reminded him of something out of a *Get Smart* TV episode. It was the size of a small suitcase, with a row of buttons, an antenna and a telephone handset attached. The reporter would have to find a conveniently located window to maximize the effectiveness of the antenna. The call would go through an operator who dialled the radio station, and the reporter filed or taped an on-location report. Then, of course, there was the phone booth. To file a phone report, Maxwell unscrewed the speaker portion of the phone and attached two alligator clips similar to the ones used to boost car batteries. Then, after dialling the CKGM newsroom, he fed the audio tape through the line. Mission accomplished, all done without Agent 86 Maxwell Smart's "Dome of Silence."

His brief apprenticeship at 'GM served Maxwell well when he moved on to CHUM in Toronto. There, he wrote and produced the morning show, before branching out into creative and promo writing for their FM station. He had a 25-year career with CHUM, which ended with him as director of new media. He then jumped aboard the satellite radio phenomenon at Sirius XM as program director for the show *Laugh Attack* on their comedy channel. All of his experiences in radio are now wrapped up in Ansell and Associates, where he now teaches others how to handle new media.

JEFF ANSELL: CKGM NEWS ANNOUNCER

Jeff Ansell was weaned on CKGM. In his Montreal home, his parents had the dial locked on CKGM in their pre-Top 40 days, with music and talk format mix, and with acerbic hosts Pat Burns, Joe Pine, and Tom Sherrington. On Sunday, his mother loved to listen to Pastor Robert Johnson, the golden-voiced minister whose shows, *Ask the Pastor* and *The Naked Truth*, were the forerunners of current affairs and advice call-in shows that enjoyed a short-lived heyday on CKGM. Then there was the inimitable Buddy Gee, who was the precursor to 'GM's full Top 40 format switch in 1970. Ansell remembers his mother taking him downtown to see Buddy Gee on location. "I was about 11 or 12," he says. "Buddy Gee was at Place Ville Marie playing rock music. They had go-go dancers, the whole '60s thing going on. My mouth was open the whole time. There he was, live. The dancers in short skirts. I was smitten."

About the time that the Buddy Gee era ended at 'GM in 1968, the downtown station had moved to 1310 Greene Avenue in Westmount. It was outside their new location that you'd see the teenaged version of Jeff Ansell hanging out after school waiting to spot a CKGM DJ or two. He wanted in. He used borderline harassment tactics reminiscent of the side-stage doors of 1940s Broadway, where aspiring actors looked for an inside connection. "Hey, are you an announcer?" Ansell would say as people went in and out of the building. He'd even do an on-street audition if the right person went by. Eventually, CHOM's Earl Jive – Live Earl Jive to his listeners – took pity on Ansell and gave him the basic CHOM internship package: he got to hang around the radio station and pick up after the jocks. He was an ace ashtray cleaner and took advantage of the opportunity to make an audition tape with CKGM equipment, flogging it to any and all English radio stations in Montreal. He fancied himself a DJ, but was willing to just get a foot inside the door behind a mic. Montreal's multilingual community station CFMB gave him that first crack, but only because Ansell had worn down the station's owner with repeated phone calls to follow up on his audition tape. He told the owner he was 19 and a university student at Sir George Williams University, a bit of a lie to make things legal and respectable. In fact, he was 17 and had dropped out of high school. For about a year, he did the morning news in English alongside his French colleague. It wasn't long before he got an offer from CKGM news and headed off to the building he could find blindfolded. This time there was no ashtray cleaning in his job description.

It was a quick learning curve in Top 40 AM radio news; you either had it or you didn't. Even though news director Dixon was a patient mentor and easy to work for, news announcers were mostly ready for action, gaining experience with on-the-run tutoring. When Ansell was not anchoring the news, he was out in the CKGM news cruiser responding to an accident or fire. He drove the cruiser, the CKGM call letters emblazoned on each side, with a certain pride. Occasionally, he took it home and parked it on the street, an open ad for the station and his newly acquired status. He was living, and driving, the dream. CKGM news leaned toward the entertainment factor of news, when other more serious news didn't get in the way. After all, their demographic was the 16 to 35 crowd.

In December 1973, it was with considerable hype that the film *The Exorcist* descended on theatres across North America. It was a must-see film, even if it was between fingers covering both eyes. Ansell was sent to check out rumours that the film was making people throw up in the aisles of Montreal cinemas. Fortunately, this was not the case on the night Ansell was there to interview people coming out of the theatre. The vomiting was left to the demon-possessed character of actress Linda Blair. *The Exorcist* was a huge hit given its horror-film label, garnering 10 Academy Award nominations. It took in some $441 million worldwide, and its soundtrack album, *Tubular Bells* by Mike Oldfield, became a standard on CHOM-FM. They played the hell out of it. Hardly hard-core news, but versatility was part of the job.

Although Ansell's tenure at 'GM was not that long, it was an auspicious beginning for a guy who just a few years earlier had been hanging out on Greene Avenue trolling for a job. Just as Dixon had done, Ansell moved over to CFCF, which took its news a little more seriously. From there, it was onto the big time in Toronto and back to Top 40 radio news at CFTR before reuniting with Richard Maxwell at CHUM-AM.

Not all radio guys have TV-friendly faces, but Ansell easily made the transition to City TV where he was a reporter/anchor. He used that experience as a platform to then produce and host his own TV shows, and pioneer media training videos before finally founding Jeff Ansell and Associates in 1995.

Now he and Maxwell specialize in media crisis communications and teach public speaking. Not bad for a guy without a high school diploma. "Working in the CKGM newsroom was a highlight of my radio career," says Ansell. "It was the most popular rock station in town. When I started at CKGM, Ralph Lockwood was doing the morning show. I had just turned 18 and CKGM was the only station my friends and I listened to. I remember driving in to work one day listening to the morning show, when Ralph told a joke about me. I must confess that just hearing Ralph say my name was such a thrill."

Another CKGM news alumnus, Murray Sherriffs, was similarly star-struck when Lockwood would occasionally drop into the matchbox-sized newsroom to offer some encouragement. "Murr," said Lockwood, using the short form of Sherriffs' first name like the hapless newscaster Ted Baxter did with news writer Murray Slaughter on the popular 1970s sitcom, *The Mary Tyler Moore Show*. "Great package, great package." Lockwood didn't much care if Sherriffs' newscast went a little over the 90-second limit of Top 40 radio. "Ralphie was very cool," Sherriffs says. "He knew what to do, when to do, and who to do. He just knew stuff."

Alas, not every jock was as laid-back about news announcers who went over the 90-second headline news, sports, and weather package. Other DJs might complain to management about the news guy cutting into their show. On Top 40 radio, the music and the DJ came first and second respectively. Sherriffs, for the most part, did not try to swim upstream. At 26, he was already a well-travelled newsman when he signed on with CKGM. In 90 seconds he could pump out six or seven headline news stories, one or two sports scores and a quick weather check. "Once you accept the fact that the music comes first, then the jock, you understand where the news goes in the hierarchy of things on Top 40 radio," he says.

The news was taken seriously by the guys putting it together, but not always by the DJ on duty. On occasion, a DJ would wander into the news announcer's booth to try and throw off his timing. Stories of DJs setting fire to news copy in the middle of a newscast are legend, but pedestrian compared to what Sherriffs witnessed one day. A DJ came into the newsroom while the announcer was in full report mode, undid his zipper, and laid his penis on the table. Without missing a beat, the news guy briefly hit the mic kill switch, then thumped his fist down on the unsuspecting body part. "The DJ is hurting something fierce but he couldn't make any noise," remembers Sherriffs. "He's hopping around holding his crotch and the news guy never missed a beat. Whoa, baby, that was entertaining."

Like Ansell, Sherriffs did not graduate from high school. He dropped out of St. Leo's Academy in Westmount after two attempts at grade 10. At 16, he worked at the Montreal *Gazette* as a copy boy, then briefly at CJAD, where he caught the radio bug and decided to take a course through the National Institute of Broadcasting. Then, he hit the radio road with stops in Medicine Hat, Peterborough, Kitchener, Victoria, Edmonton, Montreal, Calgary, and then Montreal again, where he would spend the biggest chunk of his radio news career.

There's always a news story that stands out in the myriad of stories covered in a lengthy radio career. While at CKGM in 1978, Sherriffs was in charge of assigning stories for the day. When word came in about a bus crash east of Montreal, he decided to cover it himself. He arrived to witness a grisly scene. The brakes of a school bus had failed, sending the vehicle off the road into a lake near Eastman, a small town in the Eastern Townships. There were 48 passengers on board: most of them were physically or mentally handicapped and were travelling with their church caretakers. Only seven people survived, making it the worst bus accident in Canada at the time. "To this day, I'm haunted by the memory of a priest's body being hauled up by police divers," says Sherriffs. "He was just a young guy, trying to save one of the passengers but couldn't swim. The police are trained to handle this stuff, but not reporters."

Sherriffs has been a fixture on the Montreal radio news scene for CFCF, CJAD, CJFM, and CFQR, with perhaps his best and happiest years doing news on the Aaron Rand and Tasso Patsikakis (a.k.a. Paul Zakaib) afternoon show. Sherriffs would find himself on the outside looking in at both CFQR (re-branded Q92, then the Beat 92) and CJFM (first renamed Mix 96, then Virgin Radio), as those stations changed format and hired younger, and cheaper, staff. Without a radio job for the first time in more than 45 years, Sherriffs learned how to drive an 18-wheeler and went on the road once again. Perhaps just a little too road-weary after a lifetime of moving from place to place, Sherriffs quickly parked that career change and took up home renovations. Then, in August 2014, he was back behind the news mic for BOOM 99.7 in Ottawa. "It beats the hell out of driving an 18-wheeler and doing home renos," says Sherriffs. Unfortunately, in the more unpredictable radio climate of the corporate era, Sherriffs, along with several other radio personnel under the cross-Canada Corus umbrella, were let go in June of 2016 and now Sherriffs is using his newly acquired downtime to take up writing, a lifelong passion of his.

MARY ANNE CARPENTIER: TAKING CARE OF TRAFFIC AND WORKING OVERTIME

Ralph Lockwood, CKGM's morning man, is stripped naked to the waist in the studio, the thermostat turned down to a near-hinterland temperature. Lockwood really leans into the mic and his frenetic morning pace tightens up his shoulder muscles. He introduces a song, gives a time check, turns the mic off and motions to traffic reporter, Mary Anne Carpentier. Time for his morning massage. She dutifully comes into the studio and gives him a therapeutic shoulder massage—definitely not in her job description as a traffic reporter, but she's more than happy to oblige despite the fact that, as the morning rush-hour reporter, she has to keep up with the chaos, filing a report every 10 minutes from 6 to 9 a.m. She's even checked with Lockwood's wife Lois to see if the shoulder thing is okay with her.

She and Lockwood have good chemistry, and their mildly suggestive and flippant banter is all part of the show. Ralph's a little risqué and she gently puts him in his place. Their exchanges are part of the success of Lockwood's top-rated morning show, which has taken Carpentier out of the obscurity of CKGM's record library and place her at the intersection of Montreal morning radio.

Born in California in 1947, Mary Anne McFall was something of a child prodigy in her teenage years. She attended one of the more prestigious arts schools on the West Coast, the Chouinard Art Institute, which would become the California Institute of the Arts – founded and created by Walt Disney. Attending art school in L.A. meant McFall was close to what would soon be referred to as a kind of cultural revolution – the California version – which duelled with New York City for trend-setting, fame-seeking artists. California

148

had the Beach Boys, who had striking West Coast beauties like Mc-Fall in mind when they wrote "California Girls."

The Fillmore West in San Francisco was at the epicentre of the music revolution, hosting concerts that were part "happening," part music – like the Celestial Synapse, a musical event held at the Fillmore West in February 1969 that heralded the psychedelic era of rock music. The performance began with a Tibetan Buddhist monk playing gongs and chanting, essentially the opening act for the Grateful Dead, who played the Fillmore West 64 times between 1968 and 1971. Politics, religion, and rock music had joined hands on the West Coast. California was feeding cultural cues to the young people of North America. The change swept east with the winds and soon it was a coast-to-coast shift in the cultural and musical dynamic. It was a memorable time for the impressionable McFall, who was taking it all in.

After her art school education, she began a mission towards self-discovery. She hit the road – the European route. She was inspired by Jack Kerouac's book, *On the Road*. With a couple of girlfriends as travelling companions, she headed for Paris, touring Europe and North Africa, the chosen route of thousands of young Americans, Canadians, and European travellers who were looking for adventure in the 1960s. She returned to California, not with her two girlfriends but with a French-Canadian man whom she had met in Europe. They married and had a son, then packed up the West Coast life to move to Quebec. It was late in 1967, the waning of Canada's 100th year celebrations. The marriage, unfortunately, didn't last long. Mc-Fall then met another Quebecer, Yves Carpentier, whom she married, and they added a daughter to the family mix. She had graduated from flower child to mother and wife; suddenly, she had a lot going on in her life.

With her husband and a McGill University sociology student, she set up Drug Aid, a drop-in centre which helped young people deal with drug and alcohol problems. Then along came more casualties of the 1960s: runaways and draft dodgers with nowhere else to go. At that time, in Montreal, there was a significant number of young males who sought refuge in Canada from the Vietnam War draft. Montreal had a reputation as a draft dodger-friendly city, and Drug Aid was part of a movement to support them. There was an overwhelming need for young people in Montreal to voice their anti-war sentiment by helping Americans such as singer/songwriter Jesse Winchester, who had chosen the city as a safe haven.

But working at the drop-in centre, however noble a project, did not pay all the bills. In 1972 a friend of Carpentier's, who was the executive secretary of CKGM general manager Jim Sward, told her that there was an opening in the record library. Sward interviewed her and, after a few weeks, she got the call to come in. With record librarian Bonnie Truscott as mentor, Carpentier learned the ropes but was soon "discovered" by newsman Lee Marshall who put her on the air to do traffic for the morning and afternoon rush hours. "You're a voice and you'll go far with it. This is where you belong," Marshall told her.

Morning man Ralph Lockwood had a reputation that intimidated Carpentier. He was flippant and quick-witted, and she wasn't sure she was up to the pace and pressure. She had no prior radio experience. This was Lockwood's first year at CKGM, too, but he was hardly a rookie. "So I thought, 'Okay, well, I'll do the job and try my best,'" Carpentier remembers. The simple approach is best, she figured. Marshall had advice for her: "Just be light-hearted and goof around with Ralph and stuff like that, because he's a goofy guy and he'll be good to you."

Lockwood never tried to take advantage of her inexperience by embarrassing her on air. This was his gig, but she was part of it, as was his sidekick operator/producer "Crazy" Bruce Morel. It helped that Carpentier could take a joke. "I tried to be a personality without overdoing it," she says. "It was a lot of double-entendres from Ralph, a brisk repartee, and much kibitzing. I grew up in the show business world of L.A., so I understood shtick. It came very naturally to me. Ralph was very fast and so was I. We had good chemistry."

Carpentier didn't bruise easily. She rolled with the occasionally sexist banter between her and Lockwood. They were both acting and it was good for ratings. "It was a different time," she says, and a lot of fun. "We were young. We were sexy. It was not meant to be salacious."

Mary Anne Carpentier and Ralph Lockwood (seated) with operator/producer "Crazy" Bruce Morel in background formed a triumphant CKGM morning show trio, 1974.
Photo by Garth Pritchard courtesy of the Montreal Gazette.

Carpentier was good at what she did and the jaunty back-and-forth made for good, wake-up morning radio.

Carpentier took the business of traffic reporting seriously. While she was parrying with Lockwood, there was important information that Montreal morning drivers needed to hear. Back then there were no traffic cams with views of major Montreal arteries. There were, however, the CJAD and CFCF traffic helicopters. During commercials and songs, she monitored the two competing radio stations for their traffic reports and made the odd call to the provincial police. Listeners called in, too. On one occasion, a driver was so frustrated with the traffic, he pulled over for a coffee and used a public telephone to tell Carpentier about it. Those were loyal listeners, and they got to hear their name on the radio. The "theft" of other stations' traffic reports didn't rattle CKGM's credibility. Everyone listening knew where Carpentier got her traffic info.

The traffic job came with a certain amount of schmoozing with sponsors. They enjoyed it when a radio celebrity showed up at their restaurant or car showroom. Carpentier accepted invitations to local restaurants that were clients of the CKGM sales department. Then, she incorporated the restaurant name into her traffic report. Lockwood would ask her what she did last night. It was all planned. It was good for business when she slipped in the name of the restaurant she had dined at the night before. That was one of the perks of the job. As long as she was in Montreal, the meal at that restaurant wouldn't cost her a dime.

The demands of the job were hard on Carpentier's marriage. Working the drive show mornings and afternoons made for some weird hours. She was up early, home for an afternoon nap, and back to the studio for the 4 to 6 p.m. rush hour. Personal appearances were also on the agenda from time to time. She had two children, one of whom had special needs, and services were not affordable or readily available. For her first year at CKGM, no one but one trusted colleague had any idea she was the mother of two. So, she simply played the role of the carefree, perhaps available woman. "While all else in my life was going crazy, I had my career to keep me sane," she says.

Carpentier then made a career move to Top 40 radio giant CHUM, in Toronto, a bigger market and an expanded job description, where she honed her skills by branching into producing magazine-style entertainment reportage. Carpentier calls CHUM her "palace," a place where she got to shine and mature professionally. She racked up some serious credibility in Toronto as a producer, announcer, and consultant.

Just like her male counterparts, Carpentier's career trajectory was hardly geographically linear. After her stint at Toronto's CHUM, she returned to Montreal, to CFCF Radio, to work with legendary morning man George Balcan, who had been lured away from CJAD. That's a decision she regrets to this day, as Balcan would leave after only a year at CFCF because of conflicts with ex-CKGM program director John Mackey who was hired in 1974. She would go on to work in Halifax, Ottawa, Toronto and, from 1985 to 1988, reunite with Lockwood at CKGM.

It was a different station that Lockwood and Carpentier returned to in 1985 when 'GM had abandoned its Top 40 format, going instead with something they called "Lite Rock, Less Talk," which was antithetical to the Lockwood style of broadcasting. (CKGM later changed the format to "Favourites of Yesterday and Today.")

Lockwood was under new management and under a lot of pressure to revive 'GM's flailing ratings. For Carpentier it was the same old Ralphie, except for a certain something that seemed to be missing. He was more subdued on air, without the characters he used to deliver via his vaudeville-influenced humour. There were fewer bits with less room for spontaneity. Carpentier, while returning to her familiar position of traffic reporter, was now also the station's entertainment editor. After one more move to Toronto to resurrect Oldies 1310 AM, she had finally had enough of the nomadic radio life and took refuge in her Lunenburg County, Nova Scotia, cottage, where she revived her arts school roots.

In 2003 she married a retired Air Canada pilot, the two settling into the warmth and comfort of Tucson, Arizona.

"I just loved my career," Carpentier says. "I immersed myself in it. We were all so talented," she says of her CKGM days. "We were energetic and beautiful. And we gave it our best shot and won; there's nothing better than that. Montreal was just rockin' out. When I want to feel better, I just think about all of that."

KATIE MALLOCH: FROM CKGM TO THE MOTHER CORP

Katie Malloch is just happy to be in radio, even if it means she has to get up at 3 a.m. for her 4 a.m. to noon CKGM news shift. (To this day, whenever she hears Elton John's "Philadelphia Freedom" or the Captain and Tennille's "Love Will Keep Us Together," it takes her back to those dark, lonely mornings.) She's 23, and like Mary Tyler Moore, she's arrived. The recent McGill graduate is not used to early morning hours, having lived the life of the aesthete for the past four years. This is more like the time she might go to bed, not wake up. Her first newscast won't be until 5:30 a.m., so she has time to wake up on the job, scan the morning newspapers, check the newsroom teletype machine, and make a phone call to police to see if any overnight crimes are worthy of reporting.

Top 40 radio newscasts in the mid-1970s were tightly written, headline style. They ran 70 to 90 seconds, including a quick look at sports and weather. It was still pretty quiet at that time of the radio day; the morning man, Ralph Lockwood, would be on at 6 a.m. when Malloch would do a couple more newscasts, before Montreal was at the breakfast table getting ready for the ride into work or school. The big newscast was at 8 a.m., only Malloch wouldn't be the one doing it. That job fell to news director Bob Durant. Malloch was writing his newscasts and his editorials. Though he complimented her on the quality of her writing, it was not Durant's "policy" to let a woman do the prime-time, "meaty" newscast. That, apparently, was a man's job.

Back in 1963, just before the Beatles, the Dave Clark Five, and Gerry and the Pacemakers left for the big bucks of the North American market, they were already stars in their own country. There, with them, for one pre-British Invasion year, was a temporarily displaced preteen direct from Westmount, courtesy of her father's one-year sabbatical from teaching English literature at McGill University for a temporary teaching post at illustrious Cambridge University. It was only right that Katie Malloch and her family should end their trans-Atlantic voyage in the Liverpool harbour. There they rented a car and began the drive to Cambridge. Her mother, getting into the spirit of the adventure, turned on the car radio and spun the dial until they locked in on a song that would add some serendipitous poetry to their Liverpool landing. Whatever station it was, Katie, her three younger siblings and mother were just in time to hear the strains of the Beatles' "Love Me Do." They were already beginning to feel less homesick. Their father, maybe just a little distracted, was concentrating on keeping to the left side of the road.

It was great timing, since Katie was hearing a Beatles tune a good six months before any of her school pals at Westmount High would have. Things were looking up for a girl in something of a sulk over having to leave her friends behind to go to some place she thought of as snotty and boring. "It seemed like the end of the earth to us. I remember bursting into tears when I heard I was going to be going to England for my grade 7 – a whole year! It felt like I was going to the outer reaches of Mongolia or something." She was leaving her comfortable Montreal home behind, but she was dropping in on a major musical, about-to-bust-out revolution in Britain that would soon soothe her anxiety. Rock artists yet to tap the North American market were regulars on TV shows like *Top of the Pops, Ready, Steady, Go*, and *Thank Your Lucky Stars*. She would see the Beatles, the Rolling Stones, Freddie and the Dreamers, Cilla Black, Gerry and the Pacemakers, the Searchers, and other freshly formed groups and singing artists getting major exposure weekly on the BBC. After a few months, Katie settled down to write letters home that made her Westmount High School friends green with envy. Mongolia? What Mongolia? Prof. Malloch had a happy preteen on his hands. Her homesick tears dried, she decided England was one pretty cool place after all.

Back in Canada in the summer of 1964, she was full of stories from the Old Country, her gaggle of girlfriends rapt with attention and envy as she told them of her British immersion experience. They had some stories of their own, as the Beatles had finally hit North America in February of that year, debuting on the popular *Ed Sullivan Show* in New York. In Montreal, Malloch joined the reams of instant Beatles fans who tuned into *The Dave Boxer Show* on CFCF-AM 600 to hear their favourite songs. She joined his fan club and became one of "Boxer's Bubbies," the name Boxer gave his fan club members. "Boxer Bubbie" membership qualification was simple: just listen to Dave Boxer – and only Dave Boxer. Inspiring devotion and loyalty was part of Boxer's efforts to build an audience. Malloch entered a CFCF contest where listeners had to write to Boxer to say what bugged them about his show. Malloch wrote him that she hated it when he talked over the musical intros to the songs. Her critical insight won her, and four other contest participants, a Saturday afternoon in the CFCF studio with Boxer himself. "I thought it was so exciting to be in a radio studio all afternoon," she says. "I remember how stained his fingers were from smoking, and he seemed so grown-up, his hair all Brylcreemed up – no Beatle-type haircut – with a V-neck sweater. He played great music. I was just awestruck."

As awestruck as she was, that day in the studio with Dave Boxer would be surpassed on September 8, 1964, when the Beatles played the Montreal Forum. Malloch and her boyfriend, who lived next door, went together to the evening show, the second of two the group did that day. Her hero Dave Boxer was on hand, sharing emcee duties with CKGM's Buddy Gee and CJMS's Michel Desrochers. She and her date didn't exactly have front row seats; it was eight dollars general admission, first come, first served. "We were sitting so far away that you could barely hear a thing," she says. "So this experience that I had been anticipating for so long, I didn't want to say it was a disappointment. I wouldn't admit that to anyone at the time. It was great just to be there. But, it was not a wonderful experience." George Harrison remembered the group's Montreal experience years later, as quoted in a book that is part of *The Beatles Anthology* released in 2000. "We went to Key West from French Canada, where we'd thought Ringo was going to get shot. A Montreal newspaper reported that somebody was going to kill Ringo. Because they didn't like his nose or something? Because he was probably the most British of the Beatles? I don't know. Anyway, we decided, fuck this, let's get out of town, and we flew a day early, instead of staying the night in Montreal."

Although Malloch had her own meagre collection of 45s, she was a Boxer devotee for the most part. He had his fennortinzer [as he called it], basically a dime-store plastic slide whistle he used to punctuate his patter. Malloch went out and bought one of her own. Like thousands of other Boxer fans, she wrote in to get a questionnaire sent to her, which she describes as a kind of "personality qualifier" that she filled out and mailed back, along with two dollars. A few weeks later a little wooden pendant arrived in the mail. "This little kind of tiki pendant was meant to be hung around your neck," she says. "In the middle was a cut-out hexagon or octagon that supposedly told what kind of person you were. The girls' was concave. Talk about sexual symbolism, right? The boys' was convex, so when you met someone else with one you tried to fit them together as a test of compatibility, I guess. It was complete horseshit but, hey, I was 15 years old."

Boxer had a way of bringing people together, whether it was with music, contests, or gimmicks like wooden pendants. Malloch thinks Boxer tried to come across as everybody's big brother. He would suggest to listeners that they drive to the Orange Julep on Décarie Boulevard or the Westmount Lookout. This was pure *American Graffiti* stuff – before the movie! Kids were together, either at home doing schoolwork or at some teen hangout, but never far from their radio. "He wasn't trying to be a kid because he knew (and we knew) he was older than that," Malloch says. "But he wanted to be the kind of cool uncle who brought kids together."

Meanwhile, her AM Top 40 hero, the cool uncle, was growing up on air. One night, Boxer admitted on air he had fallen in love and was getting married. Boxer had gone to Israel on holiday and had fallen for an El-Al Airlines stewardess. Perhaps some of his female fans were disappointed, their favourite, single, and available DJ was walking the aisle.

Boxer's impending nuptials might have been the topic of conversation at Nick's Restaurant on Greene Avenue in Westmount, not too far from Malloch's high school. She and a bunch of her friends were regulars at Nick's, where they could run into some of the cute boys from a local boys' private school, St. Leon Academy, an all-French Catholic school. The two teen solitudes intermingled easily at Nick's, fuelled by adolescent hormones. There she met Alain Montpetit, a student one year her senior. She was 15 when he became her first serious boyfriend. Her mother began worrying the day Katie came home with Montpetit's ring on a chain around her neck. Gone was the CFCF tiki pendant. He was her first love and it stung her deeply when he broke up with her. Strangely, though, she would remain connected to Montpetit beyond her brief teenage fling.

Montpetit had a good pedigree. His grandfather, Édouard Montpetit, was founder of the University of Montreal's Faculty of Social Science and his father, André, was a high-profile lawyer who served on the Quebec Superior Court. For the short time that Montpetit and Malloch were an item, he shared with her his interest in theatre and radio. As a 15-year-old budding radiophile, Malloch related to his artistic leanings.

157

Malloch worked at Radio McGill for her entire undergraduate years. While she was still a student, albeit a graduate student tending bar, she ran into Montpetit, who was now married and working in the CKGM-AM newsroom. During their Montreal reunion conversation, he tipped her off to a job opportunity in the news department at CKGM. After she did land a job there, they would see each other briefly, as he was on his way out the door at 4 a.m. and she was on her way in.

Montpetit's career trajectory would take him in a radically different direction after his job as newsman at CKGM. Disco was happening big time in Montreal in the mid-1970s – some say almost as big as New York where the famous Studio 54 nightclub was the kingpin of the disco phenomenon. Montpetit rode that disco wave to radio stardom at CKMF and as host of a TV disco dance show on Montreal's Télé-Métropole. He became Montreal's king of disco, with all the trappings of stardom including late nights fuelled by drugs at Montreal's premier disco destination, the Limelight nightclub.

There were plenty of women in the clubs, attracted to his smooth-talking ways, matinee idol looks, and celebrity. A relationship he had with Paule Charbonneau was floundering when one night at a New York disco, he asked up-and-coming Québécois model Marie-Josée Saint-Antoine to act as an intermediary between him and Charbonneau. Saint-Antoine was not interested in getting involved and after a heated exchange, she left the club. The next day her body was discovered in her New York apartment, the victim of multiple stab wounds. Montpetit returned to Montreal surrounded by scandal and suspicion. Though a suspect, he was not charged. A witness, who later recanted her statement, told police Montpetit had been with her the night of the murder. Although he continued to work in Montreal, his career and personal life were in a major tailspin. In July 1987, he was found dead from a cocaine overdose in a Washington, D.C., hotel room. He was 36. Malloch was stunned when she learned that her teenage boyfriend and short-term CKGM colleague had died in such a tragic fashion. She had casually followed Montpetit's career, catching the odd news story about his acting, radio, and TV endeavours. In 2002 the New York City Police

Cold Case department reopened the case and declared Montpetit posthumously guilty of murdering Marie-Josée Saint-Antoine, another piece of information Malloch had trouble digesting. The cold-case verdict was small comfort for Saint-Antoine's family, who had been devastated by her death – and by the suicide of her distraught father weeks after his daughter's murder.

Montreal's Limelight disco era was recreated in the 2011 film *Funkytown* based on Montpetit's and former CKMF colleague Douglas "Coco" Leopold's prime disco days. The bilingual film was a big hit for those remembering their 30-year-old dance floor moves. For others, it brought back some painful memories. Broadcasting the news was mostly an impersonal process, but sometimes boundaries got crossed. On March 29, 1975, a young girl named Sharron Prior went missing in Montreal. Three days after her disappearance, police told Malloch that they had found the body of a young female who had yet to be identified. Malloch decided to lead her newscast with the story, telling listeners that police had found a body but didn't know if it was Sharron Prior. In her zest to put out a kind of scoop, she thought nothing about the effect this information might have on one particular listener. Back at her desk shortly after her newscast, she took a call. It was Sharron Prior's mother asking Malloch if she had any more information. Malloch's stomach sank. "I had this sickening feeling, 'oh my god.' You forget that there are real people involved in these things. I didn't know what the proper protocol was."

The police had not contacted Mrs. Prior because they had not yet done a forensic examination, but eventually they confirmed it was the body of her daughter. "It just made me feel so badly that I hadn't understood a more graceful way to handle it, because when the mother called you could tell she was dying for someone to be able to tell her anything about her daughter." The Prior case remains unsolved.

For the two months she was at 'GM, Malloch looked forward to 6 a.m., when the station really woke up with the arrival of morning man Ralph Lockwood and his operator/sidekick "Crazy" Bruce Morel. Lockwood would turn the studio thermostat way down and

159

doff his shirt for his three-hour shift. Lockwood worked hard and, when he was on, he was razor sharp. He juggled music, news, traffic, sports, and multiple time checks for the bleary-eyed listener trying to be on time for work. He was like the Groucho Marx of Top 40 radio, with some choice, cheesy jokes, wordplay, some flirtatious banter with the traffic girl, and, of course, Top 40 music to get people out of bed. "Time to get up, sleepy heads," he would say to his mostly youthful listenership, all of whom would rather crawl back into the fetal position if not for Lockwood's early morning exhortations coming over their bedside radio-alarm clock.

Malloch loved to watch him work. "He had very positive energy," she says. "Sometimes he would come into the newsroom and say, 'How you doin', sweetie?' He wanted everything to be good for people. He had nicknames for everybody. Made fun of everybody, even the news people. He was king of the clubhouse and he could make jokes about whomever he wanted. He was what I'd call affectionately respectful. He was fun to work with. A real pro."

If Lockwood had had more time to chat, he would have found out Malloch wasn't doing fine. The early hours were killing her. After about a month on the job, her skin rebelled and she broke out in the worst case of acne, "killer acne," she calls it. She asked news director Bob Durant if she could work the afternoon shift. "The city isn't ready for a woman newscaster in the afternoon," was his reply. "It's mostly still a brotherhood out there," says Malloch. "But at the time I knew that if I wanted to do hard-core news, CKGM wasn't the place for it. Their mindset, too, made me realize I wasn't going anywhere." Rather than just hang on, she quit.

Malloch would find a new radio home at the CBC, where the hours, the pay, and the level of respect, were a lot better. Malloch moved seamlessly from CKGM to the CBC, after passing her staff announcer's test, and she soon joined Wayne Grigsby on the afternoon drive show *Sounds Unlikely*, which she later did solo under the *Homerun* banner. This is where Malloch really hit her stride, combining her AM work with *That Midnight Jazz* on CBC-FM before moving on to do four nights on a show called *Radio Active*, which featured international French-language musical artists.

Afterwards, Malloch reunited with former *Sounds Unlikely* partner Wayne Grigsby for a weekly CBC-TV arts and entertainment show, *Stepping Out*. She also worked for Montreal CBC-TV as its resident current-affairs reporter.

But it is the 23-year *Jazz Beat* run that put Malloch on the CBC coast-to-coast map, making her one of the premier jazz announcers in Canada. Her show helped promote the early days of a much more modest Montreal International Jazz Festival, by recording concerts to be played throughout the year, interviewing jazz greats, and giving Canadian jazz musicians a platform they did not have on national radio until then.

In 2012, it was time for Malloch to bring her 40-year CBC career to a close with a three-city farewell tour in Montreal, Vancouver, and Toronto. "It was the right time to go," she says. Just as it was after her brief but passionate AM news career.

CHAPTER SIX

The CFOX Years
From Country to Rock and Back Again

DEAN HAGOPIAN: THE DEAN OF MONTREAL

In the mid-50s the rural town of Galt, Ontario, had a population of 19,000. There was not much going on Saturday nights, especially for its younger residents. Seventeen-year-old Dean Hagopian and a few of his buddies drove up to a hill nearby. With maybe a mickey of rum and a few beers on hand, and the car radio on, this was as good as it got for the boys from Galt looking to pass the night without getting into any trouble. Their objective: tune into the 50,000 watts of WLAC Nashville with DJ Gene Nobles, and wait for the magic to begin. Nobles, Hagopian and friends knew, was a mid-50s R&B and gospel music trailblazer, introducing Chuck Berry, Fats Domino, and Little Richard before New York DJ Alan Freed, though the latter got most of the credit for taking black music to white listeners.

The hill outside Galt was the one portal through which they could hear recording artists who weren't getting any airtime on the local AM station. They pumped up the volume to hear Chuck Berry, Jimmy Reid, Lightning Hopkins, Muddy Waters, Little Junior Parker, the Spaniels, Sonny Boy Williamson, and Etta James. Hagopian and friends were in seventh heaven. Dean was smitten by radio, and the music he heard on WLAC was the foundation for his own playlist when, years later, he was the one spinning the discs behind the mic.

Hagopian was born in 1938, in Galt-Cambridge, after his parents fled the persecution of Armenians in Turkey, coming to Canada via

France. Along with his two brothers and sister, he went through elementary and high school in the same building in Galt-Cambridge, but Dean had some post-graduation plans that didn't include more schooling. He left home at 18. His parents were disappointed that he would not be the first lawyer or doctor in the family. At first, he didn't stray too far from home, taking a job as an operator at CKGR. It was the only radio station in Galt, the one whose classical music format put Hagopian and his buddies up on that hill looking for the WLAC signal to breeze in.

Hagopian turned out to be a gifted mimic. Comedian Jonathan Winters was a particular favourite of his and the inspiration for a character he created called Maude Fricker – a fastidious, quirky old lady whose voice Hagopian would later incorporate into his own on-air persona. Eventually, he had about 10 different voices he could call upon based on Jose Jimenez, a regular on the Ed Sullivan Show, a drunken Lone Ranger and sober Tonto, a bit inspired by a Bill Cosby routine, which turned the tables on a well-accepted stereotype of the day. "I used to drag out the intro to that joke for almost two minutes before getting to the punchline," he says. "Looking back on it now, I'm not sure how I did it, but it worked." Then there was Carlton Segura, an effiminately-voiced character roughly based on a well-known Ottawa Rough Riders player in the Canadian Football League. Anyone could drop the needle on a record, but Hagopian felt that the DJ's job was to entertain while playing music. He left CKGR and landed his first AM DJ job at a London, Ontario, radio station and unwrapped the voices he'd been practicing in his spare time. Not all station GMs were ready for his free-form riffing-with-voices routine. This wouldn't be the first time he ran afoul of management and found himself forced to move on.

Not content to just play the records, Hagopian also wanted to make his own music. In London, while working at CFPL and CKFL, Hagopian tried to throw a bunch of local guys together to play rock. One was local organ player Garth Hudson, who was snapped up by Rompin' Ronnie Hawkins before he even had a chance to play with Dean and the boys. Hudson would eventually join Levon Helm, Robbie Robertson and Richard Emmanuel as the Hawks, who were backing up Hawkins in Toronto. Hawkins eventually lost his entire backup band, who went on to work with Bob Dylan before breaking out on their own to become the Band, one of the most successful and legendary rock bands in contemporary Canadian music history.

While a DJ at CKOY in Ottawa, Hagopian helped put together and sang lead for the Staccatos for the better part of 1963, before Les Emerson eventually took over as lead vocalist and guitarist. The Dean was always an unabashed Canadian talent suporter and in the years preceeding Canadian Content regulations, Hagopian's role in promoting Canadian talent at CKOY drew the attention of management, who at one point asked him bluntly if he was receiving money in return. "The Alan Freed payola scandal was still fairly fresh in radio management's minds," he says. "I was so angry with the guy for even asking, I could have thrown him down the stairs. I never took a nickel." By 1963, Hagopian was married and his extracurricular music career with the group was gradually reduced. The Staccatos went on without him and placed nine songs on the Canadian charts, one of which, "Half-Past Midnight," peaked at No. 8. Rebranded as the Five Man Electrical Band – a name more reflective of the late 1960s – the group made a significant impact on the charts in Canada and the U.S. Their anti-establishment hippie anthem "Signs" sold a million copies and topped the charts. Thanks to Canadian-content regulations which came into effect in the early 1970s, "Signs" was one of those songs that would get serious airplay well beyond its 1971 release date, still on the playlist of 1960s and 1970s specialty radio, satellite stations, and classic rock stations. Hagopian may have missed out on a piece of Canadian rock fame, but his next radio move would be consolation enough.

In August 1965, a small radio station located on Montreal's West Island, with an unfortunate end-of-the-dial location, decided to experiment with Top 40 music, bringing in Hagopian from CKOY. They weren't quite ready to dump their current country music format completely, but they gave Hagopian a chance to go Top 40 during the prime morning show time slot, which had been the domain of owner Gord Sinclair. One morning, Sinclair, Jr. stepped away from his CFOX-AM 1470 morning show and introduced Dean

(Left) Dean Hagopian was CFOX's first all-rock morning man when the station converted from country music to a Top 40 format in 1965. First up on the turntable: the Rolling Stones' "Satisfaction."
Courtesy of Dean Hagopian.
(Right) At remote broadcasts, Hagopian was often accompanied by Miss CFOX Louise "Corky" Van Guelpen, an aspiring rock 'n' roll singer with charisma to spare. *Courtesy of Louise Van Guelpen.*

Hagopian to his audience. Hagopian and Sinclair, Jr., who was more country than rock, had some transitional banter.

Although it was pretty early in the morning, there was a lot of champagne flowing. The Top 40 party was just revving up and Hagopian was now the Dean of Montreal. He then dropped the needle on his first record of this new era in Montreal radio. The distinctive opening guitar notes of the Rolling Stones' "Satisfaction" went out to suburban listeners just wiping sleep from their eyes. The switchboard soon lit up with listeners asking, "What the hell is this? What happened to the country music?" Sorry, no more morning Merle Haggard, they were told. It was time to rock 'n' roll. Soon, the morning ratings shot up and other stations were craning their necks, wondering who the hell CFOX and Dean Hagopian were. Word on the street – mostly the tame suburban streets of Montreal's West Island – spread quickly.

Hagopian's success gave CFOX a good reason to throw caution to the wind, drop their country music programming completely and go Top 40 24/7. CFOX still retained some holdovers from their country format with "Big Daddy" Bob Ancell, a popular mid-morning-to-afternoon DJ, staying on. With more successful ratings and increasing advertising revenue, management could afford to bring in some new Top 40 blood, augmenting the lineup with Ralph Lockwood from the U.S., Roger Scott, a Brit whose accent was his ticket to ride, and motor-mouthed Charles P. Rodney Chandler. Together, they became the "CFOX Good Guys."

The "Good Guys" were often called out to do remote broadcasts from local businesses, who were also advertisers. The bane of the Top 40 DJ existence, remotes were a lot like working out of a fishbowl, but they were great PR and revenue generators. To soften the edges of the remote (not every DJ was comfortable doing them), CFOX management put an ad in the papers looking for candidates who would fit the role of Miss CFOX, who presumably would be the pretty face for the station. Without much ceremony, the crown went to a five-foot-two fledgling rock singer dynamo and Leslie Gore look-alike, Louise "Corky" Van Guelpen. Barely out of high school, Van Guelpen celebrated Canada's 100th birthday as Miss CFOX, complete with a Miss CFOX royal sash and just enough natural sass to help run interference while the DJ was doing a remote broadcast. She was a big hit in public and a breath of fresh air in a male-dominated business. When they worked together, she and Hagopian had good chemistry, Van Guelpen schmoozing the live remote crowd and giving out free albums while Hagopian plugged the business and DJed his show. The Miss CFOX gig lasted about a year when she turned her attention to finishing her teaching degree, married at 20, became a teacher, then started a family, her music career ambitions put aside permanently. Because of his love of R&B, Hagopian liked to program the in-music he thought the audience needed to hear. Canada wasn't exactly a Mecca for black music, but it caught on fast. He'd started playing Motown in 1959 and 1960 on CFPL in London, and then at CKOY in Ottawa (where he was the Dean of Ottawa). In Galt, these were records he played after trips to Detroit record stores, where he discovered that R&B was in the "Race Music" section of the store. He brought his young passion for R&B and found

Montreal a welcoming city for the soul, R&B, and Motown sound. In fact, CFOX listeners loved it, and suddenly the British Invasion groups had some major competition on the charts. The Dean was having a blast, playing the music he loved. Doing the afternoon 4 to 8 pm shift, his show overlapped with Dave Boxer on CFCF and Buddy Gee on CKGM. He was not above doing some CFOX chest-thumping. "Even though I was doing the 4 to 8 pm afternoon shift when Boxer and Buddy Gee were on, I still took advantage of this to take a few shots at Boxer on-air. It was all in good fun – sort of – but it was just what I call friendly sniping. Just to let him know I was there." CFOX had one big thing over both competing stations: They were pumping out Top 40 hits 24/7.

One of Hagopian's goals, besides throwing in a smattering of R&B amongst the hits of the day, was to make people laugh or smile, preferably both. And he was eminently successful at it. Before Top 40 DJs were reined in with the less talk and more music format, it wasn't unusual for Hagopian to take as long as he liked to construct an improvised radio routine before he played a record. In his Bill Cosby-inspired drunken Lone Ranger and straight-man Tonto routines, he could take up to two minutes to arrive at the punchline. There must have been plenty of listeners in their cars pulling up in the parking lot at work waiting for Dean to finish, then trying to replay their own version of the joke around the office water cooler. This was a DJ's greatest unspoken compliment.

To raise the public profile of the "Good Guys" (and some extra cash for the Boys), there were sock hops and high school dances to emcee. Hagopian ran his own dances – with a heavy dose of R&B for the kids to dance to – at the Manoir, a church basement club in the Notre-Dame-de-Grace area of Montreal. In the second half of the 1960s, Montreal was becoming a regular tour stop for some of the major rock acts in the world. Hagopian was on stage to introduce two Rolling Stones concerts, the Who, Led Zeppelin, Cream, and Jimi Hendrix. The first Stones concert at the Maurice Richard Arena took place on April 23, 1965, before the Stones became really big. It was a relatively tame affair compared to when they played the Forum in October of the same year. The Stones were barely 10 minutes into their set before all hell broke loose, with folding chairs on the Forum floor being tossed about. The Stones fled and some concertgoers turned their frustration on the Montreal police and the wooden folding chairs provided for ice-level seating. Montreal was not the only place where the group had trouble; they seemed to attract a more aggressive fan demographic.

Few jocks in Montreal displayed their emotions on air, but Hagopian's connection to the music, especially R&B, was intense. In December 1967, the plane carrying Otis Redding and seven others, heading for a gig in Madison, Wisconsin, crashed just miles from its destination, killing all but one passenger. It was a great blow to the soul music community and the millions of fans Redding had acquired as a result of his Top 40 exposure. Hits like "Sitting on the Dock of the Bay," "Shake," and "Try a Little Tenderness" had made a star of Redding. When Hagopian told his CFOX listeners about the crash, he wept openly on the air and played Redding songs back to back for the next half-hour.

Some of the music Hagopian was handed to play just wasn't up to his standards. A 1964 single by British singer Adam Faith repeated the words "I wanna tell you it's all right" over and over again. Less than halfway through all the "all rights," Hagopian yanked the record off the turntable. If other DJs wanted to play the song, they would have to fish the 45 out of the Dean bin. (Faith's song reached No. 31 on the U.S. charts – his only success outside the U.K.)

As a self-confessed rebel and renegade, his time at CFOX was not all smooth Top 40 sailing. He got fired two or three times, he recalls. During one of those "off" periods, Hagopian lost the prized morning shift to Ralph Lockwood, who was brought in from WHLO-AM in Ohio. Hagopian never got that shift back, but he bounced back to do the afternoon drive-home shift.

Dean remembers his time at CKOY in Ottawa and CFOX in Montreal as his best years: memorable years when his engagement with the audience was part art, part music. CFOX, particularly, invaded Montreal airwaves with a force not unlike that of the British Invasion. The station held the No. 1 English-language Top 40 radio spot for five years, and Hagopian was a crucial part of the first wave.

168

CFOX's Top 40, 24/7 format was what eventually led to CFCF dropping the *Dave Boxer Show* in 1968. CFOX was hampered by a poor signal that did not penetrate Montreal's downtown core. Its light faded when CKGM-AM went full-out Top 40 and the FOX lost a good portion of its listenership. CKGM was poaching CFOX DJs towards the end of the 60s, luring them to the bright lights of the city, along with more bucks and a bigger audience. CFOX's time in the spotlight was coming to an end. "We had a great team at the 'FOX," Hagopian says. "There was 'Big Daddy' Bob Ancell, Bill Lowell, Bob Baker, Roger Scott, Ralph Lockwood, Steve Shannon, and Jim Patton. But in the end, it was our weak signal that eventually killed us. That, and when CKGM went Top 40 in '70 with very few commercials, we couldn't compete. We had our time in the sun."

Hagopian stuck around after CFOX dropped its Top 40 format in 1971, first as a late-night talk-show host, then back to DJ when CFOX fully adopted an alternative country sound. It was not the same country music that the station had played in the early 1960s but a hybrid format, music that had been labelled country rock. There was some Kris Kristofferson, Poco, and Leon Russell. Hagopian even threw in a few country-tinged songs by the Stones. He was essentially his own music director and shopped around for music he thought would fit into the new format. He had some fun with it, not pining too much for the Top 40 sound. But it wasn't the same and somehow it just didn't seem right for him to be doing the Tonto, the Lone Ranger, and the Zelda Zorch shtick. Gord Sinclair, Jr. sold CFOX in 1972 to Slaight Communications, then Sinclair moved on to an announcing job at CFCF. The Sinclair/CFOX Top 40 era was over.

A cornucopia of jocks came through the CFOX doors, some with more staying power who permanently left their mark on a generation of Baby Boomer listeners. DJs like Bob Gibbons, Bob Baker, George Ferguson, and "Big Daddy" Bob Ancell, who were at CFOX before the 1965 Top 40 format change, made the transition to Top 40 seamlessly. Others like Roger Scott, who was the de-facto British music expert and instrumental in CFOX's live remotes from the Queen Elizabeth Hotel during the Lennon/Ono Bed-in for Peace, was part of the new wave. Hagopian said Scott had a great ear for music. (As the resident Brit, Scott was all over the "Paul is dead" urban legend and conspiracy theory that Beatle Paul McCartney had died in 1966. Like DJs on hundreds of other North America Top 40 stations, Scott played the Beatles' "Revolution 9" song backwards, where listeners could apparently decipher the line "Turn me on, dead man." It was an urban legend that had teens leaning in hard over their AM radios.) Scott and Hagopian often enjoyed some friendly changing-of-shift banter that involved Hagopian calling Scott a "steaming nit" to which Scott would come back, calling Hagopian a "steaming twit." Scott spent four years at CFOX before going back to Britain and a stellar radio career there before he succumbed to cancer at the age of 46 in 1989.

After finally leaving CFOX, Hagopian had stints at almost every English-language radio station in Montreal – CJAD, CFCF, CHOM-FM. His brief time at CHOM-FM was not the highlight of his broadcasting career, a time when he thought he was not doing his best radio. After taking a long break from radio to hang out with his dogs and inhale some pure country air in the Ottawa Valley, he was back at it in the 1980s as program director at CKGB-AM in Timmins, Ontario, one of six stations run by his old CFOX pal, "Big Daddy" Bob Ancell. He was, at the same time, following a lifelong passion for acting, with roles in films by David Cronenberg, namely *Scanners*, and Brian de Palma's *Snake Eyes*, filmed in Montreal with Nicolas Cage. He got small roles in TV series, as well as voicing characters for animation and video games. His talent for voices was still his bread and butter.

In 1981, Hagopian was diagnosed with bladder cancer, battled it and has been cancer-free since, although a misdiagnosed tick bite in 2006 would almost end his life. Hagopian, now in his mid-70s, is still taking on film and voice-over gigs. Zelda Zorch, Carleton Segura, a drunken Lone Ranger, and Tonto: they're all still spinning around in the Dean's head. Every once in a while, if the mood strikes, he'll do one of them on request.

CHARLES P. RODNEY CHANDLER: THE MAN
WITH THE MOTOR MOUTH

When two Montreal Top 40 DJs, Charles P. Rodney Chandler and Roger Scott, got word that John Lennon and Yoko Ono were coming to the city as part of their Bed-in for Peace, they hatched a plan that could potentially put CFOX in the headlines. At the airport on the evening of May 26, 1969, Scott and Chandler buttonholed Lennon's publicist, Derek Taylor, and gave him their pitch-on-the-run, as Taylor tried to expedite the Lennon entourage's escape out of the airport to the Queen Elizabeth Hotel downtown. "Ask me again tomorrow," he told them. Chandler had convinced 'FOX program director Doug Ackhurst that they could pull off a Top 40 radio coup if they could just persuade Lennon's management to let them do remote broadcasts during Lennon's stay in Montreal. The next day they did ask again and Taylor liked the idea. Soon CFOX engineers were setting up the necessary equipment for remote broadcasts back to CFOX central in Pointe Claire. For the better part of the next week, Chandler and Scott were sitting in the catbird's seat right next to John Lennon and Yoko Ono's king-sized bed. Interviews, updates, music, and even Lennon-introduced beer commercials meant CFOX was *the* station to listen to for any you-heard-it-here-first Lennon/Ono Bed-in news.

It was a seminal moment for Chandler, one that would define his life for many years to come. He was bedside with a mic in his hand talking to the most famous rock musician of the time. It was a pretty heady week for the 22-year-old DJ. He had direct access to a man and an event that resonates for many in Montreal and around the world more than 50 years later. To this day, being part of the Lennon/Ono Bed-In for Peace ranks as one of his most enduring radio business memories. Over the years – and especially after Lennon was murdered in New York on December 8, 1980 – Chandler has been interviewed dozens of times on important Lennon anniversaries. "The [Lennon Bed-in for Peace] was the most significant thing that ever happened to me in my life," says Chandler, 46 years later. "Even though I was too young to realize just how big it was at the time."

When the 22-year-old Chuck Chandler joined CFOX in Montreal in 1968, the station had been in full Top 40 mode for three years. His timing couldn't have been better. Since stumbling into the radio business at the age of 18 in Dawson Creek, B.C., he had pinballed around Canada, back and forth at radio stations in Edmonton and Halifax, then to Montreal. He put a lot of miles on his car taking in the view of Canada from west to east. Born Charles Paul Rodney Nahumko, his last name cried out for Top 40 radio revision. It was changed when he got his first full-time radio gig at CJCA in Edmonton: the station manager, as the story goes, opened up the phone book and his finger randomly landed on Chandler.

Chandler spent a very brief time in post-war Britain before his Canadian Army father and British-born mother immigrated to Winnipeg, then Edmonton – the city in which he would ultimately spend most of his radio career. But it was a move to Dawson Creek, B.C., for his last year of high school, that led to an opportunity at CJDC, the only radio/TV station in town. When he was not working as the part-time switcher for the TV side of CJDC, Chandler wandered over to the radio studio where Mike Laverne, owner, program director, and general manager, hosted the station's only weekly rock 'n' roll show, *SatMat* – a clever contraction of Saturday and matinee. Chandler watched Laverne at work. One Saturday, Laverne threw on the theme music for *SatMat*, opened the mic and said, "Welcome to *SatMat*. Today your host will be Chuck Nahumko," then disappeared into his office with his girlfriend. It was baptism by fire. But after having watched Laverne in action for weeks, he took a deep breath and waded in.

Laverne must have been impressed. Nothing went amiss with Chandler at the *SatMat* helm that day. While still holding down his job as CJDC-TV switcher, Chandler got his own show playing a combo of rock, country, and requests. Management even called on him to do the nightly TV news before they went off the air, his TV suit jacket and tie handy in the studio. He was young and keen, and he was cheap labour. This was small-town Media Immersion 101. Chandler was a cocky 18-year-old thrust into adult responsibilities. "I've got a job and a regular paycheque, so why not get married?" he thought.

Chandler was a well-travelled DJ, but his time at CFOX as the fastest talking guy in town was a highlight of his career that included covering Woodstock and the Lennon/Ono Bed-in for Peace in Montreal. *Courtesy of Don Major.*

Like many cities across Canada, Edmonton was enjoying the maturation of the Baby Boomer demographic, progressing from rural to urban Canada where there were plenty of job opportunities. It was almost too easy for Chandler and his wife. She found employment first. Shortly afterwards, Chandler was hired at Top 40 radio station CJCA after the all-night jock got sick. For a guy with no game plan and limited radio experience, he lucked out. The Edmonton gig was the beginning of the east-west pinballing of Chandler's early radio career. In the next two years, he went back and forth between CJCA in Edmonton and CHNS in Halifax four times before landing a job at CFOX in Montreal in 1968. In Halifax, he added some pizzazz to his on-air name, going from Chuck Chandler to Charles P. Rodney Chandler. His new on-air name had a ring to it, even though it violated the unwritten law of Top 40 DJ names – a one-syllable first name followed by a two-syllable last name. With all the back and forth, it's unlikely Chandler got to know Edmonton and Halifax

173

that well, at least not until later in his career when he would find himself in Edmonton more often than not. Alas, he knew even less about Montreal, but he knew that it was the big time compared to Dawson Creek, Halifax, and Edmonton.

The next two years were exciting times for Chandler who landed the prime 5 to 9 p.m. shift at CFOX – the Top 40 game in town, and he hit the ground running. He describes his on-air style as "pretty frantic." Taking his cues from U.S. jocks in major markets like New York, Chicago, and Philadelphia, Chandler was strictly a high-energy, fast-talkin' DJ. Montreal concert promoter Donald K. Donald used CFOX to advertise his concerts and would drop in to sit with DJs to do live paid commercials. Donald was no shrinking violet when he got behind a mic, but he remembers that it was hard to get a word in edgewise with Chandler. Of course, there was ego involved; after all, it was Donald K. Donald on the Charles P. Rodney Chandler show, not the other way around.

Chandler settled in quickly to the pace of Montreal living and the swagger that came with being something of a rock radio star. Although the CFOX studios were located in the suburbs, Chandler and his wife rented a home in Westmount, much closer to the temptations of Montreal's nightlife. The benefits of having a recognizable name got him gigs introducing bands at local concerts, which put more money in his pocket, free drinks, and a VIP gold-card membership at the downtown Playboy Club. "Even though CFOX was out in the sticks, people downtown never looked at us that way," says Chandler. "They never looked at us as yokels. We were fuckin' stars. There would be two or three bars I'd go into and they would be lining up drinks for me." A 22-year-old DJ with a Playboy Club gold card, Chandler didn't hesitate to sidle up to the Playboy Bunny buffet. Somehow Chandler's relationship with his wife survived those CFOX years – for a while, at least. Nonetheless, he married three times. "Life was good in those days," he says. "I have no regrets. I've had a lot of highs and lows and that's the only thing you could wish for, is to make life interesting."

And make it interesting he did. He went out and made it happen when Lennon came to Montreal: he and fellow DJ Roger Scott were making history and considerably raising the profile of CFOX. The almost week-long Bed-in for Peace became part of CFOX's daily programming. There was a parade of celebrities anxious to be a part of the scene: singer Petula Clark, comedian Tommy Smothers, poet Allen Ginsberg, DJ Murray the "K," comedian Dick Gregory, the tune-in-turn-on-and-drop-out psychologist Timothy Leary, and an angry *L'il Abner* cartoonist Al Capp, all dropped in to talk to Lennon and Ono. The whole thing was filmed and later released as the documentary *Bed Peace*. Except for Capp, Chandler remembers the vibe in the room was mostly peace and love. Although CFOX had an exclusive going for them, there were plenty of other media who wanted a piece of Lennon. He did dozens of live interviews for radio stations in the U.S. while in Montreal. There were some quiet times when Lennon would be reading, but being under constant scrutiny while in bed dressed in pyjamas must have been draining. On the wall in his apartment, Chandler has a photo of himself in bed with Lennon and Ono. It's travelled with him since 1969, easily his most treasured possession. "There's some very good memories about that whole thing," he says. "It was remarkable how it all came down and worked out." He wishes he had the tapes of his on-air interactions with Lennon, such as the commercial where Lennon read: "The next five minutes of the Charles P. Rodney Chandler show is brought to you by Molson, a beautiful ale with soul." "I felt like the king of the castle," says Chandler. "John Lennon reading a commercial on my show. I loved it."

The bed-in, as a vehicle for peace, turned out to be only a two-city affair. The fact that Lennon couldn't get into the U.S. limited the scope of his message. But the Montreal Bed-in left its mark, one that has endured through song, books, documentaries, and even museum exhibits. Chandler "played" the coffee table (so many would later claim to being part of that moment) when Lennon put together the song "Give Peace a Chance." When it came out as a single in the summer of '69, the song was on every Top 40 radio station's playlist, including CFOX's. If he listened closely to the engineered version, Chandler could hear himself pounding on the table. Or so he thought.

Chandler (along with CFOX DJ Roger Scott) had front row seats at the 1969 Queen Elizabeth Hotel Lennon/Ono Bed-in. He and Scott negotiated an exclusive with Lennon's manager, to be the only radio station with bedside access.
Courtesy of Roy Kerwood.

He was there for the whole show and, when Lennon and Ono packed up their tent and left town, Chandler was back to reality behind the mic in the tiny CFOX studio. Although he was always the consummate pro, those immediate post-Bed-in days must have felt like something of a denouement. "Give Peace a Chance" was technically the last single put out by the Beatles – writing credits went to Lennon and McCartney – and Chandler was on it.

Just three months after the Lennon Bed-in, Chandler and fellow CFOX DJ Lynda "Honey" Moffet were on a bus on their way to another major slice of rock music history – Woodstock. This, however, would not turn out to be nearly as visceral an experience as the bed-in. The CFOX-sponsored trip to Woodstock, with three busloads of fairly stoned music fans, was more *Twilight Zone* than epochal musical moment. Chandler's memory is more than a little sketchy about details of his Woodstock experience. "I'd love to hear a story about me during that trip because I have no idea, man," he says. "I remember the bus, the people, and the drugs. I wasn't a big druggie. I

176

drank a lot and smoked weed, so I can't figure it out." The buses did get within walking distance of the stage, close enough for Chandler to be able to hear the music but not to see it. He and Moffet filed a few Woodstock "lifestyle" reports back to CFOX, then hopped back onto an empty bus and told the driver to head to La Guardia Airport in New York City where they caught a flight back to Montreal. There are no photos of the Woodstock trip on his wall, but he was there . . . sort of.

Chandler jammed a lot into his two years at CFOX. When he left in 1970, it was for a job in Winnipeg as program director at Top 40 station CFRW. "The writing was on the wall [as far as CFOX's future as a Top 40 station was concerned]," he says. He hated Winnipeg and came back to do a six-month stint at CKGM, which was now positioning itself to take over the Top 40 audience from CFOX. Using a new name, Todd Young, he toned down his frenetic Top 40 patter for the tight Top 40 format 'GM was employing. Less talk. More music. The jingles said so. "I got into using my voice and developing it more at CKGM. Up until then, I was too fast. Too fuckin' balls-to-the-wall for anybody to be in love with my voice." His voice, now less hype and more style, was his vehicle until his 2008 retirement from radio (his last show was on May 24 on CKRA-FM in Edmonton), after covering a fair amount of geography and genres, including a 1980-81 gig as the studio announcer for Monty Hall's popular TV show, *Let's Make a Deal*.

Unlike his vague memories of Woodstock, Chandler remembers clearly where he was when he got word of John Lennon's death. On a day off between shooting *Let's Make a Deal* in L.A., the phone rang in his hotel room. It was CBC calling to ask for his reaction to Lennon's death. He was taken aback. This was the first he'd heard about Lennon being shot, by Mark Chapman, outside his Dakota apartment building in New York City. The phone rang more than once that day. Outside the Dakota the next day, thousands of bereaved fans gathered to honour Lennon. They sang, "Give Peace a Chance" over and over. Chandler was in on that song in a way none of the thousands of mourners outside Lennon's apartment could have imagined.

Chandler was 63 when he officially did his last radio show on CKRA-FM in Edmonton. He had his retirement all figured out, with a part-time radio gig lined up in Malaga, Spain, far removed from the vicious Edmonton winters. His two adult sons from his first marriage were professors of English in Spain. With the money he had saved for his golden years, all the stars seemed aligned for a smooth, graceful fade-out on the Costa del Sol with family nearby. With an apartment, radio gig, and retirement funds all lined up, he was ready to move onto a new phase of his life. Then, on a routine visit to his Malaga ATM, his whole life dropped out from under him. His account had been wiped out: he was apparently the victim of identity theft. He was devastated. "It's one of the only things in life that made me cry," says Chandler. "The theft just wiped me out, my retirement. It's not a story I like to dwell on."

Somehow Chandler managed to pick up the pieces with the help of his sons and left Spain for Victoria, B.C. It's not the Costa del Sol, but it is the warmest year-round place in Canada. The fall-out from his ravaged retirement plans still stings. He can take some solace from supportive friends and family and the memories of a long and respected radio career – and those heady Montreal radio days at CFOX and CKGM when he was in full Top 40 flight. "It was a great time to be a Top 40 rock 'n' roll DJ," Chandler says. "I have no idea what I'd be otherwise."

Lynda Moffet: It Was a "Honey" of a Job

Lynda Moffet is alone in the CFOX studios. It's the early-morning hours of her midnight to 6 a.m. weekend shift and her bladder is starting to speak to her. After a couple of months on the air, she has learned how to take care of this situation: play either the Beatles' "Hey Jude" or Mary Hopkin's "Those Were the Days." With a running time of 7:11, "Hey Jude" was her best bet. "Those Were the Days" gave her 5:05; not bad, considering most other 45-rpm records being played on Top 40 radio barely topped three minutes.

Just before the top of the hour when Moffet would also have

to do the news, she gave the Beatles or Mary Hopkin a spin and went for a quick round trip through the studio: first to the teletype machine to rip off the latest news bulletins, then to the bathroom, then back to the announcer's booth to figure out what her newscast would be. "Those two songs were a godsend," Moffet says. "I don't know how I would have survived without them."

As mundane as these things seem, they were the routines of the midnight-to-morning Top 40 DJ running a one-"man" late-night show. The timing had to be right on, just to meet your basic bio-logical needs, and Moffet's timing was very special. Barely 20 years old, she was Montreal's first – and at the time, only – female Top 40 DJ. CFOX management thought of her as a kind of experiment, but this was not by any means a proto-feminist statement. The all-male CFOX radio-name committee decided "Honey" would be Moffet's on-air name.

Moffet graduated in 1967 from Malcolm Campbell High School in Montreal, then enrolled at Sir George Williams University (now Concordia). Her father, she remembers, took a somewhat dim view of her post-secondary ambitions. He told her, "Girls don't do that. You go and learn to be a secretary or a teacher." But that route was not her style, and she backed up her determination by financing her way through her two years at Sir George.

"I was very confident in my abilities to hold my own in the world with men. So, when I got into radio I brought those attitudes with me. But those attitudes [like her father's] were quite common at the time, and women were being pulled one way or the other. We were trying to get into the new way of thinking and there were forces trying to pull us back into the traditional role." When Moffet did get into radio, she found some of those paternal attitudes still firmly entrenched in the culture of Top 40 radio.

It was at one of those all-male managerial meetings at CFOX that the idea to have a female DJ was hatched. At the time, it was a bold decision that pushed some long-established radio gender boundaries. So out went the call to women interested in becom-ing a Top 40 weekend DJ. Moffet got wind of the call from her two brothers, both aspiring musicians with their ear close to the ground and the radio.

Despite not having an audition tape, a standard accessory for any wannabe DJ, she was interviewed by CFOX program director Charles P. Rodney Chandler, who informed her she had some stiff competition. The station was apparently deluged with applications, including some from Playboy Bunnies working at the downtown Montreal nightclub. Moffet played it pretty cool. She didn't think she had much of a chance of getting the gig, but she tried to remain positive. It didn't hurt that she actually knew something about music, having dabbled at managing a few rock bands in her late teens. She was hired and, a couple of months later, dropped out of university to turn her full attention to her new job. Her father, by now, was used to his daughter's headstrong ways, and resigned to this new direction. He became one of her devoted listeners – for as long as he could stay awake after midnight, anyway.

Moffet stepped right into it, going out on location with CFOX DJ Ralph Lockwood and introducing a few songs at a dance-marathon contest. Chandler gave her a crash course in queuing up records and how to use the commercial cartridges. Finally, one Saturday night in October 1968, the red light came on and she was off on her own. Station owner Gord Sinclair and management thought they were looking out for Moffet when they gave her the on-air tag "Honey." They were concerned about having a woman on the air doing the all-night shift who might be hassled at home by enthusiastic male fans. She hated the name right off the bat. It just so happened "Honey" was the name of a cheesy Bobby Goldsboro tune that came out that year, a song she loathed as much as her new radio name. Moffet wanted to be considered one of the CFOX Good Guys and, for the most part, her DJ colleagues were very supportive.

But she was – and would be – the only CFOX Good Gal, and that was something she learned to live with. She would never be a part of the fraternity of Top 40 DJs; she would never be one of the "boys." Management wanted her to use a sexy, breathy, Monroe kind of voice. When she tried that, Chandler sometimes called her during her night shift to admonish her. She was confused at first, but

Lynda Moffet (here with CFOX's morning man Ralph Lockwood) was given the on-air name "Honey." For just over a year, she was the first – and only – female DJ Top 40 DJ in town in a radio world dominated by men. *Courtesy of Lynda Moffet.*

she decided to ignore management and took Chandler's advice to just be herself. "I'm not the kind of person that could do the whole heavy breathing, sexy thing," she said. "Chuck [Chandler] told me to just be like the other guys. I knew he knew what he was talking about. He was an announcer, not them. I wanted to be a Top 40 jock and I recognized that they [management] were trying to use my sex rather than my abilities. I didn't want to just be window dressing."

CFOX was a pretty tight shop with about 25 employees, a family-friendly station with the benevolent but sometimes grumpy Sinclair as the father figure. Moffet and other female employees were used to his morning hugs. He took employees out for lunch on birthdays

181

at his favourite lunchtime hangout, the Dorval Hilton. He was old school, and casual wardrobe comments were part of the agenda of Sinclair's weekly staff meetings. It was the days of the short skirt.

When Moffet was on air there were often late-night calls from men. They wanted Moffet to tell them what she looked like. More often than not, they had already conjured up an image of her. "It was always the same," says Moffet. " 'You've got long blonde hair and you wear a yellow dress,' they would tell me. It was so weird." Some early mornings just before her shift ended, when she looked out the window, there might be a few cars lurking in the CFOX parking lot waiting for her to come out. For those occasions, she had a number to call. The police looked out for her and chased the car pervs away.

In the confines of the station, she would get feedback like, "Linda, you're a good broad." She figured it was an entertainment business thing; it was as if some of the all-male management team were stuck in a Sinatra time warp.

After a couple of months, Moffet was in a groove. She teamed up with 'FOX DJs for regular Saturday morning remotes from Morgan's stores (later bought by Hudson's Bay in 1972) around Montreal. There were live fashion shows where special guests like the Guess Who stopped by to talk music. She filled in for other announcers, and got a taste of what style to use for different time slots. She emceed some local concerts for Donald K. Donald. In short, she was getting closer to being a Good Guy, more so than the "broad." On remotes, male "Honey" fans would show up to see what she looked like. It was flattering in a creepy sort of way. Their blonde hair and yellow dress fantasies took a hit, though. If any of her early-morning telephone admirers would have taken the time to see her at any of the CFOX remote broadcasts, they'd have seen a petite, five-foot-one-inch brunette with almost waist-length hair. She let the boys have their illusions.

A free record scavenger hunt attracted hundreds of kids to the back lot of the CFOX studios. There was a staged kidnapping of one of the DJs. It was always about engaging the listenership – mostly in fun – but serendipitously the station was a participant in events that went beyond simple giveaways and commercial stunts. Moffet was at CFOX for two of 1969's most seminal moments in rock history: Woodstock and the John Lennon Montreal Bed-in for Peace. CFOX had negotiated a ringside seat for Lennon's Bed-in at the Queen Elizabeth Hotel in May 1969. DJs Roger Scott and Chuck Chandler would broadcast live updates from Room 1742, along with some exclusive bedside interviews. This was a huge coup for the station. Moffet was there when the station set up right at the foot of the bed. She remembers that Lennon occasionally got out of the bed and came to watch Chandler at work, doing live reports. Lennon seemed fascinated by Chandler's Top 40 super-charged patter. "He [Lennon] couldn't believe that Chuck could talk so fast," Moffet says. "He remarked on this several times." It was Moffet's impression that Lennon didn't take to fellow Brit Scott in the same way. "Lennon kind of gravitated toward Chuck, sometimes ignoring Roger Scott."

After a few hours, bored by the Bed-in proceedings, Moffet wandered around the chaos of the hotel room and found herself in an adjoining room where Yoko Ono was chewing out two young babysitters who were responsible for her five-year-old daughter, Kyoto. There were two broken TVs courtesy of Kyoto and several empty containers of butterscotch pudding that the child had ordered from room service. Ono turned to Moffet and asked her to take over babysitting duties. "Can you do something with her?" Ono asked. "Sure," Moffet said. "I stayed with her for a couple of hours. We jumped on the bed together, had more butterscotch pudding and watched an episode of *Star Trek*. Kyoto was very bright. We had a great time." Moffet missed the recording of "Give Peace a Chance" the next day, but she remembers seeing something written by Lennon she thought, scrawled on the wall: "The 13th Commandment is Thou Shalt Make Money." A little piece of her faith in the purity and depth of Lennon's peace motives died that day.

In August of 1969, a local bus company and CFOX teamed up to sponsor a three-day trip to the Woodstock Music and Art Fair. Moffet and Chandler were to be CFOX's emissaries, with regular reports for listeners back in Montreal. Though some of the travellers on the three Woodstock Festival Express buses had come prepared with certain recreational substances, they managed to get through customs without incident. The turnpike and Woodstock exit were a clogged mess of thousands of cars by the time their buses got there. Many had to abandon their vehicles miles from the concert site, including the three CFOX buses. Concert organizers expected 50,000 people to attend, but it wasn't long before that estimate went out the window. The boys on the CFOX buses, noses pressed against the windows, were delighted to see so many braless hippie chicks. Meanwhile, Moffet and Chandler had to report back to CFOX listeners who were anxious to hear about their Woodstock experience. They reported on the hordes of hippies walking peacefully from the chaos of the road and their abandoned vehicles, undaunted, still full of the innocence and collegiality that were part and parcel of the 1960s philosophy. "The whole action wasn't the music," says Moffet. "The action was the immense number of people, which was truly peace and love." In fact, neither Chandler nor Moffet made it anywhere near the Woodstock stage. No Sly. No Janis. No Santana. No Who. No one.

The two of them hung around for two days, spending nights on the bus and phoning in reports to CFOX during the day. It must have been slightly uncomfortable for them inasmuch as none of their reports included any mention of the live music. By the third day they'd had enough and along with the bus driver, who was anxious to get out of the chaos, they headed back north. Looking out the windows, they saw a stream of abandoned cars on the interstate as thousands gave up the drive to walk to Woodstock, a biblical mass of the bearded and braless headed to musical Nirvana. Tired and dirty, Moffet and Chandler had the driver drop them off at New York's La Guardia Airport before he headed back to Montreal. With only a few war stories to tell, the assignment kind of fizzled out, another "we-almost-got-to-Woodstock" story. At least Moffet remembers her Woodstock experience; Chandler, not so much.

Back at the station, there was something in the air, and it wasn't peace, love, and understanding. Owner Gord Sinclair and station GM Doug Ackhurst called Moffet into the office in the fall of 1969 and told her the "Honey" experiment was over. It wasn't because of her ratings or on-air performance. According to them, it was the fact that it wasn't a woman's job to read the news. After the better part of almost two years as the weekend night jock, filling in for absent announcers, doing any number of station promotions and emceeing concerts, it all came down to the news. Considering the station was too cheap to hire a guy to read the news during her six-hour weekend shift and that she had, until that point in time, handled it admirably by herself, it seemed like a slap in the face. "They never really gave me any insight into why they thought that way," says Moffet. "They just said, 'No, this isn't working out. Women shouldn't be doing the news.' This was the Walter Cronkite era. They didn't look at women as having any gravitas to do news." Towards the end of 1969, Moffet's precedent-setting DJ gig ended. She was not bitter initially, preferring to take a more philosophical approach. The enlightened CFOX management further pressed the boundaries of civility by asking her to train the new male jock who was taking over her time slot. "One more for the team, Lynda. You're a great broad."

They then moved her into the traffic department where commercials are scheduled, thousands per week. It was hardly the same as her on-air job, and she soon tired of the tediousness of it all. One day she found herself in Sinclair's office making what would be her last stand. Her frustration was so profound, she began to cry. "Okay. Every broad in this station has come into my office and cried at one time or another. And now you," said Sinclair. He told her he was sorry but he had to let her go. "Being taken off the air, it pissed me off," she says. "I was heartbroken. CFOX was my world. They were all my friends." Moffet went home, fielded a few calls of sympathy from her station colleagues and wallowed a bit in the betrayal of it all. Word in the English-language radio biz travels fast, especially bad news. After a couple of days of moping around in her parents' house, the phone rang and it was Montreal impresario Donald K. Donald. He offered her a job handling concert tickets for radio stations and assorted special guests, along with booking local Montreal bands. Basically, it was a PR job that put her right back in the game.

Donald K. Donald was at the beginning of what would evolve into a brilliant concert promoter career that would make him – and

Montreal – a huge player on the music concert scene. In 1969 he helped launch Aquarius Records. One of their clients in Nova Scotia was April Wine, who in the following years became a big money-maker for the company. In 1973, the group was working out of Montreal. Guitarist Gary Moffet, Lynda's brother, joined the group and would be a mainstay of their success until 1984. Bruce Moffet, another of Lynda's brothers, would go on to play with Corey Hart, Sass Jordan, and Prairie Oyster. The Moffet family had music in their DNA.

As chief ticket manager for DKD Productions, Lynda got to move in some cool rock circles. DKD was booking some local Montreal bands that had survived the 1960s. Bands like J.B. and the Playboys, the Rabble, the Haunted and Trevor Payne and the Triangle and, from the Ottawa area, groups like the Staccatos who later rebranded as the Five Man Electrical Band. Sometimes these bands would open for big-name U.S. groups that DKD brought to the Montreal Forum.

Moffet, of course, never had any problems getting tickets and she witnessed some historic shows. There was the scintillating Janis Joplin in her early days, a wobbly Jim Morrison, the erratic Sly Stone, and Led Zeppelin mesmerizing a sold-out Forum audience. She got an up-close and personal look at some of rock's biggest and upcoming stars. "They were so young," she says of a backstage encounter with Led Zep lead singer Robert Plant and drummer John Bonham, who were only 22 when they played Montreal. "They still had pimples." Moffet left DKD after one year, when she became pregnant with her son Drew, who was born at the end of 1970. With her son just four years old, Moffet took a shot at politics, running for the Progressive Conservative Party in the the 1974 federal election, a time when female political candidates were a rarity. She ran a noble but doomed campaign in hot-bed Liberal territory, finishing a distant but respectable second. She did all this while working for a talent agency, going to school part-time, and being a mother. When the talent agency she worked for looked as if it was folding, Moffet and a few of her colleagues got together to form their own agency, Music Market. Eventually, she ran the whole show herself, before folding her tent and making her way to Toronto, where she managed bands and set up a successful indie label, Loggerhead Records. Now Moffet and her entertainment consultant husband work out of their home in St. Catharines, where she manages four bands and a solo artist. The working atmosphere of the rock business is marginally better for women today, but she uses her 35-plus years of wisdom and a truckload of experience to keep her "boys" in line. The word "broad" is not part of their vocabulary.

These days, when the subject of Moffet's DJ days come up in conversation, it's mostly about which famous rock stars she met while in the music biz. People are more impressed, it seems, by her rubbing shoulders with Jimmy Page and Robert Plant than they are with the fact that she broke new ground as a female Top 40 jock. Modest to a fault, Moffet prefers to downplay her historic role in Top 40 radio, throwing at least a good part of the credit to the man who hired her, CFOX owner Gord Sinclair, Jr. Modest almost to a fault, Moffet is reluctant to admit any trailblazer role. Today, there are many more women in radio who have her as a role model. Her career path in a male-dominated business, essentialy swimming against the current, is as good an example of perserverence as they are likely to find.

DOUG ACKHURST: CFOX LIKE WKRP IN CINCINNATI — PROGRAM DIRECTOR AND GENERAL MANAGER, 1965–1971

It's the early spring of 1988 and Doug Ackhurst and Dean Hagopian are on a plane to Cleveland to attend the funeral of ex-CFOX DJ "Big Daddy" Bob Ancell. As program director, then general manager, Ackhurst had overseen the mercurial rise of the station from a community-based, country music AM station with 5,000 watts in 1962 to a rockin' Top 40 contender.

Ancell, an Ohio-born DJ and record producer who arrived at the 'FOX in 1967 with plenty of road-tested radio experience, was an important part of the CFOX "Good Guys" era. He was the senior member of the on-air CFOX personalities and, moreover, an American jock others looked up to. A tall, robust man, his nickname was well-earned. He had also earned a reputation as a hard-drinking, hard-gambling, three-packs-of-Camels-a-day man, and it had finally caught up to him. It was the least Ackhurst and Hagopian could do, to be there at his funeral and represent the Canadian contingent for Ancell's send-off. Seriously ill with cancer, Ancell had called his old buddy Dean Hagopian who, along with his wife, took care of Ancell until he had to be hospitalized in Ottawa. Near the end, Hagopian was the only family Ancell had.

CFOX was Ackhurst's second family, a slightly dysfunctional one, but a family nevertheless. He was married into it for almost eight years as a kind of den father to the cast of CFOX characters. Ancell had given much to CFOX, mentoring the younger DJs and even the struggling-to-succeed concert promoter Donald K. Donald. The CFOX family may have been somewhat unpredictable, but that day Ancell had two members of his CFOX family there to see him off. It was the right thing to do.

Ackhurst was barely out of university in 1965. He became the program director and then general manager of CFOX within two years. He was the 22-year-old "boy wonder," said one newspaper article, after his stewardship had taken CFOX from the bottom of the ratings pile to the No. 3 radio station in Montreal. But he was hardly a neophyte pretender to the radio business. He had started with Sinclair's Lakeshore Broadcasting, which had launched CFOX in 1962. He worked every summer during his four years at a West Island high school, then repeated that cycle for the four months between each academic year in university. By the time he joined 'FOX full-time, he had amassed a legion of knowledge of the radio biz from the ground up. Really, he was no boy wonder, but that newspaper article nevertheless made him feel like he'd arrived. Behind-the-scenes radio guys didn't get much attention.

For the first four years, Ackhurst worked at CFOX part-time. The station's mandate was to be the voice of Montreal's West Island community. That was one of the main conditions to Sinclair's license from the CRTC. "It [CFOX] was a kind of extreme MOR [middle of the road] station," Ackhurst says. "Every Sunday they had a rosary broadcast from some local church at 7 p.m. They had to do all sorts of stupid things. A lot of dumb things. I'm not sure anyone was listening, but it was a start. It was a hell of a training ground for me." Sinclair decided traditional down-home country was the format to go with. At first, it was a "real tough sell," Ackhurst remembers. But he kept his comments to himself. By 1965, he told Sinclair he wanted to get into TV. Ackhurst was talked out of it by his very persuasive boss, who offered him a promotion to program director. Ackhurst had only one condition for staying: change the format, dump the country, and go solid rock 'n' roll. Sinclair, who once told Ackhurst that he would never play the Beatles, relented.

The CFOX country gentlemen were put out to pasture and in came a couple of hotshot American DJs, Bob Baker and Bob Ancell, both smooth-talking personalities with just the right amount of cachet for the times. The U.S. had a head start on Canada in the fledgling Top 40 radio format business. As station owner, Sinclair, a conservative man, must have felt he was out on a limb. But with two seasoned DJs like Baker and Ancell, and the addition of morning man Dean Hagopian, the station was off to a good start. Sinclair and Ackhurst drove down to Massena, New York, where Baker was broadcasting his radio show out of the local Holiday Inn. Baker was a master improviser and a bit of a technical wizard, and he impressed the hell out of Ackhurst and Sinclair.

"It was the first time we'd ever seen an American DJ work live," Ackhurst says. "Baker had these huge earphones we'd never seen before. He was a bear of a man. He'd throw things around; he had a terrible temper." They loved him and hired him to do the afternoon show at CFOX. Baker held down two jobs, commuting back and forth between Montreal and Massena.

Baker introduced CFOX to his homemade reverb/echo machine, a plywood box with "springs and wires" that produced a kind of sound that was hot in the early days of Top 40 radio. It also came with a button that repeated end-of-word sounds, mimicking nature's echo. A simple "Hello" would repeat the last couple of letters, HELL-O-O-O-O. Sinclair loved it and drove the staff crazy by using it continuously for days after Baker helped the CFOX engineer install it. The echo effect became a frequent go-to sound for Top 40 stations in North America. Baker had "Americanized" CFOX, and Ackhurst couldn't have been more pleased. As program director of the only Top 40 station in Montreal, one that went from nowhere in the ratings to the top three in Montreal in six months, he had bragging rights. No more apologies for replacing a format that could put a bridge club to sleep.

Ackhurst saw a lot of DJs come and go at CFOX, but he says they basically remained a family, a little like the one on the popular TV sitcom of the late '70s and early '80s, *WKRP in Cincinnati*, only more real-life weird. Whether by committee or individual revelation, CFOX decided to do a Thanksgiving promotion using a live turkey as the central character. The idea was for listeners to guess how much weight the turkey would gain by the time Thanksgiving Day rolled around. (In a famous episode of *WKRP in Cincinnati*, hapless but earnest station owner Arthur "Big Guy" Carlson decided that dropping live turkeys from a helicopter would be a great Thanksgiving Day station promotion event. "As God is my witness, I thought turkeys could fly," said Carlson in the aftermath.) The CFOX turkey promo, just like the WKRP one, went comically wrong. The resident CFOX turkey, though apparently well-fed, stank up the studios and lost weight instead of gaining. Eventually, someone won a free Thanksgiving turkey, but details of the actual turkey weight were deliberately fudged so the contest didn't completely tank. The fate of the 'FOX turkey remains a mystery.

Some of CFOX's success was a kind of "smoke and mirrors" approach to radio, Ackhurst says. Like the traffic reports on *WKRP in Cincinnati* where fictional newsman Les Nessman beat on his chest to simulate the noise of the station's non-existent traffic helicopter, CFOX too had its Nessman moments. The guy who provided them was Barry Gordon, a brand new Montrealer who was on his way back from picking up CFOX's mail at their downtown post office box. You had to multi-task in those days and on his drive back to the West Island, the station asked him to deliver a few traffic reports. He knew only one way back to the station, so he wasn't about to take any deviations. Thinking in his seat and improvising, Gordon deliberately mumbled his way through a couple of fake traffic reports.

Drivers tuned to CFOX that afternoon looking for directions were on their own. It was just another *WKRP* moment for a new member of Ackhurst's flaky 'FOX family.

Ackhurst and the 'FOX staff were having a ball and there was no dearth of wild promotion ideas being kicked around. Bring on the next weird idea. Why not have listeners mail in their radios – on and tuned to CFOX – to the station? There were no winners for this, just a bunch of loyal listeners with transistor radios they knew they'd never get back. In the weeks following the promotion, mailboxes in Montreal had the muffled soundtrack of CFOX coming from within. The post office employees handling mail that played music were a bit baffled – and upset. This was not a good time to be messing around with mailboxes and the post office. The FLQ had been using Montreal mailboxes to plant bombs. These were anxious times for post office employees and police. Ackhurst heard from authorities in no uncertain terms that this promotion was not appreciated. There was certainly a lot of publicity but, in the end, it too was a bit of a turkey promotion. "The radio business was fun in those days," Ackhurst says. "But there's good days and bad days, right? Good ideas and bad ideas, too."

While CFOX was virtually unchallenged in the Montreal Top 40 radio field of the day, from 1965 to 1970, they were ultimately done in by an ongoing problem: their 10,000 watts didn't quite reach downtown Montreal. An offer from Allan Waters, who owned CHUM in Toronto, to buy CFOX and perhaps take it to a more powerful place, didn't work out. The Canadian Radio and Television Commission (CRTC), established in 1968 and then headed up by Pierre Juneau, refused to consider CFOX as anything other than a community radio station, instead of a downtown radio station. "Our license was quite specific," Ackhurst says. "It was Lakeshore Broadcasting. You can't fight the government." Ackhurst has no love lost for CRTC chair Pierre Juneau. "He was a real asshole about the whole thing." That ruling, along with the defection of CFOX sales manager Jim Sward to CKGM (who eventually took a number of 'FOX DJs with him downtown), sank the station. By 1971, it was pretty much downhill for the little station that could.

Ackhurst wound up in Ontario, like many English-speaking Quebecers who fled the province after the PQ came to power in 1976. Ironically, he wound up managing several radio stations in that province owned and operated by Télémedia, a company based in Montreal. Ackhurst believes he was hired by Télémedia because of his background in the Montreal radio business. "I think it worked out because I understood the mentality [of Quebec] a little bit. I consider myself a Quebecer in many respects," he says, even after living more than 40 years in Ontario. Ackhurst retired from radio after finishing his career with the Fan, a sports talk radio station in Toronto now owned by Rogers.

CHAPTER SEVEN

Pioneer Montreal Rockers
Make Their Mark

THE BOYS IN THE BAND

When American rock 'n' roll filtered its way onto Canadian radio stations, the sound inspired hundreds of fledgling musicians, some with more natural talent and ambition than others. It was a time when certain innate leadership skills in teenage boys – the ones who would put the whole thing together – would surface. All one needed to do was find three or four other guys who were similarly hooked on rock, and had a guitar and amp of their own. Finding a drummer with the necessary equipment was always the most difficult. The next problem would be to find out which member of the newly formed band had parents cool and patient enough to allow them to use their garage or basement to rehearse.

After a moderate amount of rehearsal time, the next step would be to find a place to perform, which, in the early to mid-1960s, meant high school gymnasiums, YMCAs, church basement dances, or pool and park gigs. A band might even hire a manager, who probably did not have any experience. He would be the guy who was not failing high school math, had some elementary experience with all things electric and was not afraid to cold-call adults. There were never enough gigs to go around relative to the number of bands sprouting up on the early Montreal rock 'n' roll scene. Friendships and alliances were made and broken. Bands came and went. But some, like the Haunted and J.B. and the Playboys, still enjoy legendary status.

193

At his home in Montreal, Bill Hill listened to whatever was on the radio and what he could find in the home record collection. He grew up in a musical family; his father was a musician and his two older sisters were graduates of the London Conservatory of Music. As the junior member of the family, he deferred to his sisters' musical tastes and listened to the sounds of Elvis, and Bill Haley and the Comets – hits of the late '50s and early '60s. Thanks to them – and to his next-door neighbour, who owned an acoustic guitar – Hill began a love affair with the guitar that has lasted decades. When he finally got one of his own, it changed the way he listened to music forever. He cued in on Presley's lead guitarist, Scotty Moore. "People would come into our house and say, 'Wow, you have a lot of Elvis records. You must be a fan,'" Hill remembers. "I'd say, 'Well, I'm a fan of the guitarist.'" There weren't many Elvis fans honing in on the singer's lead guitarist, though Keith Richards of the Rolling Stones called Moore one of his earliest influences.

In the late 1950s, well before the British invasion, Hill put together his first rock group: the Del Cappos. (A capo is a clamp that is strapped onto the neck of a guitar to raise the guitar's pitch). Hill had a new electric guitar thanks to a deal with his father that involved a haircut. He was also gigging with his part-time musician father's jazz band, where he got to stretch out his young fingers beyond the limitations of the Del Cappos' early 1960s rock songs.

The Del Cappos didn't last long and, while attending Monkland High School in Montreal's west end, Hill joined a band with guys a couple of years older, who were playing club gigs. It was a step up from the weekend church basement circuit and Hill found himself playing much more often, getting home at 3 a.m. and getting up for classes the next day. The band, Dave Nicholls and the Coins, wanted to hit the road. But Hill was still in school and was not inclined to make the serious move to full-time musician. It was a wise decision, despite the disappointment of his bandmates. "I enjoyed that band," says Hill. "We were making pretty good money for the time and I thought we had a great sound." Then he got a call from

Dave Nicholls' younger brother Allan. He wanted to start up a new band, one that would soon have Hill putting aside any regrets about leaving his former band behind. Nicholls would be lead singer with Hill on lead guitar; Andy Kaye (born Kajachanei) on rhythm guitar; Lou Atkins, who, like Kaye, eschewed his given surname Yachnin for a more rock 'n' roll friendly version, on bass. Backing it all up on drums was Doug West. In a small basement studio below the B-Sharp Music Bar, using a three-track movie recording machine, the group, under the name Al Nicholls and the Playboys, put out their first single, "Cheryl," Nicholls' ode to his first girlfriend. The B-side was a cover of the Beatles' "All My Lovin'."

Their first manager, Lionel Pasen, was hardly steeped in the business of rock 'n' roll; he was in the vitamin and perfume business, but the group was impressed with his credentials enough to think maybe he'd be their Brian Epstein. The first order of business was a name change. "J.B." was a frequent cartoon character in *Playboy* magazine, so ultimately the band drew heavily from the popular adult magazine of the day to become J.B. and the Playboys. Their mascot/brand symbol was a stick man in a top hat with a cane, leaning jauntily to one side. J.B. was featured on West's bass drum and on the cover of their first album, a brilliant but simple form of marketing. In later years, many bands would adopt a similar kind of branding or styling of the band's name or sound. Dressed alike in their shiny suits and pointed-toe Beatles boots, they soon became a fixture on the Montreal rock show circuit, playing Beatles tunes before many had even seen or heard of them, thanks to Nicholls' rock music-loving aunt, who lived in Britain and sent him pre-North America-released records. Like many start-up bands of the day, they performed mostly cover versions of other established artists. Soon after their 1964 start, Kaye, Hill, and Nicholls came up with some original material to mix with cover songs.

In the early-to-mid 1960s, most local Montreal rock 'n' roll bands were in charge of their own promotion, but Pasen made sure to nurture the relationship between the Top 40 DJs of the day and the band. At first, it was next to impossible to get any radio airplay. The rock band word-of-mouth grapevine was the next best thing.

After gigging Montreal's church, high school, and dance club circuit, word got around that J.B. and the Playboys were contenders. It was a brilliant promotional move when the boys had hot, new Top 40 CFCF-600 AM DJ Dave Boxer emcee one of their appearances at a local Montreal high school. Boxer had a following of his own. When he showed up to introduce the band, his radio fan base and J.B.'s combined to make a pivotal event. It didn't hurt, either, that Boxer mentioned them on his show the next Monday. A shout-out on Boxer's 6 to10 p.m. Top 40 hits show was more than equal to slapping up hundreds of posters advertising their next gig. The clean-cut J.B. and the Playboys were Boxer's idea of what a rock 'n' roll band should sound and look like. He became a J.B. booster, playing their singles and having them as guests on his show. Likewise, CFOX DJ Dean Hagopian joined the J.B. fan club when the station went to a full Top 40 format in 1965. Well before any Canadian-content regulations came into effect, the burgeoning Montreal rock band scene was impossible to ignore, even for radio stations whose music content was almost 100 percent American.

Riding the post-Boxer promo buzz, the band got an invitation to play Montreal's local version of Dick Clark's *American Bandstand, Like Young* – a teen-oriented dance show broadcast on CFCF-TV every Saturday. These shows called for groups to lip-synch along with an in-studio recording. But the band, who had yet to record any singles, came into the TV studio and set up as they would for a live gig and sang one of the songs they had written. "We set up our equipment in a really neat kind of way," says Hill. "They [CFCF] were really behind the times as far as recording live on that show. And the way we set up, we sounded not too bad for TV." They sounded good enough to get the attention of RCA Records, who called them a few days later and signed them to a recording contract. So far, the whole ride had taken less than a year to unfold.

As the front man of J.B., Nicholls had all the charisma and voice of a natural performer. The group tried not to take themselves too seriously on stage, and led by the stellar guitar work of Hill and Nicholls, the band became one of Montreal's favourite live acts. With the simultaneous release of three singles on RCA, something the record company had never done before, the boys quickly found a home on Dave Boxer's CFCF charts. "Those three singles charted in the Top 10 on CFCF in April 1965," said Nicholls. "And we started to get airplay in eastern Canada." One of the singles, "My Delight," got good airplay on both CFCF and CFOX. It was a simple, danceable, catchy rock song that blended the early Brit-invasion groups with a little Buddy Holly. Hill's brief, but crisp, guitar solo punctuated the opening notes of the song. The Kaye/Nicholls lyrics were simple, no-nonsense rock love songs:

> I love her with all of my might
> And I'm yearnin' to hold her tight
> And I hope I'll see her tonight
> Because she's my delight

> (Lyrics used with permission)

It was the power of Top 40 radio that put the group's name on every teenager's must-see list. Writing in his *Rosemère Journal* column under the pen name Willy Spots, Donald Tarlton (a.k.a. Donald K. Donald) called Allan Nicholls the "most promising Canadian singer" and the band the "best Canadian group."

They became one of the hottest Montreal-based rock bands of 1965. At one point, there was a line of suits, shoes, and shirts named after the band being sold at Eaton's department stores. Hill thought the group had arrived when, on a trip to the signature downtown store, he got on the elevator to check out the J.B. fashion line. On one whole wall of the elevator was a poster of all five Playboys dressed in their Eaton's finery, pointing to their footwear. Hill lingered for a bit, savouring his rock 'n' roll living-colour moment.

Having exhausted different places to play in their hometown, the group set out on the road, with Hill driving one of the two J.B. vehicles (with a U-Haul behind each). The boys toured Ontario and Atlantic Canada. Despite their presence on the Top 40 charts in Montreal, there was never any guarantee that people coming to their concerts in other towns had heard the group's recently released singles. Rock groups starting out in the 1960s in Canada often had a local following with limited geographical reach. While the band played before crowds of 3,000 people at the Bonaventure Curling Club in Montreal, their fan base was still a work-in-progress in towns like Moncton and Fredericton.

When the Rolling Stones came to the Maurice Richard Arena on April 23, 1965, for their inaugural North American tour, J.B. and the Playboys were on the bill. It wouldn't be the first time they brushed shoulders as an opening act with some of rock's bigger attractions. These included the Dave Clark Five, the Mamas and the Papas, and the Beach Boys when they toured eastern Canada. When the band arrived to set up their equipment on stage at the Stones concert, they thought they would be the last act before the Stones came on after an intermission. "Not so," said the promoters. "You guys are going on first." In a move that could have been a career killer, the boys decided that if they couldn't open for the Stones, they weren't going to play at all. Though there were apparently some important music execs in the crowd that night looking to check J.B. out, they held firm, in a moment of pride that Donald Tarlton still thinks was a mistake.

Looking back, Hill has no regrets about the group's decision. "I would do the same thing," he says. "We were headliners in our city," and he reminded the CKGM concert organizers of that backstage. "We were probably the biggest act in Montreal at the time," Hill says. "Playing the show would not have enhanced our popularity." So the group made their stand. At the end of the concert, after the Stones finished their set, all five members of J.B. came onto the stage for the final bows, just to let their Montreal fans know they were there.

Dave Boxer went to bat for his favourite Montreal group on his show, saying the band should have opened for the Stones. As a DJ for a competing radio station, he had everything to gain by calling out CKGM's apparent lack of concert protocol and sloppy promotional skills. When J.B. and the Playboys moved on with the Stones' tour to three Canadian concerts in Ottawa, Toronto, and London, they were the unquestioned openers. While in London, the group drew some unexpected bad-boys-of-rock cred. The city's police chief blamed J.B. and the Stones for a riot that took place about 15 minutes into the Stones' set and police cut power to the stage. "Our instruments

J.B. and the Playboys, with their trademark slick, Beatles-influenced suits, cut their first and only LP in 1965, which had four songs that made the Top 40 charts in eastern Canada.
Courtesy of Allan Nicholls.

wouldn't work, and the place was dark. There was a riot but it wasn't our fault. We're always the ones to get the blame," Jagger said of the affair. This time they shared the blame with the clean-cut boys of J.B. and the Playboys. "We were thrilled to death," says Hill.

In the summer of 1965, the band went to Toronto to record what turned out to be their only album. RCA decided most first albums were the equivalent of an introduction and titled it *J.B. and the Playboys,* with a cover photo of the boys and their "mascot" J.B. in his rightful place beside their name. Unfortunately, the album wasn't the defining moment they thought it would be. After just a year and

By 1967, rock group styles and music had changed dramatically and J.B. and the Playboys were no different when they morphed into the Carnival Connection. The hair was longer, the matching suits gone, and the sound leaning towards the psychedelic.
Courtesy of Allan Nicholls.

a half together and in a kind of touring quagmire, RCA sent them to New York, where it was assumed new opportunities would arise. Under new direction and with a new studio producer, the band went after that elusive song that would put them on the U.S. charts. They needed a hit record. First, there was a problem with their name. So as not to be confused with Gary Lewis and the Playboys, whose "This Diamond Ring" was a hit on the charts, RCA recommended a refit. Trying to not lose the name-recognition momentum they had, they decided on a safe iteration of J.B. for their new name: the Jaybees. There was no time to mourn the transformation; this was a business decision. They'd do whatever it took to be successful in the U.S. Despite the name change making some noise back home, in the U.S. they were a brand new product. Still, the name change had some promoters explaining on advertising posters underneath the new name, "Formerly J.B, and the Playboys."

Their NYC studio work just didn't yield the hit they were looking for, though four singles were released from those New York sessions. "When you left the recording studio in those days," says Hill, "you assumed you'd recorded some sort of hit. Something that's going to make some noise. And there's a million reasons why it doesn't become a hit." They just didn't make the dent in the U.S. charts they were hoping for. It was unsettling being in New York and some of the band members got restless. Bassist Lou Atkins and rhythm guitarist Andy Kaye were let go from the band after manager Basen discovered they had brought marijuana with them across the border. There was to be one more band transformation.

By 1967, the Beatles had stopped wearing their matching suits, going for a much more individualized, casual look. Then, with the release of *Sgt. Pepper's Lonely Hearts Club Band*, any preconceived notions of the Fab Four went out the door. Thousands of bands changed their look, and in some cases their names. The Jaybees were also caught up in the sweeping changes of the look and sound of rock 'n' roll. They had already been growing their hair and now, with yet another name change, the Jaybees resurfaced as the Carnival Connection, in full psychedelic '60s mode. As the Carnival Connection, they looked nothing like the boys in the shiny, slim-legged matching suits and Beatles boots.

Hill and Nicholls formed the core of the Carnival Connection. They released the single "Poster Man," composed by the songwriting team of Artie Kornfield and Steven Duboff, who had written "The Rain, the Park and Other Things" for the Cowsills. It was pure pop, a dressed-up studio effort with backup singers, brass, strings and a catchy singalong chorus. The song had a Cowsills feel to it and Nicholls remembers the recording session as something of a soul-sucking experience. "By now we had a new manager and a new producer in New York who took control of the whole process. None of the songs came from us. It was as if we were spectators," he says. "Poster Man" did reasonably well on the charts, but was hardly a game-changer for the group. In fact, this would spell the beginning of the end for J.B. and the Playboys/The Jaybees/Carnival Connection. Near the end of 1969, Nicholls got an opportunity to audition for the Broadway musical *Hair*, and eventually went on to play one of the leads for the next two years. Eight performances a week meant any thought of continuing to be part of the Carnival Connection ended. Except for a brief appearance with Montreal group Mashmakhan, Nicholls was now on a stage of a different kind, appearing in three other Broadway musicals before moving to Los Angeles where he learned the film business at the feet of legendary director Robert Altman. Now a permanent resident of Burlington, Vermont, for the past 20 years, Nicholls keeps busy with his company, Mr. Nickles Music, and tours with his trio, the Hokum Brothers, music still running through his veins.

After the dissolution of the Carnival Connection, Hill played briefly with the band Life, then Freedom North, who released an LP of the same name (produced by Hill) on Donald K. Donald's newly minted Aquarius Records, with two singles, "Ordinary Man" and "Doctor Tom," making the charts in Quebec and eastern Canada in mid-1970. As usual, rock band lineups were fluid and at one point in Freedom North's tenure, the Haunted's Bob Burgess stepped in to play bass. Rare for the time, the group had a female lead singer, Frankie Hart, who later would occasionally sing backup for the Wackers, a California-based band who found a home – and cult status – in Montreal in 1971. Headed up by Randy Bishop and Bob Segarini (and later with ex-Jaybees guitarist J.P. Lauzon), the Wackers were a CHOM-FM favourite whose four albums and two-month, eight-sets-a-night shows at Norm Silver's Moustache, next to the Montreal Forum, are still talked about in the rock-purists-of-a-certain-age circles. The Montreal rock music scene was, at that time, a series of shifting, interchangeable parts.

Freedom North's album was produced in association with CHUM Ltd.-owned Much Productions (with Hill as producer), a decade before it morphed into Canada's first all-music video channel MuchMusic in 1984, launching a new kind of DJ, the VJ. Hill was then hired by Much Productions as a producer, before opening up his own studio, Montreal Sound, which Hill calls a "major league disco studio." He sold Montreal Sound in the mid-1980s, but now he still toys with engineering the odd album and has a small production company with his son. The Nicholls and Hill friendship has survived a long time in rock 'n' roll years, which has been witness to any number of broken relationships. Along with assorted guys from the old NDG days, they still get together on occasional weekends to jam, swap revisionist rock history stories, and share progress updates on grandchildren.

The Haunted: Montreal's Bad Boys of Rock

If J.B. and the Playboys were the yang of Montreal's 1960s rock band scene, then the Haunted were naturals for the yin. The Haunted had way more hard edges, yet the two bands' career trajectories had much in common.

The Haunted and J.B. were at the very top of the Montreal rock music vanguard in the mid-to-late 1960s. Both bands benefitted from Montreal's Top 40 radio jocks Dave Boxer of CFCF, Dean Hagopian of CFOX, and Buddy Gee of CKGM, who gladly played and promoted their music and emceed some of their shows. Boxer's involvement went a step further when he and the Haunted founder Jurgen Peter teamed up to form their own concert booking agency, GASS – Groups and Sound Service – as well as the biweekly newspaper *Music Trend*.

J.B. and the Haunted both travelled to New York to record, and exploded out of the gate with 45s: the Haunted with "1-2-5" and J.B. with "My Delight." Both songs were played in heavy rotation on Montreal Top 40 radio and on eastern Canadian radio. The groups had about the same lifespan, though, with 15 musicians who could call themselves members of the Haunted by the time the group finally imploded in 1971, they had J.B. beat in the revolving-musicians'-door department by a mile.

Jurgen Peter, Pierre Faubert, Glen Holmes, and Peter Symes were the nucleus of the Haunted's early lineup. In 1963, the boys were a band without a singer, struggling just to find a place to play and make a few bucks. Lachine native Bob Burgess alternated over the years as bass player and singer, before settling in as the Haunted's lead singer. By 1965, Faubert had left the band and was replaced by Al Birmingham, who quit McGill University after one semester to become a full-time rock 'n' roll guitar player. Birmingham was a serious blues fan and had picked up the guitar in his early teens. Like thousands of other wannabes, he listened to legendary guitar instrumental wizards like the Ventures, wearing out his turntable trying to replicate their sound. "My first 'real' band was the Centuries," says Birmingham. "I had a Gibson Les Paul, Jr. guitar, which I traded in for a Fender Jazzmaster because it had the cool vibrator lever that the Ventures used. We'd play sock hops at my high school [Beaconsfield High on Montreal's West Island] and the Coop (sometimes called the Red Barn by locals) in nearby Baie d'Urfé." Birmingham had Chuck Berry, Jimmy Reed, and Muddy Waters as his early blues/rock heroes. While he was lead singer in a band called Muddy Waters, Jurgen Peter and Bob Burgess came to check him out. By then, he had switched back to his Gibson (better for blues and rock), and the vibrato-levered Ventures sound was retired. Peter and Burgess were impressed with his version of Chuck Berry's "Oh, Carol," and he was as good as in and along for a ride that would take him well beyond the world of high school sock hops.

The Haunted did not deliberately decide to be the antithesis of most Montreal bands that were Beatles-style cover bands. The original band members were all weaned on blues, as were British groups like the Rolling Stones and the Animals. In the early Montreal rock band scene, there was a plethora of bands that took the matching-wardrobe approach to live performances, but the Haunted were a more street-casual band. There were no trips to Eaton's for a makeover. "The Haunted were a gritty blues-rock band," says Birmingham. They were a garage band, even a proto-punk band – a category that includes such diverse names as the Kingsmen, the Shadows of Knight, the Doors, and Lou Reed. Comparisons to the Rolling Stones persisted, and the band was flattered, though lead singer Bob Burgess was hardly a Mick Jagger clone. After dropping out of Lachine High, much to the dismay of his Pentecostal minister father, he was just kicking around the 'hood in a blue-collar part of Montreal at the

The Haunted were regulars at the Bonaventure Curling Club on Saturday nights during the mid-60s. As headliners, they drew crowds of up to 3,000 dedicated, and sometimes unruly, fans.
Courtesy of Bob Burgess.

time. The whole hair issue was a big deal in 1965, essentially still a clean-cut time in Montreal. Burgess was going against the blue-collar grain when he let his hair grow, taking plenty of razzing on the streets. He had the Brit mod-rocker look down, with just the right amount of attitude and swagger.

Unlike a lot of casual rock bands who gigged only on weekends, the Haunted were full-time rock musicians, a requirement set down by Peter who, though the band went through a couple of hit-and-miss managers, eventually became the de facto manager/leader of the group. People had to quit their day jobs. Peter was older by a few years and had an innate sense of how to handle bookings and promotions. As the self-designated COO of the Haunted, his business-like approach would not always sit well with some band members, especially lead singer Burgess, who had his share of disagreements with his bandmate over the years.

Entering a battle of the bands competition at the Montreal Forum in early January 1966 turned out to be a pivotal decision. Dubbed a most uncool "Bring Your Lunch Hopsville," the event was an all-day affair sponsored by Quality Records and hosted by CFCF DJ Dave Boxer. There was some significant competition from other Canadian bands like the Staccatos, a pre-Blood, Sweat & Tears with David Clayton-Thomas, and J.B. and the Playboys, among others. Each band had two 20-minute sets to impress. "We showed up and that was it, the place went nuts. There was something there that the crowd liked," says Burgess. The Haunted prevailed, taking the top prize: free studio recording time with Quality Records. The 45 they recorded with Quality had the song "1-2-5" on the A-side and "Eight o'Clock in the Morning" on the B-side. The A-side song, written by Peter and Burgess, turned out to be a bargain for Quality Records in terms of studio time, with the group wrapping up the song in just a couple of hours – an investment that worked out well for both the band and Quality Records. The lyrics for "1-2-5" had a raunchy edge to them.

> Walking down the street on a foggy night
> I saw a young girl standing under a light
> Her face was pale and her skirt was tight
> Had a five-dollar bill, I felt alright

(Lyrics used with permission)

The song soon found its way onto Dave Boxer's CFCF Top 10 hits in May 1966, sandwiched at No. 2 between the Mamas and the Papas' No. 1 hit "Monday Monday" and the Stones' "Paint It Black." For a week or two they weren't just a Stones knock-off, but better. "Not bad for a song about a hooker and drugs," says Burgess.

The song "1-2-5" has enjoyed legendary status since it peaked on the charts some 50 years ago. The band had other singles that made the Top 40: five all together, including a French version of the

Jimi Hendrix song "Purple Haze," titled "Vapeur Mauve." None had the lasting impact of "1-2-5," which sold 15,000 copies despite little help from Quality Records. (Someone was asleep at the switch when early pressings of the group's first 45 had their name misspelled as "the Hunted.")

The buzz from the song meant other Canadian Top 40 radio stations wanted to play it. Quality Records suddenly became more interested, after hearing the ring of the cash register. The single was then re-released by other labels in the U.S., Australia, and Europe. The song's lyrics, particularly the third verse, which made reference to the exchange of money for sexual services and Mary Jane, the coded words for marijuana, had Quality Records nervous. So, the Canadian-released single had a sanitized version while other markets got the raw version of "1-2-5." The song opened with Burgess' harmonica and an organ brought in just for the recording session, all topped off by a memorable Gibson fuzz-tone-driven guitar solo by Birmingham. It came in at two minutes and 31 seconds.

The Haunted singles, especially "1-2-5," have shown up on various compilation albums released many years after the band dissolved in 1971. The song has rated a spin or two on *Little Steven's Underground Garage*, the popular nationally syndicated Sirius Satellite Radio show hosted by Steve van Zandt, lead guitarist for Springsteen's E Street Band. That single has given the band a seemingly unlimited expiry date as online music enterprises resuscitate edgy, garage-style '60s and '70s music with a whole new generation discovering it for the first time. The Haunted even garnered a half-hour on the 1967 CBC-produced centennial TV series, *The Restless Years*, featuring the boys playing one of their hits, "Mona," a cover of the 1957 original by Bo Diddley. While other Canadian rock groups groped for ways to get noticed, the Haunted were blessed by the rock gods.

As co-writer, Burgess still occasionally gets royalty cheques for "1-2-5." "They're small cheques," he admits. "My wife jokes, 'Geez, I could have married Paul McCartney.' Listen, I tell her, I get the same cheques as McCartney, only all my zeros are at the beginning as opposed to the end." Burgess did very well with the Haunted, though by the end of 1966, he bailed out and moved on to form another band,

Our Generation. There was one too many arguments with Peter, artistic or otherwise, and Burgess decided to move on. Today they're still in touch, but the subject of Burgess' departure remains a delicate topic.

When the Haunted played the Bonaventure Curling Club, they soon became headliners in front of some big Saturday night crowds. They had a loyal fan club (Peter even arranged to have school buses get them to Haunted gigs, including the Bonaventure). As a Lachine boy, Burgess could look out into the crowd and see some of his hometown acquaintances, pre-stoked on beer and pot, ready for some Saturday night action. Haunted fans were not big dancers. They were there to support their favourite band but, for some of them, that wasn't a passive kind of activity. They were there to let off steam and, inevitably, there were some altercations. Word on the street was that a Haunted night at the Bonaventure meant there were risks involved. The band just seemed to naturally attract guys who were more '50s than '60s, with cigarette packs tucked under the sleeve of their white T-shirts, hair short and greased back, *Rumble Fish*-style. Between sets, the band mingled easily with the crowd; no backroom, between-sets retreat for these guys. Still, at the Bonaventure, security was rudimentary and they often had a front-row seat to the various fracases that broke out. "Every time we played, there were big scraps right up in front of the stage," says Burgess. "We just kept on playing. Sometimes guys would get a little too close and we had two roadies, one of whom, George Durocher, was a big guy. Nobody challenged him."

Our Generation didn't last long for Burgess, but the group didn't have to wait as long as the Haunted to play in front of a big crowd. In 1968, the new group was on the same bill as Burgess' former band at Montreal's first "International Pop Festival," sponsored by CFOX and East/West Productions at the Autostade – a god-awful outdoor stadium that stood as a monument to concrete, built as part of Expo 67. It was a wild day, with the Who as headliners, along with Procol Harum, Mitch Ryder, the Troggs, and the Ohio Express. Our Generation had the hit "I'm a Man" going for them, but the Autostade's tiny sound system didn't do them any favours.

The local bands had all been booked early in the concert lineup, but the Haunted got two kicks at the can that night, playing the second set using the Who's sound system that had more oomph to it. Procol Harum was missing in action and the Ohio Express gave Montreal's fickle fans a live taste of their then current hit "Yummy Yummy Yummy (I've Got Love in my Tummy)." Fortunately, the crowd was too stoned to boo. These kind of concerts were icing on the cake for the Haunted, who were very busy playing some 300 gigs around the city, the province and eastern Canada. Both francophone and anglophone audiences embraced them. They sang in Toronto before that city was closed to bands who were not based there. They did not feel the need to explore possible fame and fortune in the U.S. "We thought we were on top of the world right where we were," says Birmingham. "No foreign touring required. It was a lifestyle thing for me," says Birmingham. "I lived on the waterfront in suburbia, drove a souped-up Mini-Cooper S, then a Corvette Roadster, partied continuously, and gigged in arenas all over Quebec and eastern Canada. Who needs musty hotel rooms in faraway places with unknown audiences?"

Birmingham was more laid-back than Burgess and left the band on good terms. He came back one more time, in 1968, at Peter's behest when the group's bass player was too ill to play at Place des Nations in front of their biggest crowd ever. That same summer, Birmingham decided Vancouver was the place he wanted to be. Having managed his money well, he bought his first house at 21. Then he returned to Montreal where, inspired by Peter, he studied for his helicopter license. Birmingham eventually bought his own helicopter, on which both he and Peter trained, and after he was fully licensed, he would occasionally ferry members of his old band to nearby gigs. This was first-class travel for a band used to jamming five guys into a beat-up van. Today, he is back on the West Coast with his wife and three adult children who live in the Vancouver area. Music he recorded with his band Aeon between '74 and '76 in Montreal – with Burgess and ex-Rabble guitarist Rick Metcalf – has recently been released digitally. He makes regular visits to Montreal, where he reconnects with some of the Haunted and other assorted musicians to plug in and once again rattle the walls of a suburban garage.

Burgess is one of the musicians Birmingham gets together with when he's in town. He still calls himself a musician, though his CV reveals his transition from a blue-collar rock guy to a straight, white-collar success story. He took on his first 9 to 5 gig as music director at CFCF radio, then to its FM side at CFQR. After getting squeezed out in a round of budget-cutting layoffs, he worked in print sales in Vancouver, Ottawa, and Toronto. For Burgess, giving up the biz of making music was borne from a realization that he needed a day job. "Necessity being the mother of invention," he says. "I had to think about my future. All your friends tell you that you can sell. I didn't think so, but apparently, I can."

Now retired and living comfortably in an off-island Montreal suburb, Burgess doesn't dwell too much on whether the Haunted could have been bigger. After he left, replaced by lead singer Johnny Monk, the band moved towards a more psychedelic sound, and bought into a more Hendrix-influenced style, mixing in their trademark songs. Peter stopped playing live and took up managing the group, eventually leaving. The flashbacks are self-generated. "I do occasionally wonder what it might have been like to make it big across Canada and in the U.S.," says Burgess. "We could have been like the Guess Who. We could have been *that* band. But you know what? Egos being what they are, you're young. It's just the way it goes."

CHAPTER EIGHT

El Primo Promoter

DONALD K. DONALD: THE P.T. BARNUM
OF ROCK CONCERTS

There are some uncanny similarities between Montreal rock concert producer Donald K. Donald (born Donald K. Tarlton) and his mentor, legendary concert and theatre promoter Samuel (Sam) Gesser. Gesser was *the* pioneer music impresario in Montreal, starting in the early 1950s. He was the first to bring folk singer Pete Seeger to Montreal, in 1953, when Seeger was blacklisted during the McCarthy era in the U.S. The music promotion business is all about taking chances, and a young Donald Tarlton took his cue from a master like Gesser.

Gesser was only 23 when he booked Seeger. He was even younger when he took a shine to folk music, eventually founding Allied Records in Canada to promote Canadian folk music, something no one else was doing at the time. Tarlton and partner Terry Flood co-founded Aquarius Records in 1969, the same year that Gesser brought in an unpredictable but prodigiously talented Janis Joplin for a concert at the Montreal Forum. Gesser was no rock 'n' roller. His taste in music ran along the lines of artists like Harry Belafonte, Liberace, Canadian opera singer Maureen Forrester, pianist Glenn Gould and Greek singer Nana Mouskouri, all of whom he brought in to perform at the newly constructed Place des Arts. He made a star out of Mouskouri, who still sells out when she travels to Montreal. When Tarlton's concert promotion company DKD Productions was in high gear, Tarlton made Montreal the Mecca of rock for groups like Pink Floyd, Genesis, Jethro Tull, Gentle Giant, Supertramp, Yes, and Emerson, Lake and Palmer.

211

Backstage at the Forum one night, Gesser was showing Tarlton the ropes as he dropped by to greet Janis Joplin before her concert. Gesser had dabbled in a few rock concerts, producing Canadian folk singer Gordon Lightfoot, and the Band, who were in the throes of making their mark on the rock music scene. When Joplin came out of her dressing room to meet Gesser and Tarlton, she was already well into her pre-concert warm-up mode which consisted of heavy doses of Southern Comfort. What happened next became Montreal rock concert folklore. "It was the beginning of the rock 'n' roll era and Sam had a hard time relating with the culture," says Tarlton. "He hired me as the stage manager. Janis was drunk, and as she and Gesser were introduced, she promptly threw up all over his shoes. Sam was horrified, looked at me and said, 'Donald, you can take over all the rock stuff from here.' And that was it. I became the rock promoter of Montreal." Janis didn't even apologize and, feeling somewhat refreshed, went out on stage and dazzled a full house. Less than a year later, on October 4, 1970, Joplin was dead. She was 26, the same age as Tarlton the year he, Joplin, and Gesser shared their memorable backstage moment.

Gesser knew when to step aside, but his career as an impresario was hardly over. He just changed gears, pursuing his passion for music and theatre until his death at 78, in 2008. After Gesser passed him the rock concert baton, Tarlton blossomed into one of the major players on the North American rock concert circuit. Tarlton remembers Gesser as "Mr. Show Business." No doubt as Gesser watched his protégé flourish over the years, he saw a lot of himself in Tarlton. Despite the cutthroat nature of the concert promotion business, Tarlton managed to keep his mentor's motto in mind: "It's all about the art. And, oh yeah, making a few bucks wouldn't hurt either."

If there was money in being a carnival barker, Donald Tarlton would have made millions. He was an unapologetic self-promoter from the get-go. That's where he and Gesser differed in style. Tarlton became a brash personality, something he'd been refining since his teenage introduction to rock 'n' roll. Where Gesser was a much more understated promoter and impresario, Tarlton quickly learned that one had to shout over the noise of the rock 'n' roll business to be heard.

Tarlton wasn't exactly born into the chronological heart of the Boomer Generation. The year he was born, 1943, was the big-band era of Tommy Dorsey and Glenn Miller. Artists like Bing Crosby and the Andrews Sisters were topping Billboard's hit charts of the day. In the 1950s, the Tarlton family radio was tuned to either CFCF or CJAD, the two stations of choice for Montreal's English-speaking adult population. A very young Tarlton must have heard the big-band sound leak out of his family radio, but by the mid-1950s, rock music was seeping its way onto radio, TV and into magazines as well as into Tarlton's heart.

On the cusp of adolescence, Tarlton was hearing Bill Haley and the Comets' "Rock Around the Clock" and Elvis' "Heartbreak Hotel," both of which topped the Billboard charts in 1955 and 1956 respectively. After school and on Saturdays he was glued to CJAD when Mike Stephens' Club 800 show was rock-based refreshment from the station's otherwise mature audience programming. "When Elvis came out with 'Heartbreak Hotel,' we'd all phone CJAD and request the song, over and over. We couldn't get enough of it," he says. Soon, Tarlton was off to the local record store cruising for his favourite 45s. When his collection became substantial enough, he took his records and himself on the road to local high schools, churches, youth clubs and YMCAs. Employing American DJ patter, he introduced himself as "Dimpled Donny, the Daffy DJ Making the Scene with My Record Machine." He was a portable jukebox, dimple and all, with two homemade turntables, spinning his own version of the Top 40. He cranked out a teen-oriented column for the *Rosemère Journal*, a weekly newspaper for residents of the northern off-island suburb of Montreal. It was an ideal format to promote his own appearances and include his Top 10 hits package and teen gossip under the pseudonym Willy Spots. Like many Top 40 DJs of the day, Tarlton had a flair for using alternate identities.

Using his newspaper column as leverage to get on major record labels' mailing lists, he received hundreds of free promotional records. He threw out the duds (and there were plenty) and kept the best to play at dances. He had all the latest hits, and he could meet almost any request at events he DJ'ed. Meanwhile, as Willy

Spots, he reviewed the records he received, well before any of Montreal's newspapers or magazines devoted any space for rock music critiques.

Just as the British Invasion was hitting North America, Tarlton and his blossoming record collection landed a job as the Friday-night DJ at a privately owned station, CKJL in St. Jerome, a no-frills operation that was a kind of a test ground for young DJs. He called himself Don E.T. – the E was for Excellent and the T for Terrific. Clever, bold,, and somewhat risqué, Tarlton loved to ask his CKJL audience, "Every record I play has a hole in it, how 'bout you?" The station, which had a mostly French-speaking audience, was hot for the Beatles and the request line often had calls for either "I Wanna Hold Your Hand" or "She Loves You." One Friday night, he decided to give the people what they wanted: he played both Beatles songs over and over, introducing the songs differently each time. He thinks he may have played both about 35 times in a row, after which the request line went silent. A couple of days later, station owner Jean Lalonde got wind of Tarlton's antics and fired him.

He rebounded as an operator at CKGM during its talk show/music mix days of the 1960s, screening calls for the Joe Pine talk show. Then he took on more odd-shift operating and producing gigs at 'GM. He still had DJ ambitions and auditioned several times at the station. Alas, management told him he had "bad diction," not good enough for prime time. It was an epiphany of sorts and he decided to turn back to what he knew best: organizing and emceeing dances. He was stung just a bit by the thwarting of his fledgling radio DJ aspirations, but he didn't look back. Soon, Montreal would hear him on the radio, this time as Donald K. Donald, bad diction and all.

First, it was back to basics. Back to the church basements, youth clubs, school gymnasiums and YMCAs whose mandate it was to keep idle youth off the streets on weekends. With the arrival of the Beatles, dozens of live bands formed around Montreal, all looking for a place to play. Tarlton was happy to oblige them. As one of the few basement impresarios in town, he fielded calls asking if he could line up a band for a Friday or Saturday night dance. The boys in the bands were happy to have some representation. Most newly formed groups had no idea how the music business worked. That's where Tarlton came in. To complete the circle, he lobbied DJs at CFOX, CKGM, and CFCF to make an appearance at a Tarlton-organized dance to introduce the band and hang out for about 15 minutes, before moving on to do another dance – sometimes six in one night. Tarlton gave the jocks 15 percent of the gate and in return they would hype the event, and the music, on their shows. It was the accepted, symbiotic relationship of promoter and DJ at the time.

Everybody came out a winner, especially the DJs, who relied on the extra income to supplement their meagre paycheques. The local bands, Top 40 radio stations, and Tarlton all thrived, riding the wave of a brand-new live Montreal music scene. "The jocks got out into the community," says Tarlton. "It was good for the stations. It was good for business in general. Sharing the gate revenue with the DJs was a trade-off. It was an 'I'll scratch your back, you scratch mine' kind of set-up. Everyone was working for their money."

Switching into high gear and dumping his Dimpled Donny, Willy Spots and Don E.T. personas, he was now Donald K. Donald. The K Tarlton borrowed from famous U.S. DJ Murray the "K" (Kaufman), the self-proclaimed "Fifth Beatle" because of his blanket coverage of the group's first appearance in New York City. The repeated first and last name came from Boston's WMEX Top 40 DJ Melvin K. Melvin, who was also known as the super wound-up, prototypical, fast-talking DJ, J.J. Jeffrey. Tarlton was a DJ at heart; he knew this was a name people would remember. He was now representing some of the hottest Montreal bands like the Haunted, J.B. and the Playboys, the Rabble, Bartholomew Plus Three, and M.G. and the Escorts. To clients he sold not only the bands but also a complete production package, including lights and sound, and even a generator to supplement the rudimentary wiring in the average church basement or high school gymnasium. He could throw in a between-sets DJ if the event could afford it. The bands wanted some punch to their sound, and many couldn't afford all the equipment, so DKD Productions was happy to fill that need, for a price, of course. The Rabble's lead guitarist Mike Harris and vocalist John Pimm remembered their first encounter with Tarlton in a 2008

Montreal *Gazette* interview. "I don't recall the exact details of our meeting Don Tarlton," said Pimm. "He turned up at a gig we were doing, but we all liked him right away because of his enthusiasm and integrity. He was energetic, industrious, honest, and loyal to his acts. A young man in a shirt and tie, Don was intent on building a circuit and reputation from the ground up. He took us on as one of the vehicles with which to accomplish this feat."

Tarlton provided the venues, the PR, and the punch. The infamous Saturday night concerts at the Bonaventure Curling Club (a.k.a. Saturday Night at the Fights, produced by CFCF DJ Dave Boxer) were Donald K. Donald groups for the most part. Popular Montreal bands found themselves rising stars in no time flat, playing to big crowds after auditioning to mostly family and friends in their parents' basement or garage. What they may have lacked in finesse was more than made up for in enthusiasm.

Tarlton recycled his concert profits into buying advertising time on the air to promote his concerts, often in the studio with the DJs talking up his upcoming concerts. "I built all my initial connections, all my initial network, through parlaying my influence and connection to the disc jockeys," Tarlton says. "It was the DJs who provided me with the publicity to bill the acts so they played the record which made the acts stars. They built the image of the artist so the kids would be willing to spend money to come to the shows. If we were going to bring in a big act, the DJs would start focusing and playing their records."

Besides the local Montreal band scene of the mid-to-late 1960s, Tarlton was looking at the bigger picture – bringing American acts to Place des Arts (PDA) and small arenas like the Paul Sauvé. Tarlton brought 1950s rock 'n' roll pioneers Fats Domino and Bo Diddley to PDA one night and, with both on the bill, there were some logistical problems. Tarlton went into Diddley's dressing room before the show and welcomed him to Canada. Then he asked him nicely if he'd start the show. Fats Domino was up after, so Diddley had to be out of the house and his band's equipment dismantled. Diddley, however, was in no hurry to go on stage, at least not until one issue was settled. Diddley aimed his index finger at Tarlton's chest and said,

Donald Tarlton (a.k.a. Donald K. Donald) was into the rock business first as a DJ, then moved to producing local dances before becoming a major player on the international rock concert scene.
Courtesy of Donald Tarlton.

"Mr. Donald, Bo don't go 'til you hit him with the dough." Diddley was a songwriter through and through, even in negotiation mode. This was Tarlton's first experience with a black artist with so much mileage on him; Diddley had been in the music biz since 1943. Many younger black rock and blues artists had been stiffed by shameless promoters over the years, and Diddley was understandably wary. He wasn't a fan of "the cheque is in the mail." Tarlton scrambled to accommodate him and paid in cash. By the time Tarlton brought in James Brown, he was a wiser promoter. Brown had a reputation for being temperamental, and he too did business in cash. This time Tarlton was ready. What he wasn't ready for, however, was Brown's tour manager, who instead of bringing out the requisite calculator and pen, pulled out a gun and laid it on the table, as Tarlton handed over the money. "It was an interesting way of asking someone if the bill is legit," Tarlton says. Brown, who called himself the "Hardest Working Man in Show Business," was full value for the money.

By the end of the 1960s, young music consumers wanted to see the big U.S. rock acts, and Donald K. Donald was happy to accommodate them. He brought in Steppenwolf as the headlining act at the Montreal Forum for his first foray into rock concerts in the big arena. The Forum, with over 16,000 seats, was a far cry from the modest capacity of other venues. Steppenwolf was a hot commodity with their hit "Born to be Wild" in heavy rotation on Top 40 radio, and their music as part of the soundtrack to the classic 1969 film *Easy Rider*. It was quite the night, with Quebec singer Robert Charlebois, Triangle, and Life as the opening acts. Depending on who you talk to, Charlebois stole the show from headliners Steppenwolf that night in June 1969. Donald K. Donald had billed the event as Montreal's "Bicultural Rock Show," a deliberate nod to the significant portion of the crowd who were already Robert Charlebois fans. With his wild, frizzy hair, bulbous nose, Montreal Canadiens sweater and his lyrics sprinkled with joual, he worked the crowd like a pro. With 10,000 seats sold, it was an auspicious Forum debut for DKD Productions.

Tarlton successfully sold the Montreal Forum management on the idea that rock concerts were money-making ventures and they moved to help bankroll Donald K. Donald Productions. The Forum had dabbled in rock concerts, but they were mainly one-off events. U.S.-based promoters would come and offer up a package of artists who were blazing a brand-new touring trail in the early days of rock. In May 1958, Danny and the Juniors, the Diamonds, Buddy Holly and the Crickets, Billy Ford and the Thunderbirds, Jerry Lee Lewis, and Frankie Lymon were all on the Forum bill. Years later when the Brit groups invaded, it was the Beatles, the Rolling Stones, and the Dave Clark Five who headlined with two or three opening acts – all for about five bucks. There was money to be made in rock 'n' roll, so Forum management was more than happy to work with DKD. When Tarlton rolled out his first Forum rock concert, tickets for Steppen-wolf, Charlebois, and Life were seven dollars and 50 cents. Tarlton was not looking for short-term gains; he was a long-term investor and his patience and dedication would eventually pay off. For the next 27 years, DKD and the Montreal Forum enjoyed a happy and mostly profitable promoter/concert-venue marriage.

It was a quick ascension for Tarlton, all things considered. He had done his time in the trenches of the germinating rock music scene in Montreal. At Expo 67, Tarlton had gotten the booking rights for the Garden of Stars concert venue, introducing Canadian rock groups to Montreal's youth market. When Expo ended, many of the pavilions on the site continued to be called *Man and His World*. Tarlton partnered with Terry Flood and turned the former Expo Youth Pavilion into a dance hall, charging 25 cents per person for one hour of taped music and dancing. Taking full advantage of the flexible parameters of capitalism, Tarlton turned that meagre cover charge into bags of quarters by gonging out dancers after one hour, only to have them dance around back to the entrance to cough up another quarter to boogie again. Tarlton had met Flood at Snoopy's, a Montreal dance club that Flood owned. They hit it off and Tarl-ton bought a one-third interest in the club, beginning a partnership that would endure all the bumps and bruises of the rock music biz. Meanwhile, Tarlton opened a club of his own in 1968, Laugh-In, named after the popular comedy TV show of the late 1960s, where he brought in CKGM DJ Ralph Lockwood to add some local ce-lebrity buzz. Laugh-In featured mostly local live bands but, after

Tarlton's Forum-promoting career took off, club-goers there might catch Johnny Winter, Steppenwolf, or the Doors jamming live after a Forum concert appearance.

In 1969, with Flood as president, Tarlton teamed up with Bob Lemm, and Dan and Jack Lazare to found the independent label Aquarius Records, signing up April Wine (then based in Halifax), Mashmakhan, and the Rabble, among others. Of all the early garage bands to come out of Montreal, Tarlton thought the Rabble had the rawest talent, but it was April Wine that turned out to be Aquarius' biggest meal ticket. By the 1980s, they added Corey Hart to the label, who had spectacular success with his hit single "I Wear My Sunglasses at Night." Tarlton has sold his interest in Aquarius but still supports current and classic independent Canadian artists.

It says something about Montreal that by the time the Forum closed for good in 1996, Rush and Céline Dion had accumulated the greatest number of Forum appearances at 16 apiece. The city had an ongoing love affair with Rush, and Dion was one of their own who had made it big. For DKD, this merely proved that Montreal was an open music market: a flexible, sophisticated audience not hung up on the language fault lines. Close behind Rush and Dion in Forum appearances were prog-rock British bands Yes, Emerson, Lake and Palmer, Genesis, Jethro Tull, and Supertramp. Tarlton found that Top 40 groups could not sustain a concert on their own. He would have to package at least three of them on a bill, but that was unwieldy.

Genesis, at first led by Peter Gabriel, played the Forum 12 times. When Gabriel left to pursue his solo career, Phil Collins moved up front for Genesis, before he then moved on as a solo performer, appearing seven times at the Forum. Tarlton was growing up with the Baby Boomer crowds that were his concert meat and potatoes – the same ticket buyers who, in their late teens, fired up a joint before heading out to see Genesis were coming to see Phil Collins years later. DKD brought Britain to Montreal: Rod Stewart, Elton John, David Bowie, Eric Clapton, Led Zeppelin, the Kinks, George Harrison, Ten Years After. and more. They all came to the Montreal Forum.

He gave the Montreal rock concert-going crowd what they wanted and they had favourites like Frank Zappa. Zappa went from

Frank Zappa had a loyal Montreal following and DKD Productions were happy to oblige. After one Montreal Forum concert, Zappa and Robert Charlebois hooked up backstage and a few days later Zappa contributed to the Charlebois song, "Petroleum," which was released as a single, then on the album, "Swing, Charlebois Swing."
Courtesy of Donald Tarlton.

playing before a couple of hundred people at the New Penelope club on Sherbrooke Street to seven Forum concert appearances. Zappa was a very special and single-minded performer. Tarlton recalls telling Zappa before one Forum gig that union rules required there be an intermission in every Forum show. Zappa (then playing with his group, the Mothers of Invention) was not happy. He was a musical free spirit and didn't like the idea of interrupting his momentum for an intermission, then having to crank it up again, after the requisite bathroom break and beer refill. On stage, he did pause – for about a minute or so – telling the audience that this was the intermission. Then he resumed playing. That cost DKD a $5,000 fine. Nonetheless, despite his prima donna behaviour, Zappa had such a loyal Montreal following that Tarlton didn't hesitate to bring him back.

Of course, rock music had its share of divas, but most artists DKD dealt with honoured the terms of their contracts with professional cool. Tarlton learned on the fly how to deal with sensitive musicians. When Johnny Cash came to town, the first Donald K. Donald Productions show at the Forum, there were no special riders in his contract, no "only blue Smarties" for Cash's dressing room. In fact, Tarlton had nothing special in mind for him when he arrived at the Forum the afternoon before he was set to go on. Tarlton came with his own deli sandwich and beverage, only to find it gone when he came back to eat it. Chatting with Tarlton before the show, Cash thanked Tarlton for providing the food. Apparently, the country singer was not used to such pre-concert perks. From that point on Tarlton made a mental note to provide catering to performers; it was the little things that bands remembered about the cities they toured.

Folk-rocker Cat Stevens, flower child that he was, wanted a greenhouse in his Forum dressing room. Rock group Kiss had a standard rider in their contract that said every promoter had to dress up in Kiss makeup and costume. A big man, well over six feet tall, Tarlton was reluctant, but understood the importance of the contract. He must have cut quite the figure parading around the Forum in his Gene Simmons regalia. He freely admits to being a people pleaser. "I was always respectful of the artists and believed in the art of the deal," he says. "It was part of my responsibility and future as an entrepreneur to be hospitable and provide as comfortable an environment as possible so the artists would want to come back to Montreal." If that meant putting on garish makeup and an unflattering, tight Kiss costume, then so be it.

The art of the deal sometimes involved heading off potential problems, especially with unpredictable performers like Jim Morrison of the Doors. After a September 1969 CNE concert in Toronto, the Doors were scheduled to perform in Montreal the next night. Morrison wanted to take the train, while his bandmates chose to fly. Taking no chances that the star of the show might go AWOL, Tarlton had three members of his staff meet Morrison at Montreal's Central Station and make sure he got to the hotel. At the Doors' Toronto concert, a one-day pop festival, John Lennon and the Plastic Ono Band had made a special guest appearance. After meeting with Tarlton

Part of any Kiss contract was that the concert promoter had to dress up in full make-up and Kiss regalia. Tarlton fit right in alongside Kiss lead singer Gene Simmons and DKD Productions marketing director Leisa Lea.
Courtesy of Donald Tarlton.

in Toronto, Lennon asked him to take a special message to the Montreal Forum audience the next night. So, before the Doors came on, Tarlton did something he had never done: he went out on stage to address the crowd. He explained to the audience that he had a message from John Lennon, who had just three months earlier landed in Montreal to stage his Bed-in for Peace. Tarlton had a visceral connection to that event and the crowd grew quiet at the mention of Lennon's name. "John Lennon wanted to be here tonight to deliver this message to you himself," Tarlton said to the sold-out Forum audience. "But he wasn't able, so he asked me to deliver it for him. He sends his love and asks one favour, 'Give Peace a Chance.'" The crowd went crazy. About 15,000 Bic lighters lit up the Forum as people chanted "Give peace a chance" over and over again. Tarlton remembers this as the most spiritually moving event he was ever part of in his lengthy career as a promoter. He was deeply moved by the crowd's response and rode that high – and a great Doors performance – for about 24 hours.

Unfortunately, that high came crashing down the next day when Tarlton and his staffers checked out the review in the Montreal *Gazette* by rock music critic Juan Rodriguez. "Donald K. Donald," Rodriguez wrote, "has found a new way to count the house. Just have everyone light up a lighter and then multiply it by $7.50." Rodriguez had cultivated a reputation as the curmudgeonly rock critic. Tarlton was stung by his cynicism, downgrading a simple message of peace into something crass and misanthropic. There would be another run-in with Rodriguez when DKD Productions (along with Top 40 radio station CFOX) brought Led Zeppelin to Montreal for their first concert appearance, in April 1970. That night, Tarlton saw his biggest Forum crowd yet, almost selling out all of the 17,872 available seats. There were no opening acts and Led Zeppelin dazzled the crowd, many of whom had clearly been preparing for the 7 p.m. concert well in advance. Zep did not disappoint, playing for almost three hours. That concert is still called the greatest live concert ever held at the Montreal Forum. The crowd, DKD, his staff, Zep's management, and band members thought the almost three-hour marathon of blues and rock had hit the bull's eye, but not everyone was on the same page.

The *Gazette*, anticipating the significance of Led Zeppelin's premier Montreal appearance, sent two critics to take in the show: Rodriguez and his colleague Herbert Aronoff. The next day their reviews ran side by side. Tarlton was once again deflated when he read both critics, who took potshots at the show. Rodriguez, in particular, called Zeppelin's performance "ridiculously monotonous," "sluggish" and "miserable." Aronoff was less brutal, but was almost as unimpressed as his *Gazette* colleague. "What came across at the Forum was more expertise than honest excitement, a tired, almost automatic performance that hardly did justice to the two Zeppelin albums," Aronoff wrote. Tarlton, burned once again by Rodriguez's harsh words, was bent out of shape. At Dorval Airport the next day, a CFCF-TV camera crew cornered Zeppelin lead singer Robert Plant and asked him about the *Gazette's* negative review. Plant was not happy; like most in attendance, he thought the band had laid it all out for Montreal the night before.

Over the years, out of necessity, Tarlton developed a thicker skin. However, he got his chance to confront Rodriguez on the CFCF-TV show *Like Young*. Host Jim McKenna invited both Rodriguez and Tarlton to debate the disparity between the rock critic's view and popular opinion. How could Rodriguez be the only one who disliked the Led Zeppelin concert? Tarlton came to the show armed with his populist promoter perspective, ready to do verbal battle. Any momentum and anger he had stored up for this confrontation was depleted when, in a brief pre-show conversation, he discovered that Rodriguez had a serious stutter. When the two of them went live, Tarlton had already decided to shave the edge from the angry promoter routine he had rehearsed in his head. Both would move on, and many years later the hatchet was buried, though Rodriguez remained a hard man to please.

Among other crowning achievements of the hundreds of DKD-produced rock concerts is the 1977 Pink Floyd concert at the Olympic Stadium. Pink Floyd were virtual prog-rock gods in Montreal thanks to CHOM-FM, which played their music in heavy rotation. Even Top 40 radio got into the act when the 1973 single "Money" off the *Dark Side of the Moon* album became the group's first U.S.

hit. Though FM rock radio was making inroads and eroding AM's traditional market domination, it was still common for artists to put out a 45-rpm single version of a popular album cut, pared down especially for that format. In the mid-1970s, there were still plenty of homes and cars without FM radios. Coming on the heels of their 1977 European and North American tour – a rigorous and lengthy stretch – to support their album *Animals,* the Pink Floyd Montreal concert was booked for July 1977. "The Big O," as the Olympic Stadium had been dubbed after the 1976 Olympics, had an official capacity of 62,000. But with room on the field in front of the stage, the available seats spiked to more than 80,000. Tarlton says there were probably even more there that night, with some side-door deals being struck with security personnel. He likes to peg the crowd at somewhere close to 100,000. This was Montreal's first rock concert extravaganza, complete with inflated puppet figures, a pyrotechnic waterfall, and a huge inflatable pig hovering over the stadium.

It was a hot July day and thousands of fans had waited hours to get in, getting pumped and primed outside the stadium. There were some backstage problems, as DKD staff scrambled to find the keys to the stadium's lighting-system control room. Bad vibes hung heavily in the air by the time ticket buyers settled into their seats and staked their concert field turf. Pink Floyd's David Gilmour and Roger Waters were in a foul mood too, apparently – as bassist Waters would soon demonstrate. The crowd was tired, restless, stoned, and drunk by the time the band hit the stage. About four songs into the set, Waters was singing "Pigs on the Wing," a quiet number that required a certain level of audience patience. Some in the audience lacked patience: fire-crackers popped as Waters tried to build the song. He stopped singing and ripped a strip off the crowd. "Oh, for fuck sakes, stop letting off fireworks and shouting and screaming," he told the crowd. "I'm trying to sing a song." There was some cheering from those who could actually hear Waters' rant as it bounced off the concrete canyon that was the Olympic Stadium.

Waters, however, was into his dark side and crossed a line he would remember for years afterwards. Making eye contact with one fan who had been annoying him near the stage, he motioned the fan forward. The young man thought he was about to have a golden moment on stage with Pink Floyd. Once he got close enough, though not completely on stage, Waters spat in his face. The fan, understandably surprised, retreated. Before the night was over, the giant inflated pink pig hovering over the Big O was somehow knifed, and near the end of the concert the crowd had surged forward to the stage, knocking down the barrier in front. That incident would later inspire Waters to write *The Wall,* the 1979 album that sold 30 million copies.

A wiser and better-prepared Tarlton brought Pink Floyd back to Montreal in 1987, 1988, and 1994 – all concerts were without Roger Waters, who left the band in 1985. Pink Floyd was a gold mine and DKD knew it. Their 1988 North American tour, even without Waters, was the highest grossing tour of that year at $60 million. It's a testimony to Montreal's love affair with Pink Floyd that 22 years after that hot and rowdy July 6, 1977, concert, the group sold out the Big O three nights in a row. Fans who were there in 1977 were now pushing 40, a much more manageable and mature crowd for Tarlton and Olympic Stadium security. Pink Floyd had established the paradigm for major rock events in 1977, like the Rolling Stones' "Steel Wheels" tour and U2's "Zoo TV" tour – all elaborate stage productions. The Rolling Stones, David Bowie, Emerson, Lake and Palmer, Primus, U2, and Pink Floyd all played the Olympic Stadium. Montreal is still a Floyd town, and not a day goes by without a Pink Floyd tune being played on some Montreal radio station, though those 1977 fans are now pushing 65.

Tarlton had proved that Montreal was a major rock concert destination; the time had passed when Canada was perceived by U.S. promoters and agents as some kind of backwater country. In fact, Canada was the breeding ground for promoters like Toronto-born Michael Cohl, who famously stepped in to save Michael Jackson's 1984 "Victory Tour" from financial disaster, then hitched his wagon to international tours by groups like the Rolling Stones, Prince, U2, and Pink Floyd. Then there's Ottawa-born Arthur Fogel, now chairman of Global Music and president of Live Nation's Global Touring Division, who got into the rock promotion business with Cohl when he formed Concert Productions International (CPI). If Canadians didn't know who Fogel was, they found out after seeing the 2013 documentary, *Who the F**k is Arthur Fogel?* Fogel, when he was with Cohl at CPI, locked up the Rolling Stones' "Steel Wheels" tour in 1989–90, a major coup. Tarlton's Donald K. Donald Productions would do business with CPI when the Stones brought that megashow to the Big O. As one of the senior members of Canada's small rock-concert impresarios' club, Tarlton is featured in the Fogel documentary. Both Cohl and Fogel credit Tarlton as a major influence in their success; they knew what he had accomplished in Montreal, and then in the rest of Canada. Regrets? Tarlton has had a few. One is that he didn't get into the music publishing business sooner. "If I had to do it all over again, I would have expanded my focus from just trying to sell that $10 ticket. The bigger game would have been in music publishing. I just wasn't visionary enough at that time. I didn't know enough, wasn't knowledgeable enough, about the whole workings of the business." Tarlton eventually did buy his way into the music publishing business: one-quarter of the revenue from any April Wine or Corey Hart song goes to Donald K. Donald Productions.

For reasons not necessarily based on any misguided sense of nationalism, Tarlton's rock concert promotion business has been Canada- if not Montreal-centric. Over the years, he's had job offers from agencies in New York and L.A., as well as offers to merge with U.S. promoters. "I always liked my situation in Montreal," he says. "Some people say I was scared to move out of my comfort zone." But he did move out of his comfort zone, developing a Canadian rock concert circuit with Michael Cohl and teaming up with him on the international leg of the Rolling Stones tours. "I didn't have the same desire to function internationally as Arthur Fogel or Michael Cohl. I was content to stay in Canada. They [Cohl and Fogel of CPI] abdicated all the Canadian responsibilities to me and I was happy to have it."

In 1991, Donald K. Donald became the exclusive promoter for Céline Dion who, though already a major star in her home province of Quebec, wanted to break into the English-Canada and U.S. markets. She did that with her 1991 album *Unison* and subsequent tour of the same name, produced by DKD Productions. It was a very productive relationship for Tarlton; Dion's husband and manager, René Angélil, chose Tarlton as the man who could take Dion's career to North America, and he delivered.

There was more than a little of his old mentor Sam Gesser in Tarlton, when he ventured outside his comfort zone to team up with New York City producer Mel Howard to put together four Broadway productions, two of which enjoyed major success. In 1986, *Tango Argentino* picked up three Tony Award nominations, while in 1989 the musical *Black and Blue* took home three Tonys for producers Howard and Tarlton. He fit right in with the theatre crowd, better-dressed than the rock crowd, but it was still all about the entertainment factor.

At 72, Tarlton has slowed down from his former frenetic pace, fleeing to Florida for the winter, golfing, and occasionally indulging his recreational poker habit with his old Montreal cronies. Divested of his concert promotion business after selling DKD Productions to Michael Cohl's CPI in 1998, he turned his attention to Aquarius Records, developing acts and expanding that part of his business into the 21st century. He is, allegedly, now fully retired. His wife of 40 years, Ann (dubbed Annie K. Annie by CKGM DJ Ralph Lockwood) would probably disagree. The DKD Group, as his business is now called, is a habit he can't give up. In his home office, an array of awards is on display: his 1982 Félix for Producer of the Year in Quebec, his 2000 Order of Canada medal, and his 2007 Walt Grealis Special Achievement Award, which recognizes an outstanding individual who has contributed to the growth and advancement of the Canadian music industry, given to him at the Junos. In 2012, he and his friend and associate Terry Flood shared the Pioneer Award from the Music Managers of Canada.

But, perhaps, his favourite award of all time is the "Above and Beyond the Call of Duty Award" from the Rolling Stones after the group's 1972 appearance at the Montreal Forum. Tarlton scrambled at the last minute to replace equipment that was damaged in an explosion in the group's trucks parked outside the venue. There was no hardware involved in the Stones award, but a full-page ad in *Billboard* Magazine thanked Tarlton for his extraordinary efforts. At the time, barely a few years into the big-time rock concert promotion biz, Tarlton couldn't have been more honoured to have the Stones salute him. He was, after all, a people pleaser.

CHAPTER NINE

CKGM-FM/CHOM
Here Comes the Sun

DOUG PRINGLE: OFF THE ELEVATOR AND INTO THE SUN

Doug Pringle is on his way to the Ritz-Carlton Hotel in the heart of what was once Montreal's Golden Square Mile, his head spinning with a rehearsed pitch – and the after-effects of the previous day's acid trip. He has an appointment with Geoff Stirling, CEO of Maisonneuve Broadcasting, owner of CKGM-AM and FM. Pringle is the prototypical long-haired hippie of the day, dressed in jeans and T-shirt with a faint odour of patchouli oil, the perfume-du-jour of the male counterculture free spirit. The Ritz doorman gives him a sideways scowling once-over as he opens up the door. Pringle is not the typical Ritz guest.

He's already given his pitch once to the general manager of CKGM, Don Wall, who set up the meeting with the boss. Pringle wants to drag Stirling's CKGM-FM station from its current elevator-music format into the world of Jimi Hendrix and Ravi Shankar. Pringle made his pitch, his vision for what CKGM-FM could be. Stirling was intrigued. "We immediately hit it off," Pringle says. "He was into Eastern philosophy. He'd dropped acid in the [Arizona] desert. We were on the same wavelength and he was very excited about my ideas."

"I've been wanting to do something with my stations," Stirling told Pringle. "And here you are and this is exactly what I want to do. Can you start tonight?"

Pringle didn't see this coming. "Well, I can't really start tonight," said Pringle. "I'm just coming down off an acid trip. But I can go on tomorrow." This was probably the first time Stirling had this excuse from a prospective employee, but he was unfazed.

It all seemed so organic, Pringle remembers. Stirling, though a free-thinker, was also an astute businessman. He told Pringle to do a four-hour show live at 11 p.m., tape it, and then replay it at 3 a.m. "I'll give you eight hours," said Stirling. "And I'll give you three weeks. If you're full of shit, you're outta here."

CKGM-FM was suddenly off the elevator, at least for one-third of its programming day. True to his word, Pringle was in the studio the next night, October 29, 1969, with a clear head and a stack of his own records. He started with one minute and 46 seconds of Robert Strauss' "Also Sprach Zarathustra," an emotional piece of music that starts quietly, then builds into a bombastic brass and kettle-drum crescendo, famously used in the 1968 Stanley Kubrick film, *2001: A Space Odyssey*. Then Pringle segued into the Beatles' "Here Comes the Sun." It was just after 11 p.m., but a new sun was rising in the FM Montreal radio scene. Word would soon get around and Pringle's three weeks stretched into months, then years.

Born in Calcutta, India, then educated in South Africa, Belgium, and England, Doug Pringle was already more worldly than the average young man when he boarded a ship in England to visit his sister in Boston with hopes of eventually living in the U.S. He ended up doing the trans-Atlantic Ocean voyage twice more, but it was his trip back to England that turned out to be a pivotal point in his life. His second voyage back to the Old Country would sail from Montreal, and with a couple of days to kill before the ship departed, he managed to fall in love with the city. He deep-sixed his U.S. immigration dreams, then applied and was accepted to Sir George Williams University and was back in Montreal by the summer of 1968. Change was in the air. At Sir George, he got involved with the university radio and TV stations, both of which were running on a student-directed free-form style. As program director of Radio Sir George and founder of its closed-circuit TV station, he had fertile training ground. About a year later, he was part of an FM radio experiment that took his newly adopted city into a whole new era of radio that came to be known as progressive, alternative, even underground radio.

Pringle grew up hearing the music that would take North America by the crotch and make it listen. A Beatles and Stones fan at first, he later leaned towards the blues-influenced sounds of edgier bands like Cream, Led Zeppelin, Traffic, Small Faces, Humble Pie, Jethro Tull, John Mayall & the Bluesbreakers, David Bowie, Elton John (long before he went all "Candle in the Wind"), and his personal favourite, T. Rex.

A trip to San Francisco ultimately inspired him to adopt the progressive FM radio idea, bring it back to Montreal and take it to a broader audience than the Sir George cafeteria and student lounges. On the West Coast, Pringle tuned into KSAN-FM, with former Top 40 DJ and Rock and Roll Hall of Famer, Tom "Big Daddy" Donahue, who made his Top 40 sentiments clear in a 1967 *Rolling Stone* article titled "AM Radio is Dead and Its Rotting Corpse is Stinking Up the Airwaves." The list of FM radio-station pretenders to the throne – being the first to introduce the free-form format – is long, but it was KSAN that inspired Pringle. Like CKGM-FM, it was a classical music station lumbering along in maudlin mediocrity. Almost overnight, it became a beacon for a brand-new adventurous FM sound, playing rock album cuts, blues, folk and psychedelic – distancing itself as much as possible from the "rotting corpse" of AM radio. Moreover, KSAN was West Coast hip, a station that became the paradigm for every new aspiring FM station looking to break out of its safe music format. Change was working its way from west to east, via San Francisco with flowers in its hair. That's the pitch Pringle took to Stirling that night at the Ritz-Carlton Hotel. Why couldn't Montreal have its own KSAN?

Pringle played the music he loved with no playlist and no program director. In those early days, he was his own boss. A few weeks after going solo, Pringle got the green light to add another announcer, Greg Schifrin, a blues devotee with his own stack of Howlin' Wolf, Lightnin' Hopkins, Mississippi John Hurt, and Sonny Boy Williamson, among many others, on his personal playlist. Stirling had given

Pringle three weeks. By the end of three months, CKGM-FM was completely off the elevator, now programming alternative radio 24 hours a day. "The reaction in Montreal was amazing," says Pringle. "The reason it was so amazing was because of all the incredible music. It was probably one of the greatest times in the history of mankind in terms of the quality and quantity of amazing music. But it wasn't just the music; it was the lyrics that carried the spirit of the time. The music and lyrics were carrying ideas around the world."

Indeed, cultural and political revolution was a work in progress when Pringle took to the airwaves. Young people seemed to talk about "the revolution" with no particular plan in mind. But the music spoke for them. The Beatles released "Revolution" (the B-side of "Hey Jude") in 1969, but the song's lyrics hardly called for an armed uprising. "But when you talk about destruction / Don't you know that you can count me out," Lennon sang. Jefferson Airplane, a band that came out of the blooming San Francisco psychedelic rock sound, released the song "Volunteers" that had a little more edge to it. Responding to campus peace demonstrations that had swept across America, lead singer Grace Slick wailed, "Look what's happening in the streets / Got a revolution / Got a revolution." With the U.S. knee-deep in Vietnam, even Motown artists couldn't ignore what was happening in the late 1960s. Protest songs were hits, No. 1 in the case of the 1970 song "War," sung by Motown's Edwin Starr. "War, what is it good for? / Absolutely nuthin.' / Say it again, y'all." Folk singers Pete Seeger, Bob Dylan, Phil Ochs, Joan Baez, Arlo Guthrie and Country Joe McDonald weighed in on war and peace. In 1963 Sam Cooke sang "A Change is Gonna Come," addressing the civil rights movement of that time. By the late 1960s, the black pride movement became a natural progression of the civil rights battles in the U.S. James Brown proclaimed, "Say It Loud, I'm Black and I'm Proud," in his 1968 song that made the Top 10 in the *Billboard* Hot 100 of that year. John Fogerty of Creedence Clearwater Revival wrote "Fortunate Son," an anti-Vietnam War anthem, and Neil Young wrote "Four Dead in Ohio" after the National Guard was called in to quell demonstrations on the Kent State campus in early May 1970, shooting and killing four students. "Tin soldiers and Nixon comin',

Doug Pringle pitched the idea of an "alternative" rock station to owner Geoff Stirling, turning CKGM-FM into what Pringle called "Tribal Radio" in 1969. For a time, he was a one-man show, but the idea caught on big time and now, as CHOM, the station has 45-plus years of history behind it.

we're finally on our own," was the song's opening line. Some U.S. radio stations refused to play protest songs, but not in Montreal. "If there was a real revolution going on, it was in the music of the '60s and '70s," says Pringle. "Many of those artists of that time were new. Now they're legend."

Pringle's CKGM-FM sidestepped bold political talk or outright support for one cause over another. But it was understood that this new, alternative FM station was radio by and for the people. It was, as it soon came to be known, Tribal Radio, a slogan hatched in Pringle's fertile mind. "We were very much of the Woodstock generation. We were a tribe. Everybody had one vote, from the receptionist to the announcers, everyone who worked there."

The word on the streets of Montreal was, "Hey, man, you got to check this new station out." Many had to get an AM/FM radio/stereo set first, and in those nascent CKGM-FM months, stereo retailers did a brisk business. CKGM-FM was in stereo and with a pair of headphones, some solid, dependable weed, and Led Zep cranked up, it was sonic heaven. When the station promoted its first concert, the Band at Place des Arts, Pringle came out to introduce the group and got a standing ovation. Modestly, he prefers to think the standing "O" was not for him but the station. He was, nevertheless, taken by surprise. "When you're in the studio, even though you're getting a lot of calls, you don't really know what kind of impact you're having. We weren't sure how popular we were, but we believed what we were doing was important to people."

Radio historians might argue about whether CKGM-FM was the first Canadian station to convert its programming to progressive rock. Both Vancouver's CKLG-FM and Toronto's CHUM-FM made the leap from easy-listening formats to rock starting in 1968, at least giving up some of its programming day to rock while still hanging on to some of its safe standards. What separated the men from the boys in Pringle's opinion was the fact that CKGM-FM had a strong spiritual component to its vision. The station's CEO was a middle-aged hippie who had embraced the precepts of Transcendental Meditation (TM). The Beatles had just come back from a trip to India to meditate with the Maharishi Mahesh Yogi. They had gone with their wives and a few other luminaries like Mike Love of the Beach Boys, rock/folk singer Donovan, and actress Mia Farrow. That garnered a lot of publicity for TM and the Maharishi himself, a funny man given over to easy fits of giggling who warmed his way into the hearts of North Americans.

CKGM-FM bought into this new Eastern-style spirituality. Pringle had a Sunday afternoon show called *The Spiritual Hour*, an hour that ran more like four depending on the guests. "I had everyone in the studio. I had swamis, yogis, Tibetan lamas and Catholic priests. And if we ran out of guests, we ran tapes by [former Timothy Leary

Harvard colleague-turned-guru, Richard Alpert] Ram Dass." This separated CKGM-FM from the two other pretenders in Vancouver and Toronto, Pringle says. It was too early in the FM free-form game to claim bragging rights as to who did what first. Competition was not part of the progressive rock radio ethos of the time. Everything, everybody was cool.

By early 1970, CKGM-FM was offering up 24 hours of unpredictable, unscripted, and almost unsponsored radio. Initially, Geoff Stirling was pleased with the impact of his "new" FM station, but while it was making new fans, it was hardly a cash cow for Maisonneuve Broadcasting. Nor for that matter was its AM station. All that was about to change. The CKGM-FM collective studiously and philosophically rejected any major corporate sponsors. It was a group decision, voted on according to the doctrine of Tribal Radio. "Coming from our position of the time," says Pringle, "we didn't understand the commercial aspects of radio. We were just doing art. So pretty much anything corporate [cars polluted so no car ads were allowed] we didn't accept." CHOM fittingly did support the independent, even underground, economy of Montreal. The coolest, hippest record store in Montreal, Phantasmagoria, became one of the station's major clients.

On November 22, 1968, the Beatles released their ninth studio album, famously called the *White Album*. Six days later, a young Montreal university dropout, Eric Pressman, opened the doors to his brand new record store, Phantasmagoria, on Park Avenue near McGill University, in a former laundromat. With an $800 loan from his father, Pressman bought 100 copies of the *White Album*, which promptly sold out on his first day of business. Two days later and with another 100 *White Album*s sold, he paid back the $800 loan. As if the serendipity of his record store opening wasn't enough, Pressman just happened to have a good friend, and eventual roommate, in Doug Pringle, whom he'd met during his first and only year at Sir George University. "Phantas," as it became known, was a natural fit for a radio station that eschewed corporate advertising. The relationship between the record store and radio station was a handy, symbiotic one, though Pressman did pay for his ad time. Phantasmagoria and

CKGM-FM were linked at the musical hip, selling and playing the same stuff. Pringle would introduce Pressman to some new music, give it an on-air spin and soon that album was sold in the store. "I think it was more CKGM-FM (and CHOM) that created the demand," Pressman concedes. "We certainly were creating music tastes, too. We'd listen to so many albums, then decided which to buy more of. But if FM was all over one artist, we'd buy multiple copies for customers. The store was just a purveyor. I dare say that Doug had a hell of a lot more influence than we did. But, ultimately, CKGM-FM (particularly Doug) and the store went hand in hand." For a time Phantas was the hippest record store in town, a warm, welcoming spot where music enthusiasts could hang out on couches and rocking chairs and watch the fish circle in the huge fish tank. Throw in a little greenery, add a psychedelic, painted-glass storefront window and a more than tolerant approach to all who spent hours staring at the fish, and Phantas was like a YMCA drop-in centre. There was no pressure to buy. Pressman knew young rock music lovers were on a pretty tight budget. They bought when they could. That one album they might leave the store with likely meant another week of Kraft Dinner.

CKGM-FM now stood out enough on the FM radio landscape for *Time* magazine's August 1970 Canadian edition to take notice, after interviewing Pringle about his meeting with Stirling and the station's half-year-plus progress.

"Stirling is not interested in a profit, only in breaking even," the article said. "Last October, he began his experiment in free-form radio by hiring Doug Pringle, an Englishman with a Home Counties accent and Pre-Raphaelite hair. Now, the station has six announcers, who are given $125 a week and complete freedom on their four-hour slots. Stirling will send the occasional memo quoting Guru Kahlil Gibran to the effect that money is not love, then telling his staff to cut costs. They in turn have created the authentic and fashionably incoherent voice of a subculture." (The same article claimed that CKGM-FM catered to only English-language listeners, which was hardly the case.)

The article quotes Neil Compton, English professor at Sir George Williams University, who was more positive. Compton liked CKGM-

FM, the article said, and saw the "almost ostentatiously clumsy and inarticulate" approach of the announcers as "a movement away from confidence in language." Such use of language, he concluded, was "preferable to the use of language in commercial hype stations." Whatever the reviews, CKGM-FM was building a whole new audience, some of them Marshall McLuhan wannabes.

By 1970, CKGM-AM was gearing up to become a full-format Top 40 radio station after juggling a number of formats since coming on the air in 1959. Stirling wanted to make some money. Even though he had put CKGM-FM on a long leash, when he rolled into town, he exhorted Pringle and the other announcers to accept more commercials. "Look," Pringle remembers Stirling telling the assembled FM staff, "you're happening. There's people listening. I don't want to go on about this, but I do want to break even. So can you guys broaden your policy a little and accept more commercials?" Like the proverbial substitute teacher, no one seemed to seriously heed what Stirling was saying. He'd leave town and the station would continue on its merry ad-averse ways. Eventually, Stirling ran out of patience. On one trip to the station, he pulled the ultimate power gambit: he threatened to fire everyone. Pringle remembers the meeting well. "Now, I've got this amazing station," Stirling said, "where you get to play whatever you want. You get to do and say whatever you want. There's one slight catch: you have to accept commercials. Now, who would like to work at my radio station?" Every arm in the room went up. "That was the beginning of the commercial phase of CKGM-FM," says Pringle.

Although it was upsetting for the FM radio purists, CKGM-FM's growing pains were part of the process of any new radio station. The move to make the station a more viable commodity may have rattled some of the announcers' artistic sensibilities, but there was no slowing the ship down. Pringle had brought in a number of francophone announcers, who introduced Montreal to brand new Quebec musical artists (like Harmonium, Gilles Valiquette, Michel Pagliaro, Offenbach, and Beau Dommage), helping to make stars out of them all. Announcers like André Rhéaume (breaking ground as the station's first francophone announcer), Claude Rajotte, Denis

Grondin, Bob Boulanger, and Bob Beauchamp, flouted the boundaries of the station's English-language license. A good percentage of its listeners were French-speaking and Pringle knew that it would be folly to ignore the reality of Montreal's two linguistic communities and cultures.

What the station really needed was a separate identity. Pringle had nothing against the sister AM station but having different call letters would separate church and state. Pringle and Stirling had made a pilgrimage to India at Swami Chidananda's ashram. The swami's name conveniently had the first two CRTC-approved letters allowed for Canadian radio stations. So how about CHID-FM? The new call letters had to reflect the spiritual leanings of the owner and his new "project." Then again, there was "om," a popular mantra and mystical Hindu sound that fit Stirling's meditation practices. CHOM-FM? It had a more attractive sound to it, less harsh than CHID, which sounded more like a disease or ugly facial growth. A committee of two, Stirling and Pringle wisely settled on CHOM. Gone was CKGM-FM, just a little over two years after Pringle took his first show to air. Cutting the umbilical cord completely, CHOM then moved across the street from its Greene Avenue location to an abandoned three-storey building. Stirling purchased the Victorian-style house for a song, as few buyers wanted in on a sale where the previous owner had committed violent suicide. There was talk of a CHOM ghost but after a facelift and a ceremony that cleansed the building of any bad vibes, CHOM had its own headquarters featuring what became their iconic door inset with a red stained-glass heart symbolic of CHOM's spiritual mission.

The new CHOM brand name took on a life of its own when Pringle saw the 1971 Sergio Leone spaghetti western *Duck, You Sucker!* (also billed as *A Fistful of Dynamite* and *Once Upon a Time... the Revolution*) with Rod Steiger, and James Coburn as protagonist John (Seán) H. Mallory, an early IRA explosives expert who flees to Mexico and gets caught up in the 1913 revolution-torn country. The musical score by Ennio Morricone has a three-minute-38-second title piece as part of the soundtrack. Sitting in a movie theatre, Pringle listened to the whistling intro with haunting flutes and soft strings, followed by the chanting of Coburn's Irish first name, Seán, sung three times, then again and again in groups of three. It didn't sound like the name Sean, but rather uncannily similar to the word CHOM being sung over and over. Pringle took his discovery back to the studios and had the sound engineers add a creaking, closing door and the sound of a laughing baby to the film's opening theme. With all the CHOM, CHOM, CHOMs being repeated several times, the edited version became the station's adopted musical ID. It was pure magic. Even in today's heavily programmed FM format, the *Duck, You Sucker!* theme still makes the odd appearance, perhaps to reassure aging Baby Boomers and loyal listeners that CHOM remembers its humble roots. It was not cool for progressive rock stations to have pre-manufactured jingles. This little bit of music sounded so right for the image CHOM was projecting. Just like their new call letters and studios, the CHOM, CHOM musical chant served to help brand the station and distinguish them from their AM cousin. CHOM was the new mantra of every self-respecting Montreal hippie.

Some CKGM-FM/CHOM announcers found their lack of freedom constricting. A few of them grumbled in private that the station's mission statement (though there was nothing in writing) was being lost in search of the almighty advertising dollar. But Pringle remembers the transition from free-form to a more commercial style as being fairly smooth. It was an adapt-or-leave environment, but the soul had hardly been ripped out of the station at the expense of more advertising. Eventually, the station would be fully programmed and jocks who didn't like it, or didn't fit in, left or were asked to leave. In fact, Pringle was one of them: he left for England to pursue his fledgling songwriting and singing career.

He hooked up with fellow countryman Marc Bolan, lead singer for the group T. Rex, on a promise that he could record on Bolan's new independent label, the T. Rex Wax Company. Lured by the possibility of recording with Bolan, Pringle left CHOM, this time by air, and returned to England. Unfortunately, his timing couldn't have been worse. Bolan, like other high earners under Britain's Labour Party tenure in the 1970s, became a tax refugee. The Stones had fled to the south of France. The Beatles referenced the U.K.'s 83-percent tax rate in their song "Taxman." Almost as soon as Pringle arrived in Britain, Bolan left the country for the U.S. and Monaco, where he would spend up to three-quarters of the year to avoid having a good chunk of his income taken by the government. Pringle was adrift. "I was basically in limbo," he says. "Bolan would fly me to some chateau in France, supposedly to work on my album, but the whole thing was just limping along going nowhere." He wound up recording a few songs in French but, after three years of increasing disappointment, Pringle had learned a hard lesson. "I realized you can't be in the recording side of this if you're just good. You can only be in it if you're great. And I was smart enough to know that I was a million miles away from being great." Slightly humbled, he went back to Montreal and into the Greene Avenue CHOM studios, home again.

The CHOM he returned to was a much more streamlined operation. Gone were the head-shop ads, replaced with clients who had much more significant advertising budgets. The music still had some diversity to it, but four-hour blues shows had disappeared. No more *Spiritual Hour* either. For all intents and purposes, CHOM was evolving into what would soon become known in the quaint par-lance of marketing as AOR (album-oriented rock.) "It was more like a normal money-making machine," Pringle says. "For some people that was a negative. The heyday of FM radio for them was the very early days. Some people lamented that, but not me." The practice of announcers bringing in their own records and playing what they wanted faded. "You've got to play the stuff that had mass appeal," Pringle says. Ironically, CHOM had become more like their AM counterpart, where the jingles said, "Less talk, more rock."

Not content to rest on his pioneering FM radio laurels, Pringle set about breaking yet more new ground by producing a four-hour syndicated show, *The Pringle Program*, which he sold to 80 stations across Canada, including CHOM. It was an expensive, but artistic-ally rewarding venture. Hours of tape had to be couriered across the country, then back again to re-use. He flew to L.A. and London to interview the rock stars of the day, then back to Montreal to do the editing. After about three years of doing a little better than breaking even, he turned his sights on TV, employing the same approach he took with his syndicated radio show. This time he videotaped interviews with big names on their home turf. He visited Roger Daltrey of the Who in his Kent, England, manor house and went horseback riding with Nancy and Ann Wilson of Heart. Tapes in hand, he and his producer edited them in a Montreal TV studio.

Pringle's *Profiles in Rock* was the first non-music video played on the new MTV U.S. station, then picked up by NBC, which ran his video interviews after their popular Saturday *Midnight Special* rock show. He stacked up an impressive musical portfolio while in Montreal, managing bands (for a time Supertramp's Roger Hodgson was one of his clients), recording songs in French, writing a syndicated national music column and starting his own radio consultancy business. Now pushing 70, he has moved up the chain of command to become director of programming after joining Rawlco, a Saskatchewan-based, family-owned company that operates seven radio stations. Fortunately, with his accumulated seniority, the job description doesn't include having to endure the harsh prairie winters, so he and his wife Heidi lounge comfortably now in the more manageable climes of Victoria, British Columbia.

Pringle and CKGM/CHOM-FM are inextricably bound together. Not that he is mired in past glories, but he did make radio history in Montreal. And in the midst of it all, Pringle and other early CKGM/CHOM announcers were blissfully unself-conscious of their impact. If only they had some of it on tape. When Geoff Stirling talked John Lennon and Yoko Ono into coming to Montreal for an exclusive interview two years after their celebrated 1969 Bed-in, it was Pringle who went down to meet their train in Central Station and conduct what turned out to be a three-hour interview that was broadcast live on CHOM. Lennon was flogging another cause, his "War is Over, If You Want It" campaign. Sworn to secrecy by Lennon, listeners had no idea where the interview was being held. Lennon had a special relationship with Montreal and especially with Stirling, who had the pull and power to get the duo to make a special trip. After the interview, John and Yoko went right back to New York. Pringle knew he had what amounted to a scoop. What he didn't have was a tape of the interview, as it was not uncommon for tape to be re-used and taped over. "I had no idea it was going to have the historical importance that it had later on," he says. "Don't get me wrong, it was a big deal to interview Lennon, but I was not a collector in those days."

Pringle now has the luxury of looking back at those pioneering CKGM/CHOM years and putting them straight in his memory, even if there is no concrete archive that has survived. There's no taping over; these memories are permanent.

"I think in the CHOM days anything was possible and there was such hope that the world was going to be remade into a wonderful place and everything we dreamed of would come to pass. There was so much hope and good feeling. Very little bad stuff happened around CHOM. It was all good and positive," he says. "We were part of the counterculture. It had no boundaries. The music went everywhere and the message [of peace] went everywhere. The leaders of the day were not the kings, queens or popes or prime ministers; the leaders of the day were named Bob [as in Dylan] and John [as in Lennon]. When Lennon sang 'Give Peace a Chance' we believed it was possible because we had stopped the war in Vietnam. We had the power to change things."

ANGUS MACKAY: IN ON THE GROUND FLOOR

It wasn't uncommon for the newly minted free-form CKGM-FM studios to have any number of hangers-on and friends milling about. Newly hired copywriter Angus Mackay at least could claim squatting rights amongst the unofficial guests keeping the DJ company on the night of October 10, 1970. Mackay was just settling into his new job and soaking up the atmosphere. He would soon get his chance to be behind the mic. But, for now, he was taking mental notes for the future.

CKGM-FM was a mellow place at night, a great drop-in centre with good music and a measure of recreational drugs. Outside, it was much less mellow. The Quiet Revolution in Quebec had exploded for good when the FLQ kidnapped British trade commissioner James Cross and Quebec Liberal cabinet minister Pierre Laporte. The cool music coming from CKGM-FM belied the political heat on the streets.

Neither Mackay, studio guests, nor the night-shift DJ would have heard the commotion downstairs in the 1310 Greene Avenue lobby. About a dozen or so Quebec nationalists entered the lobby and proceeded to badly beat up the nighttime security guard. Then they headed to the third floor where CKGM-AM and FM were located. There, they shut down the AM station, then headed for their true goal, CKGM-FM, the more suitable platform for the pro-separation rant they were soon to share with CKGM-FM's early morning listeners. As they burst in on MacKay and the on-air announcer's show-in-progress, they looked a motley crew, ordering the DJ away from the mic. They were taking over. Stunned, Mackay and the others in studio willingly backed off, surrendering the mic to the more vocal leaders in the name of self-preservation. "Be cool, man," MacKay told them. "Take over, if that's what you want." Once on the air, it was all Quebec nationalistic rhetoric and manifesto-driven choler going out to a surprised CKGM-FM audience. Listeners may have thought, "Man, this free-form radio is full of surprises. But hey, how come there's no music?" But then, one of the intruders spotted the new Led Zeppelin album. "They expected some resistance," says MacKay. "After a while, they were just happy to have their own show. It was more guerrilla theatre than anything else." (It was less guerrilla theatre for CKGM general manager Jim Sward, who has an entirely different perspective on the events of that night.)

There were no windows in the Greene Avenue studios, so no one inside was aware that the police were gathered outside the building just waiting for the green light to go in. There were unconfirmed reports that some of the intruders were armed, but Mackay never saw any weapons; otherwise, the atmosphere in the studio would have been radically different. Eventually, when they were out of gas – and albums – the group surrendered. Not a word of this was ever reported in any Montreal newspaper. Ironically – and to the amusement of the station's management – CHOM received a letter from

245

the CRTC admonishing it for letting the separatist rant on the air, while just two days before, the CBC and Radio-Canada had aired the FLQ manifesto as part of the group's demands to release James Cross. These were strange times. Nevertheless, with a certain blissful ignorance and hippie nonchalance, the free-form boys of CKGM-FM had headed off a kind of hostage-taking that could have ended badly.

CKGM-FM's conversion to alternative radio was in full flight when Angus MacKay decided he wanted in on the action. With a background at the Loyola College radio station (serving one cafeteria and two student lounges), MacKay was doing free-form radio before anyone gave it that label. Listening to CKGM-FM, he thought it could go even further and shared this sentiment with management when he applied for a job. MacKay shot from the lip when he told CKGM-FM manager Don Wall that the station, even with its hip new format, was "elitist." "The people who were on the air were intentionally uninterested in what people listeners wanted to hear," he says. "They insisted they were going to play music that they the listeners *needed* to hear. Guys [announcers] were playing music that was obtuse and unrecognizable. As a listener, I wanted to hear music that was at least vaguely popular." This kind of sharing at a job interview would normally sink any candidate's chances of employment, but this was experimental radio and MacKay got away with his moment of critical bravado. So, perhaps in a kind of sink-or-swim human resources manoeuvre, they put him to work writing copy for the meagre number of paying advertisers and tested his chops by letting him record what he wrote.

What he really wanted was his own show. And what better shift to begin with than Sunday morning from 6 a.m. to noon, talking to a numbers-thin audience still nurturing their Saturday night partying buzz. MacKay prepared diligently for his first show, knowing that amongst the listeners would be CKGM management interested in how this experiment was going to go. A late-in-life family starter, MacKay is the father of two elementary-school-aged children and has watched his share of kids' TV. Today, he likens his Sunday morning

Angus Mackay (pictured with fellow announcer Denis Grondin) took the mandate of alternative radio seriously. His show on CKGM-FM (CHOM) could feature readings from *Le Petit Prince* to full sides of newly released albums.
Courtesy of Rachel Irwin.

gigs to *Treehouse TV*, a YTV cable show aimed at young kids who are up at the crack of dawn. No violence, no commercials, and plenty of stories. For his debut CKGM-FM show, he rolled out some Carl Sandburg poetry records, mixed in a few Aesop's *Fables,* along with Joni Mitchell, to gently nurse listeners into a new day.

"It was like a show for kids, only grown-up kids," MacKay, who also answered to the nicknames "Gus" or "Goose," says. "All of the stoners who hadn't yet gone to bed flocked to the show, which I thought was unlike anything on the radio." If management was listening, MacKay didn't hear from them. It's likely that during his shift any official ratings source was still in bed and inoperative: "Nobody [management] seemed to give a shit. I played 15 minutes of *Le Petit Prince* in French, then asked people to tune in next week for another part." It was asking a lot of buzzed-out listeners whose memory span was questionable, but free-form radio held its audience's IQ in high esteem. There were expectations. Nevertheless, MacKay got some feedback from listeners still riding a high from whatever their stimulant of choice was. "Man, I stay up," one caller told MacKay. "We're all as high as kites at 6 a.m., anyway, wondering what you guys are gonna play next." That was the beauty of FM radio at that time. "You never knew what we were going to do next," says MacKay. "It was so accidental and spontaneous."

Eventually, he graduated from the existential Sunday morning hippie wake-up show to a regular, five-day-a-week shift in the afternoon when *Le Petit Prince* and Aesop's *Fables* didn't go down as well. No matter. MacKay was flexible and adaptable, with a more than solid musical knowledge that stretched across tonal boundaries. Brought up on the rock 'n' roll of the mid-to-late-1960s, jazz and blues, his record collection was an esoteric smorgasbord. When he'd play Led Zeppelin's "Good Times, Bad Times," he felt comfortable about following that up with an appropriate Miles Davis tune. "I was never trying to show off," he says, "or prove how cool I was. It was to show that there was a connection between the Zep song and Miles Davis." There was nothing accidental about that; MacKay was learning on the job and getting better along the way. The more popular CKGM-FM became, the more visits the station got from record company A&R (artists and repertoire) reps looking to promote their next big star. As it was in Top 40, there was a lot music that didn't meet the standards, as informal as they were, of free-form FM radio. With no programming director or playlist, it fell to the announcers to peruse album cuts one by one to see if they were air-worthy. Sometimes, it was like unwrapping a gift. MacKay recalls one particular album brought in by an A&R rep from Columbia Records of Canada.

"The A&R rep told me, 'This is a new guy and he's really cool.' No one had ever heard of him before. If you got a brand new album and you didn't know what to play, you skip-tracked," MacKay says. "So with this new one, I said let's just start at the beginning and play it. See what it sounds like." It was Bruce Springsteen's first album, *Greetings from Asbury Park, N.J.* "I played the whole side. As I was listening, I thought, 'I can't take the needle off here. This is just so out there.' We were just saying to our listeners, 'Goddamn, this is so cool.'"

CKGM/CHOM would break out other great music for a hungry audience. In fact, the station was a launching pad for groups that were starving for attention and radio play, their musical careers taking off after Montreal FM radio exposure. Quebec groups like Beau Dommage, Harmonium, and Offenbach were in heavy rotation. Local folk artists like Kate and Anna McGarrigle and Jesse Winchester, Montreal's favourite adopted draft-dodger, found a home on FM radio. Early in their career, Supertramp played before a few hundred people in U.S. cities on the first leg of their North American tour. But when they came to Montreal, they were surprised by thousands of fans coming out to their first concert – exposure on FM radio had created an anticipatory Supertramp fan base. Likewise, British groups Genesis, Gentle Giant, the Strawbs, Pink Floyd, Emerson, Lake and Palmer, and Yes all owed their initial North American success to CKGM/CHOM. Album cuts like "Radar Love" by Dutch group Golden Earring and "The Mexican" by British group Babe Ruth were huge Montreal hits that were picked up and added to other FM radio playlists. More acoustic artists like Chris de Burgh (with his album *Spanish Train and Other Stories*) and Shawn Phillips (with his single "Woman" from the album *Second Contribution)* found a home in Montreal that they could come back to anytime, welcomed by loyal fans. They first became known on CKGM/CHOM, when no other stations would give them the time of day.

When CKGM-FM became CHOM in 1971, with its own identity and location, success meant inevitable programming changes. Management brought in a consulting firm from Toronto, and CHOM's format took a more corporate turn toward what was eventually called AOR music. Playing popular album cuts, not an entire side, was the new approach. There were more sponsors. Although he did not participate, MacKay recalls a sponsor's promotional event in which some CHOM announcers jumped into a pool filled with

Jell-O. "That may have been the day I knew things were gonna head south, pretty damn quick," he says. He preferred the contest where listeners were asked to draw or create an image of what they thought the CHOM announcers looked like. They got thousands of drawings and even some clay-crafted sculptures – much more dignified than doing a swan dive into Jell-O.

The out-of-town consultants and ensuing album-cut playlist sucked more than a bit of the free-form out of CHOM. MacKay felt CHOM's ratings grab ran contrary to the groundwork he and other early FM DJs had built. "The consultants said, 'Okay, let's get serious. We're going to become a corporate entity and it has been determined by a focus group that this is the list of songs that people want to hear.' I looked at this and thought, 'Man, if I ever play this stuff and actually used my voice to authenticate it, then maybe it's time to move on.'" Mackay wasn't the only one who had trouble adjusting. Announcers with particular tastes in music found themselves marginalized. MacKay had issues with the standardized music format, but he was bent out of shape when one francophone announcer was unfairly let go. "It [the confluence of sticking up for a colleague and the new CHOM playlist] was counterproductive to the work we had done," he says. "Counterproductive to the philosophy we espoused, that we lived by. It was clear to me, and others, that the writing was on the wall." In the end, MacKay had a philosophical falling-out with CHOM. Although he didn't leave in a huff, his gig was over almost four years after joining the station.

However, it wasn't quite a clean break. After moving to Britain, for two years MacKay was CHOM's foreign music and culture correspondent. He phoned in a weekly report to listeners from England, still the reigning rock hot spot in the world. Then he came back to Montreal and had a short-lived gig on the emerging FM competitor to CHOM, CJFM, which was taking a run at the FM youth market. CJFM would soon be rebranded Mix 96, where MacKay was brought in to co-host the long-running Sunday night *Rhythms International* show, at first with Richard Lafrance, then solo, when pioneering world-music broadcaster Daniel Feist fell ill. After a salary disagreement, MacKay left Mix 96, taking the *Rhythms*

International show to the Internet and logging 120 archived podcasts before calling it quits.

"At the time, I really didn't think of radio as a career. But it grows on you. I was lucky to be there [at CHOM] at the time I was. We were so lucky that the people who were making music were constantly creating and inventing new things that we could be a part of. The music just got better and better. When I got some new music to share, I would think to myself, 'Man, people got to hear this. You're gonna cream yourself when you hear this!' "

Postscript: I did two interviews with Angus, one of them by phone, the other on the patio of his Montreal West home on a beautiful early-summer day. I knew he had been battling cancer for years but he was optimistic when I spoke to him in the summer of 2015. At the time I interviewed him, I had no idea when my book would be published, but he asked me to not mention anything about his medical situation. But in late 2015, the cancer returned and Angus died on January 3, 2016. His funeral was a fitting tribute to the music man and fan he was. He was 67 years old, with two children, Callem and Liam, from his marriage to Neomie, as well as a son, Henry, from his first marriage.

Dave Marsden: From AM Stardom to FM Pioneer

In the early 1960s, Dave Mickie had all of the swagger and chutzpah of a Jerry Lee Lewis. Sporting a major, pumped-up pompadour to go with his shiny, straight-legged suits, he must have cut quite the fashion swath when he sauntered along the streets of conservative Chatham, Ontario, into the modest studios of CFCO-AM. In 1963, CFCO was playing the safe sounds of the day, echoed by most AM stations across Canada that had yet to give in completely to the force of nature that was rock 'n' roll. Mickie, who adopted the last name Marsden when he took a radio job in Montreal, went along with the format because he badly wanted into radio. For a while he played the music he was told to play, that is, until one day when he brought in some of his own personal music library and threw caution to the wind with a lot more

Chuck Berry than Pat Boone. He was in uncharted territory, outside the square-head boundaries set down by management, and rockin' Chatham to its core. Pretty much the only radio game in town, word got around quickly that night. Teens got on the jungle lines. "Hey, there's this crazy guy on CFCO. He's playing nothing but rock and talking a mile a minute." In teenage bedrooms around Chatham, the dials shifted to 630 to see what all the fuss was about.

One unhappy listener, the station manager, promptly fired Mickie the next day, then un-fired him after he was told ratings had jumped during the previous night's all-rock show. The "ratings" came in the form of phone calls and word on the streets of small-town southern Ontario, where news travelled fast. Mickie was the people's choice, and that night was the beginning of a brilliant Hall of Fame radio career.

Strangely, Marsden's radio career, almost to the year, follows the same trajectory of legendary Canadian media writer Marshall Mc-Luhan's 1964 book, *Understanding Media: The Extensions of Man*, in which Marsden (as Mickie) is one of the subjects of the author's analysis of "hot and cool" media. McLuhan's book was re-issued in 2014 to mark the 50th anniversary of its publication, roughly marking the same number of years in Marsden's media career.

For the record, Mickie was both hot and cool. His frenetic, motor-mouthed DJ patter, a phenomenon McLuhan felt he could not ignore, had quickly garnered Mickie some instant radio fame in a very straitlaced, Protestant Toronto-area market. In an attempt to explain the difference between the spoken and written word, Mc-Luhan referenced one of Mickie's rapid-fire radio patter bits that came from his natural-born AM musical mouth that moved much faster than the 45-rpm records he was playing. Legend has it that he set an unofficial radio record, reeling off 700 words in one minute. Mickie spoke in jazzed-up Top 40 paragraphs with little punctuation. His intros and extros had all the information listeners needed and wanted in 30 seconds or less; the artist, the time, some rhymin' hip talk and the hit-line number: "That's Patty Baby and that's the girl with the dancing feet and that's Freddy Cannon there on the

David Mickie Show in the nighttime ooohbah scuba-doo how are you booboo. Next we'll be Swinging on a Star and sssshhhwwoooo and sliding on a moonbeam. Waaaaa how about that . . . one of the goodest guys with you . . . this is lovable kissable D.M. in the p.m. at 22 minutes past nine o'clock there, aahhrightie, we're gonna have a hitline, all you have to do is call WAlnut 5-1151, WAlnut 5-1151, tell them what number it is on the hitline."

McLuhan's book was famous for coining two frequently used terms, used mostly by the many who hadn't been able to get through his entire book without dozing off. "The medium is the message" and the "global village" became part of the 1960s lexicon and, like good rock songs, they had staying power decades on. McLuhan put his media microscope to Mickie's patter, writing that he "alternately soars, groans, swings, sings, solos, intones, and scampers, always re-acting to his own actions." Mickie was flattered by the literary shout-out. McLuhan did have a way with words.

Like many Top 40 AM DJs, Marsden created a kind of alter ego in Dave Mickie, but no Canadian DJ has ever been referenced as both personalities in Cleveland's Rock and Roll Hall of Fame. First as Dave Mickie, then as Dave Marsden, his entertainment credits had few boundaries. Dave Mickie outgrew Chatham quickly to move to the big city for a brief stay at CKEY in Toronto – all in one year. Since then, he's made an impact in every major Canadian radio and TV market from CHUM-FM, CFNY (The Spirit of Radio) in Toronto, Coast 800 in Vancouver, *The Dave Marsden Radio Show* (a.k.a. *The Marsden Theatre*), to his present gig as founder of NY-TheSpirit.com radio. Sprinkle in some TV work as Dave Mickie, hosting the CBC-TV national teen music show *Music Hop* in 1965, then *Mickie a Go-Go* on CHCH-TV in Toronto, and later producing CBC's *Pilot One*, a late-night entertainment show aimed at the teen market. That's Marsden's 50-year career, so far, which earned him a place in the Canadian Music and Broadcast Industry Hall of Fame in March 2011 with the Allan Waters Broadcast Lifetime Achieve-ment Award.

Stuffed into Marsden's prolific radio travels was a side trip to Montreal in 1968, a part of his career that gets little notice. Even

Dave Marsden (Dave Mickie) with unidentified woman. In Toronto during the mid-60s Dave Mickie was a genuine radio and TV star. When he came to Montreal to work at CKGM-AM (and then FM) in 1968, he adopted the on-air name of Dave Marsden, leaving behind the Mickie caricature forever.

Photo by John Cosway.

Marsden is not completely sure why he made the move to CKGM-AM. "I was doing well in AM radio [in Toronto]," he says. "CKGM wasn't even a real rock station at that time, it was more MOR [middle-of-the-road.]" In fact, Marsden was looking to distance himself from the Dave Mickie persona. As a result of the exposure on the two TV shows he hosted, he was living the life of the celebrity, which had its perks. But after a while it closed in on his personal life, restricting his freedom to move about in public. He was Canada's first radio/TV star personality, the Dick Clark of Toronto. Montreal was certainly not his town, but there he could at least walk down the street unrecognized.

CKGM also wanted a reborn Mickie, not the hotshot Top 40 Toronto DJ version, but a more reserved, rebranded model for the Montreal radio market. The station manager asked him what he wanted to go by. "How about Marsden?" he said. He had grown up in foster homes, never knowing either his birth mother or father. "I pulled Marsden from what I thought my birth mother's last name was," he says, unconsciously borrowing the last name of Gerry of Gerry & the Pacemakers fame. When later in life, he did meet his birth mother – and acquired his original birth certificate – he found Marsden was hardly even close to his real name, one he prefers not to disclose. The acquisition of his birth certificate and his first meeting with his mother was revelatory. "I've dealt with this [not knowing my real name and parents] for a number of years. Since I found out my actual birth name, I feel more comfortable," he says. "I remember flying around my condo saying, 'I've got a real name, I've got a real name.' It was a moment of pure joy and bliss."

Mickie didn't have an easy childhood. Raised in a number of foster homes, his identity was informed by a sense of feeling somehow different. For a young boy, often picked on and the victim of schoolyard bullying, he was at a loss to define and understand his feelings of isolation. "It wasn't until I was nine years old that I realized I was gay," he says. "I was in my late teens before I realized I wasn't the only one who felt this way." Marsden endured any number of homophobic epithets. There was no "coming out" in those days. Years later in an interview, he flippantly told a Toronto journalist who asked him about his coming out, "I didn't know I was ever in." There was plenty of pain on that journey, never letting his guard down, always concerned his sexuality could hurt his career. In fact, it did cost him his job once when a radio station manager fired him based on what he assumed about Marsden's sexual preferences. There was no recourse; he just moved on. As a high-profile DJ and TV personality, he had to be especially careful, keeping a low profile when he was out for the night at one of his favourite Toronto gay clubs.

In early February 1981, he got an urgent call from the CFNY radio general manager asking him to come down to the station immediately. It was a Saturday morning, an unusual time to call. Alarm bells were going off in his head.

On February 5, Toronto police executed "Operation Soap" with some 150 officers raiding four bathhouses and arresting almost 300 men. Police tactics included taunts and some heavy-handed destruction of bathhouse property. Many lives were turned upside down that night as men (some married) had to endure the arrest procedure and explain where they'd been all night. It was hardly a coming-out party. The next day, thousands of protestors marched on the Toronto provincial legislature building. the *Globe and Mail* wrote an editorial slamming police tactics. CHUM-AM news director Dick Smyth called the police "pigs" on air, calling their methods "ham-handed brutality and lunk-headed vandalism." Like the riots after police in New York City raided the Stonewall Inn, a gay bar in Greenwich Village, this was Toronto's Stonewall moment, marking the beginning of a long battle for respect and recognition for the city's gay community.

In the CFNY studios Marsden met with general manager Pat Hurley. In Hurley's hand was an editorial he wanted vetted. "The station never did editorials," Marsden says. "I still wondered why he had called me to come down, and I was even more nervous when he told me the subject of his editorial." Hurley explained to him what had happened with the police raids and that he wanted to go on air with an editorial. "I didn't know where he stood on this, but when

256

I read his editorial, I saw he was against what the police had done. I felt like a thousand pounds had been lifted off me. It was then that I realized I could be myself at work, that I wouldn't be fired for being gay." The Toronto police, unfortunately, would still be slow learners. More bathhouse raids came after February. Ultimately, very few of the charges laid stuck, though the damage had already been done. Marsden is not a big rainbow-flag waver, but if asked by the community, he'll help. A number of his friends were not around to savour the changes in attitude in the 1990s. AIDS had taken a toll on the gay community. "I hope it's easier for young gay people today," he says. "But they should be aware that others went through hell to get where we are today."

On the air in 1968 at CKGM-AM, he had toned down his "Mickie" shtick and worked on being relaxed, just trying to blend in. CKGM-AM was trying hard to be something to all demographics in 1968, some phone-in talk shows and some rock, but it was not yet prepared to go to full-time Top 40. Marsden was briefed on management's expectations. "I remember the station manager Don Wall telling me, 'We don't want people to think we're going Top 40, so you have to change your name.' The name Mickie was synonymous with Top 40, so that's when I went with Marsden. I was never one to put myself into a little box anyway. I was quite ready to move onto something else," he says. Marsden had been hired at 'GM-AM to pull double duty as DJ and salesman. He thought that the sales part of the gig would add more margins to his strictly on-air radio credentials. He was thinking ahead; maybe a management position would come up. He hated it. "Every morning I would get up, put on my suit [not the shiny Dave Mickie TV model] and go out trying to sell commercial time. It just wasn't me, but I knew I had to learn what it was about." Later in his radio career, he found himself selling his new radio ideas. By then he was embracing the hard sell when he believed in the product.

Right across the hall from the CKGM-AM Westmount studios was its FM partner, still cranking out Ray Conniff or Mantovani. While Marsden was labouring with his dual AM role, changes were in the air – changes he would eventually cross the hall to be a part of. As it is with a surprising number of Top 40 DJs, the music they play on air isn't the same as what they listen to at home. So it was with Marsden, who had more esoteric tastes in rock 'n' roll than the stuff that was in heavy AM rotation. He was as hip, if not hipper, than many Top 40 DJs across Canada. So when he heard the rumblings of a new sound for the FM side of CKGM, he was interested in getting in on this new experiment. Like a parliamentarian who loses faith in his party, Marsden pulled off the radio equivalent of crossing the floor to the other side of the House. It wasn't a long crossing, nor did it have much ceremony to go with it. There was, however, some resentment from his AM colleagues, who saw themselves as being deserted. Moreover, Marsden recalls, they thought he was making a bad career move. "When I moved from AM to FM, I didn't really have friends on either side because the AM guys thought I was crazy to go over to the FM side for hardly any money. And the FM guys thought of me as your typical AM DJ," he says. Marsden is nothing if not adaptable, a showman at heart capable of quick costume changes. On FM radio, the Mickie persona was buried forever; even the toned-down Marsden AM version was put aside. "I guess I went from the guy who talks 700 words a minute to the guy who is just talking casual-like," he says.

Before CKGM-FM built up its own record library, it was every man for himself in the early days, before management would require adherence to a particular playlist. Marsden brought a lot of his own music into the studio. He compares the transition from AM to FM free-form as being like a kid in a sandbox – plenty of freedom and some self-indulgent choices. "I would say we all were going down a road that was not well-lit and we were finding our way along," he says. "The idea, I think, behind the original progressive rock station was to play the music you loved. The concept that I think I created there [at CKGM-FM] – and that idea is something I've carried through since – was to figure out how to take all this music that I loved and make it fit all together to create some kind of musical tapestry." Marsden has been weaving that tapestry for almost 50 years in alternative radio, and Montreal was his training ground.

Marsden, as it turned out, never really felt totally comfortable in Montreal. Even at CKGM-FM, he felt a bit like an outsider. The political atmosphere didn't help much either. His inadequacy with the French language, combined with the escalation of violence in October 1970, made him uneasy. Still, being part of a pioneering FM radio station, he felt he was in the middle of something important. But a phone call from CHUM-FM in Toronto changed all that, and he packed up to join Canada's other alternative FM station. "I didn't leave for a negative reason," Marsden maintains. "Someone said to me recently that radio guys move around a lot for no other reason than they were going where the new action was. I suppose that's true." When Marsden headed back to his hometown, he returned as a guy miles removed from his Dave Mickie days. Complete with beard and long hair, he had no trouble walking down Toronto streets unrecognized.

There are parallels between CHOM and CHUM in terms of their evolution from the early free-form format of the late '60s and most of the '70s, until both stations took a turn away from their early, democratically designed programming to the more commercial AOR approach. In 1977 CHUM-FM told its announcers there was a new playlist. Play it. Marsden quit and started up CFNY (dubbed the Spirit of Radio by Marsden and later the inspiration for the 1980 Rush song of the same name), which went back to the early roots of alternative FM. In his capacity as program director of CFNY, in 1981 he and the station came up with the idea a national award to recognize independent and alternative music—the U-Knows (a pun on the mainstream Juno Awards). In 1985, renamed the CASBY Awards (Canadian Artists Selected by You), some of its early winners included Rough Trade, the Payolas, Teenage Head, Parachute Club, and Martha and the Muffins. Today, his *NYthespirit.com* radio show continues the traditions and essence of alternative radio.

Marsden is coy about his age, but he's been around long enough and done enough to safely be called a Canadian radio legend, something that happens when you're one of four DJs featured in the full-length documentary *I Am What I Play*, which premiered in Toronto in May 2015. Marsden joins DJs Meg Griffin (New York), Charles

Laquidara (Boston) and Pat O'Day (Seattle), all in one broadcast Hall of Fame or another, in a look back at a time when radio had personality.

Radio pundits with a sense of history bemoan the fact that radio has taken a corporate turn over the last 20 years. Rumours of its current irrelevance abound. Is anyone listening anymore? Marsden has a different take on the state of the radio nation. "I don't understand why people say radio is dying. I don't see any kind of death," says Marsden. "I see evolution."

Denis Grondin: The Bilingual Master of Music

In 1968, the Jimi Hendrix Experience was on a brutal mega-city North American tour, which began at the Fillmore Auditorium in San Francisco in February and ended in December after the group played the Chicago Coliseum. On April 2, they played to a packed house at the Paul Sauvé Arena in Montreal's east end. In the crowd, there were two long-haired Hendrix fans from Collège Mont Saint-Louis, a private Montreal high school. Denis Grondin and his friend Pierre Richard had just graduated and were preparing to go into Quebec's newly minted pre-university program (or CEGEP). The psychedelic music era was in full swing and Hendrix was at its epicentre. His fan base, mostly young males, was mushrooming in the wake of his seminal, break-out performance at the Monterey Pop Festival in June of 1967. He had bedazzled the audience with a set that included "Foxy Lady," "Purple Haze," and an interpretation of The Troggs' 1966 hit "Wild Thing." When Hendrix sang, "Wild Thing, you make my heart sing / You make everything groovy / You move me," something stirred in the loins. He finished his Monterey set by kneeling at the altar of his guitar lying on stage, pouring lighter fluid on it and setting it afire, then picking it up and bashing the shit out of it on the stage. The California-cool crowd went nuts.

So there was great anticipation when Hendrix, drummer Mitch Mitchell, and bassist Noel Redding came to Montreal. Grondin and

Richard, as co-founders of the school's campus radio station, were ready to make this concert an experience they would never forget. They had fake press IDs made and carted along a cumbersome reel-to-reel tape recorder, determined to get backstage and interview Hendrix after the concert. Security in those days was not nearly as intense as it is today and to the rent-a-cops guarding the dressing-room door, they looked like all the other long-hairs milling about. In the sweaty hockey dressing room, there are two 17-year-olds looking for a scoop amongst the band, groupies, hangers-on and assorted legitimate press. It wasn't difficult to spot Hendrix with his oversized 'fro, bright bandana with frilly, flowered blouse, embroidered purple suede jeans and pointed snakeskin boots. Grondin spies Hendrix, decompressing and seemingly sitting alone for the moment, and warily approaches him. This is his first interview and it's big. There is no front-man running interference, no PR man to go through.

"Jimi, can I ask you a few questions?" says Grondin, while Richard handles the reel-to-reel. He could have gone with the "Mr. Hendrix" approach to show respect, but after repeated plays of his music, he felt somehow close to the artist. "Jimi" seemed the more organic way to go. "We're from our school radio station, we'd like to do a little interview. Would you mind?"

"No, that's OK," said Hendrix. (Grondin remembers Hendrix looked a little "spaced.") The interview lasts about 10 to 15 minutes and Grondin is determined to ask some heavier questions. As a 17-year-old fledging radio enthusiast, he's taking himself very seriously.

"Where's rock going?" he asks Hendrix. "What's gonna be next in rock music?"

"Well, there's gonna be rock music from around the world," he says. "Rock was born in America but you have rock musicians from everywhere that are gonna be coming out and making good music." (Hendrix, as it turned out, was not just a brilliant guitarist and singer but also prescient.) The Jimi Hendrix Experience shone brightly – putting out three memorable albums in just two years – but all too briefly when Hendrix died, only two years after his Montreal appearance.

The boys, riding a natural buzz from the night before, came into school the next day and played the entire Hendrix interview for the students in the cafeteria. It's doubtful the interview was fully appreciated over the din of conversation and clattering cafeteria trays. But the seed, nevertheless, was sown. Grondin would not have to wait too long before people actually did listen.

If you were a French-speaking child of the 1960s in Canada, U.S. rock music was hard to ignore. It was everywhere, including on the big Montreal Top 40 station of the day: CJMS, where DJ Michel Desrochers ruled the night, just as Dave Boxer and Buddy Gee did on CFCF and CKGM-AM. Desrochers and CJMS, however, had two Top 40 charts to play from, one featuring the "palmarès américain" and the "palmarès canadien et français." The U.S. Top 40 chart had the usual assortment of artists like Les Supremes and Les Rolling Stones. The Canadian and French chart of the 1960s had hits like "Demain" by Les Baronets (with Céline Dion's husband-to-be René Angélil) or Les Classels (four Beatle-like guys with dyed white hair and suits to match) with "On dit que l'on sait." Desrochers was part of "l'équipe de bons gars de CJMS," the equivalent of CFOX's "Good Guys."

Growing up in Montreal's Villeray district, Grondin listened to CJMS and CKGM, picking up a little rock 'n' roll English while doing some dial hopping. "I didn't understand everything because I didn't understand English that well back then," says Grondin. "I was listening to CJMS, and Michel Desrochers was like the typical American Top 40 DJ, only he was doing it in French. But I was listening to the English stations that played rock, too [CKGM, CFCF, and CFOX], perhaps more than CJMS. But mostly, I was just listening for the music, the popular music." The idea of being on the radio had all the romance a teenage music-lover like Grondin needed. In his room at home, he had a portable record player; he became a regular one-man bedroom DJ, the operator and announcer of his own Top 40 radio show, *The Denis Grondin Radio Show*. Occasionally, he and his buddies would wander downtown to the CJMS studios on Berri Street (now the site of Montreal's Grande Bibliothèque) and press their faces up against the big CJMS windows to see the inner workings of the station. "You could see the studio and the DJ and news guys working," says Grondin. "I used to stand there for a long time and just watch them work. It was like, 'Mmmmm, I'd like to go in there.'"

For the moment, he'd have to settle for a peek at the studios of Verdun community radio station CKVL, which often invited the public in for live shows. Grondin was wide-eyed as he checked out the oversized turntables (gigantic compared to his modest portable model), the mics and then the live broadcast itself. It was all gift-wrapped for an impressionable teenager smitten with music and radio. Riding that early love affair with radio, he and a few of his equally enthusiastic school friends lobbied the school's administration for some financial support and soon the school had its first campus radio station delivered live every noon hour over a couple of cheap speakers hung in the corners of the cafeteria. That set-up continued as the Collège Saint-Louis campus became part of the CEGEP Vieux- Montréal, only now with a larger budget and more radio toys to work with. And although neither Grondin, his pals nor his parents knew it, his academic life was about to end somewhat prematurely.

Thanks to the community-minded spirit of CKVL, he and his Collège Saint-Louis radio pals landed a three-hour Sunday midnight show, part of the station's student program. The station manager was impressed with Grondin's voice and offered him his own midnight to morning show on Friday and Saturday. He logged quite a few absences for any Monday morning classes he may have had because he was in bed sleeping off the all-night shift. It was the beginning of the end of his pre-university career. "I eventually dropped out altogether," he says. "I was so much into radio it was like my head was somewhere else. I was not in school at all." CKVL was the real deal and Grondin had fun playing the Top 40 DJ for a little over a year. He was a 19-year-old long-haired hippie DJ with wads of all-night freedom, slipping in album cuts by Emerson, Lake and Palmer's "Lucky Man," or "Questions 67 and 68" by the Chicago Transit Authority (later to become Chicago), both clocking in at well over four minutes and pared down for commercial AM airplay. "The bosses didn't seem to be listening," he says. "They were most likely in bed. I was doing my best impression of the DJs I had heard on radio. I had a very tight show with jingles that sang my name. It was great."

263

Grondin picked up his English on the streets, radio, music, and a heavy dose of TV shows like *Bewitched* and *Hogan's Heroes,* two of his favourites. He was, without any formal training, fairly comfortable in English. So, when another radio opportunity popped up, Grondin's comfort level in both French and English would serve him well. As usual, word of mouth was important in the radio business, and it was through a CKVL contact that he heard that the newborn underground, free-form CKGM-FM was looking for a bilingual announcer who knew his music. It wouldn't hurt to give CKGM-FM pioneer Doug Pringle a call. When he did call, Grondin was surprised to actually get Pringle on the line. He couldn't have known that CKGM-FM, just barely over a year old, was a pretty small operation. Still, his timing was perfect. "I called the station and Doug was on the line in about 30 seconds. I'm really nervous but I give him my presentation, tell him I work at CKVL and I heard you guys were looking for a French jock that knew music," says Grondin. "I tell him I'm really into the music they're playing. So he says, 'What are you doing tonight? Can you come on the air tonight?' 'Um, yeah, sure.'" That night Grondin, with some of his own records and albums from the station's record library in hand, followed Dave Marsden and settled in behind the mic at midnight. "That show was a bit of a blur. I can't remember what I played, but after about an hour and a half, the program director came into the studio and told me I had the job." He broke the news to CKVL's station manager who was disappointed to see him go. "We had plans for you, Denis," he said, but wished him well in his new job. In late August 1971, Grondin left Top 40 radio behind. Now he could really get into the meatier music of the day.

Though Grondin didn't settle into any one particular time slot at first, he felt he did his best work on the all-night shift when it was play-what-you-want time on CKGM-FM. There wasn't any overt pressure to be the francophone DJ, but he knew that was one of the reasons they had hired him. "I never really calculated how much French and English I was speaking on air," says Grondin. "If it was a French song, I'd usually introduce it in French. I was bouncing back and forth, but I never said one thing in English then the same thing in French, like a kind of translator. I tried to have the language and the music flow. That's what people wanted." They wanted him to play Quebec-grown music artists, and, as it happened, the progressive rock scene in Quebec was just catching fire. There were the already established artists like Robert Charlebois, whose 1968 album *Lindberg*, with Louise Forestier and the single of the same name, was in heavy rotation on CKGM-FM (though it came out almost three years before Grondin went on the air). Quebec rock artists had some catching up to do with the U.S. and British rock scene in the early 1970s. But Quebec artists like Diane Dufresne, Gilles Valiquette, Lewis Furey, Mississippi-raised Nanette Workman, Michel Pagliaro, and Plume Latraverse (considered Quebec's Frank Zappa) got airtime on Grondin's show. He'd throw in the odd French rock artist to give a little international flavour to his listeners.

Then, much to the delight of music fans, came groups like Harmonium, Octobre, and Beau Dommage. Grondin was fortunate to have one of the first pressings of Harmonium's debut album before it was released in early 1974. He had the band, led by singer/lyricist and guitarist Serge Fiori in studio for an interview, put the needle down on side one of their self-titled album and simply let it run, chatted a bit, then flipped it over to side two. "I didn't know these guys at all," says Grondin. "I started to play the first cut in the studio and I said 'Wow, this sounds really good.' So, I just let it go. We chatted a bit and I wound up playing the whole album. I was free to do this. No program director calling me up and asking me who the hell I was playing. Harmonium was like the Crosby, Stills & Nash of Quebec."

The folksy, Beatles-inspired guitar intro (more than a little similar to "Here Comes the Sun") and catchy chorus of the cut "Pour un instant" by Harmonium got heavy airplay on CHOM (renamed in October 1971, just a couple of months after Grondin was hired) for years, even after the group put out three more albums before disbanding in 1978. Harmonium was huge in Quebec and CHOM could take at least some of the credit for that. The band's second album, released the next year and popularly known as *Les cinq saisons* (formally as *Si on avait besoin d'une cinquième saison*), was nominated for a Juno as Best Selling Album of the Year (1976). That same year, in the same category, was Beau Dommage's first

Denis Grondin sported the laid back look of CKGM-FM/CHOM. As an aspiring jazz drummer, he had eclectic tastes in music, making his show something of an educational experience for listeners.
Courtesy of Denis Grondin.

self-titled album – the only year that two Quebec groups would have two best-selling albums up for an English music award. April Wine, who had by then relocated from Halifax to Montreal, were also up for a Juno with their double-platinum-selling fourth album *Stand Back*. Meanwhile, Gino Vannelli picked up Best Male Vocalist. It was a banner year for Quebec popular music with artists like Maneige, Lewis Furey, Raoul Duguay, Aut'Chose, and Jean-Pierre Ferland all getting Juno nominations.

Rolling Stone magazine ranks Harmonium's *Les cinq saisons* No. 36 on their Top 50 Progressive Rock Albums of All Time. *Les cinq saisons*, released in 1975, had only five songs on it, with two running over ten minutes in length, a '70s trend with groups who were categorized as "prog rock," (progressive rock.). A 1976 follow-up album *L'Heptad*, had even more success. The group, who recorded only three albums (excluding one double-live album) disbanded in 1978, but within a short period of time their music made Beatles-like impact in Quebec. And CHOM gave Harmonium the radio exposure that most groups would kill for. Canadian music journalist Bob Mersereau has his own list in his 2007 book, *The Top 100 Canadian Albums*. Harmonium's *Les cinq saisons* and their 1976 album *L'heptade* come in at Nos. 56 and 76 respectively, keeping company with such greats as Joni Mitchell, Neil Young, the Band, Leonard Cohen, and Stompin' Tom Connors.

Grondin's early days at CKGM-FM/CHOM coincided with the release of several monumental concept albums, which the station was more than happy to play for its listeners. These albums were tailor-made for the dope-smoking crowd who could just drop the needle on one side, then sit back and enjoy. If you couldn't afford the album or didn't have a stereo of your own, that's where CHOM came in. They dropped the needle for you. Pink Floyd, Styx, Genesis, Marillion, Yes, King Crimson, and Emerson, Lake and Palmer (ELP) all put out concept albums in the early 1970s. Even former lead guitarist for the Monkees, Michael Nesmith, got in on the act. Groups like Floyd, Styx, Genesis, King Crimson, and ELP all became Montreal favourites as a result of CHOM's prog rock format. King Crimson's 1969 album *In the Court of the Crimson King* is widely considered to be the paradigm for prog rock albums. CKGM-FM, then CHOM, gave album cuts "The Court of the Crimson King" and "21st Century Schizoid Man" extensive airplay. Montreal was a frequent stop on the band's tour list, even recording an album entitled *Absent Lovers: Live in Montreal* in 1984.

On one 1971 stop in Montreal, the group wandered into the CKGM-FM studios for a live, post-Café Campus concert interview (the group would soon move up to play the Forum) with Grondin.

At the time, he was barely a couple of months on the job, mostly doing his shows in his "okay" English just to get in the practice. He had two mics set up for the interview and played a few cuts from their fourth studio album *Islands* as Crimson lead guitarist Robert Fripp rolled a huge joint. "They were very nice and polite, the British way," remembers Grondin. "I put my two microphones up and stood to interview them. When they spoke to me I could not understand a word they were saying, they had such heavy accents." Fripp was concentrating on rolling the joint and hardly seemed interested in the interview. "Okay, where are the girls in this city?" he asked Grondin while a cut from *Islands* played in the background. "Where can we go? Any clubs or dances?" Grondin is panicking a bit. Not only does the leader of the group look uninterested, he's having trouble understanding their thick southwest England accents. "Fortunately, the group's lyricist, Pete Seinfeld, could see I was having trouble and basically took over the interview," says Grondin. "There I was on live radio, winging it, faking it." He was doing a kind of stand-up in his second language, learning how to think on his feet. It was an English-as-a-second-language immersion lesson. With a little help, he passed the test with flying colours and was relieved when the group left the studio for a taste of Montreal's nightlife.

The King Crimson interview was not the only time Grondin would find himself in a pressure-packed situation. One night, on one of his famous late-night unannounced visits to his station, owner Geoff Stirling came with a radio consultant in tow to watch Grondin at work. No words were exchanged. In fact, this was only the second time that Grondin had met his enigmatic boss. Stirling and the consultant simply came in and watched him work the turntables and mic. Stirling may have been showing off CHOM's new digs in the renovated mansion on Greene Avenue, but more likely it was because he wanted the consultant to get a glimpse at how the station worked – and at Grondin's bilingual chatter. After midnight, CHOM's playlist consisted of whatever the announcer felt like playing. Stirling, who kept weird hours, stayed for the whole shift. Grondin's concentration was only momentarily shaken; having the chief watch you like a fish in a bowl didn't seriously faze him. At one point in the evening, the consultant had some observations to share with Grondin. "There's not too many radio stations in the U.S. doing the kind of show you're doing," he told Grondin. "Your show is great." There was something ominous about what should have been a simple compliment, Grondin thought at the time. "I got the feeling he was telling me to enjoy what I was doing now because things were probably going to change."

In its early years CKGM-FM, then later as CHOM, was a mostly male-dominated radio station despite the new freestyle socio-sexual politics of the day. There were some exceptions like Shelly Smith (arguably the station's first female announcer) and Rachel Irwin who had gravitated to the station naturally, part of a crowd who used CKGM-FM, then CHOM, as a place to hang out. At McGill, Irwin had made fast friends with Heidi O'Carroll, who would eventually become Doug Pringle's wife. Pringle and station owner Geoff Stirling were both transcendental meditation initiates. On a trip to an ashram in Big White, British Columbia, Irwin became acquainted with Stirling and his son Scott, also a convert and devotee of Swami Shyam. Back in Montreal, her Stirling connection led to the occasional house-sitting job at Stirling's Westmount home and probably didn't hurt her employment opportunities at CHOM. After some volunteer time at the station, she found herself on the air as Lady Rachel.

Irwin had no problems negotiating a mostly male-dominated business. This was hardly the hustle of AM radio where the office/radio dynamics might be more sexually charged. It was a very laid-back working environment. "It was just a real camaraderie," she says. "It was a brother-sister situation there [at CHOM]. I didn't feel like it was a chauvinistic environment at all, even though it was male-oriented. It was family." Change was in the air for Irwin, Grondin and more than a few other stations announcers. When CHOM management decided to tighten up the free-form format, Irwin was one of the casualties. Her time slot went to Reiner Schwartz, an announcer with a big voice and bigger vision, who came to Montreal via alternative rock station CHUM-FM in Toronto. "Few of us [at CHOM] were professional DJs," says Irwin. "We were all counterculture, just lucking into something at the moment. Not many of us thought of radio as a career."

Grondin, however, left the station in 1974 for a very personal reason: he was getting bored. His early enthusiasm for radio was waning while his inner musician was telling him it was time for a change. Grondin had a passion for the drums, something he'd toyed with since his youth. It was time, he thought, to go back to school, not to get that CEGEP diploma he never got, but to learn how to play the drums. He had played casually in bands with his musician friends, but now he went about learning his craft as he had when he started in radio, by immersing himself in learning and playing. For the next nine years, playing the drums became his new passion, attending music school by day and playing the clubs at night. He played anywhere, anytime he could: a little jazz, Sinatra, swing, some easy-listening stuff for gigs at Bill Wong's on Décarie Boulevard, a then-popular dining and dancing destination for the mature crowd. He slept in sleazy hotels and shared a van with whoever needed a drummer on any given weekend. Though he was making decent money, the life of the musician had its drawbacks. Life on the road was further complicated by his marriage in 1979 and his first-born on the way. Still, he hung on for three more years before his role of husband and father took centre stage. In 1982, he called CHOM program director Rob Braide to ask if he had anything available. "My schedule and my personal life were conflicting," says Grondin. "I figured going back into radio would be a good thing." His wife agreed, though when her husband settled into the all-night shift, she may have had second thoughts. "I remember coming home in the morning after working the all-night shift and she had been up with our second child all night," he says. "I would tell her to go to sleep and I'd take care of the kids. The bed didn't get made very often in those days. There was always someone in it."

Back at CHOM in 1982 and humbled by life on the road, any interview he did with musicians in town gave him a perspective few radio announcers had; he knew the language of the musician and the inherent fatigue that comes from constant travelling. Still, it was a different music scene, one he was slightly out of touch with. And

270

CHOM had changed, too. The format was tighter, but Grondin was a quick study and he was soon back in step. Benoît Dufresne was music director; he was also doing his groundbreaking *New Music Foundation* show featuring alternative music. Claude Rajotte, who did double duty on CHOM and as a VJ (the TV version of a DJ) on *MusiquePlus* in the 1980s, was also part of the CHOM staff. Braide asked Grondin to produce a weekly French-language music show called *Premier souffle* (First Breath). CHOM was trying to straddle the 1980 CRTC ruling that had been expected since the late 1970s: when both CHOM and CKGM-AM were doing bilingual programming, many of Montreal's French-language radio stations took their complaints to the commission. Though CHOM and CKGM-AM had been warned, the CRTC didn't officially step in to curtail the use of French at both stations, whose audience was heavily (anywhere from 60 to 70 percent) francophone. That meant the end for CKGM-AM's "La Connection Française" with Marc Denis, Scott Carpentier, and Rob Christie, although Denis soldiered on bilingually until he left the station in 1980. As for CHOM, they skirted the boundaries set out by the CRTC, though even with Rajotte, Dufresne, and Grondin on the air at various times, CHOM's bilingual days were pretty much over.

Still, Grondin's show *Premier souffle* introduced a whole new set of Québécois artists. "It [the show] was really positive for me because I didn't know anybody in the French record companies. I started to find out about them and asked, 'I'm producing this new show on CHOM. Do you have any records you could send me?'" Indeed they did. He got to meet some new artists, some of whom he is still in touch with. He interviewed some of the established Quebec artists like Robert Charlebois and Beau Dommage, but also newer ones. At first he did the one-hour show in French, but switched to English, not because of any repercussions from the CRTC but because he felt more comfortable with the language of an English radio station. The heyday of Québécois music had cooled somewhat after the success of Harmonium and Beau Dommage. Disco music was a major interruption in creativity. But in the mid-1980s, the Audiogram label resurrected artists like Octobre, Jean-Pierre Ferland, Paul

Piché, Michel Rivard (formerly of Beau Dommage), Richard Séguin and Zachary Richard. Grondin even played demo tapes by Quebec artists looking for some radio exposure.

Grondin left CHOM in 1989 and went back to some familiar territory in Verdun, where he got his start at CKVL-AM in 1969. CKVL's FM side, now renamed CKOI, was a major player in the Montreal radio market when Grondin took up duties there in 1989. With a massive 307,000-watt signal (the most powerful in North America), CKOI had captured a huge chunk of the young francophone listenership when it changed its format to progressive rock in 1976. By the early 1980s, they had seriously outgunned CHOM. By 1991, they were the No. 1 station in Montreal with over one million listeners, the first Montreal FM station ever to top the ratings. In 1998, however, Grondin was a numbers victim when he was one of eight people to lose his job at CKOI due to budget cutbacks.

From there Grondin's work portfolio takes a number of twists and turns: Internet radio with Iceberg Radio; producing shows for Air Canada's inflight music channels; starting a new commercial radio station with Maritime Broadcasting in Moncton, New Brunswick; creating programming for Radio-Nord's Abitibi operations; a one-year (2003–04) return to CHOM; starting Montreal's first all-jazz radio station, "Couleur Jazz" (an experiment he wishes had gone a different way); then XM Satellite radio; producing 100th-anniversary shows for the Montreal Canadiens; a part-time job at Corus Media, which owned 98.5 FM, while doing research for Vox-TV; then he was fired and rehired as the digital consultant for Cogeco radio stations network in Quebec. Somewhere in between, he sold TVs and stereos.

At 65, with two adult children, Grondin is gearing down, but not necessarily by choice. Recently he found a new radio home on Radio-VM (CIRA-FM), a volunteer-run station in Montreal that also has frequencies in Sherbrooke, Trois-Rivières, Victoriaville, and Rimouski. Grondin has a Saturday night rock-oriented show followed by his Sunday night gospel feature. It's a chance for him to continue in the business and music he loves. And perhaps share the story of his 1968 interview with Hendrix.

272

Postscript: Denis Grondin died suddenly at home on March 14, 2017. A renaissance radio man, he was fluent in all genres of music. His warmth and good heart were appreciated by all who knew him at CKVL, CHOM, CKOI, and 98.5 FM.

Robert "Tootall" Wagenaar: CHOM's "Four Decade" Man

After apprenticing in radio stations in Regina and Vancouver, a young Robert Wagenaar decided to head east to Montreal, hoping to catch on with CHOM-FM. The progressive FM radio scene in Canada had caught hold in several major markets but CHOM had garnered a special reputation in the Canadian radio mosaic. He hadn't phoned ahead. It was a kind of scouting mission. He had no Plan B beyond a possible job at CHOM.

First, he knocked on program director Rob Braide's door. The doors were always swinging open and closed at any given time at radio stations. Maybe his timing was right. Braide had no on-air job for him, so he moved into the production department where they wrote advertising copy and recorded commercials. There, the manager asked if he could write commercials. In a moment of rare job-hunting honesty, he told the manager he had no experience writing ad copy. Nevertheless, they asked him to write a 30-second spot for Pascal's, the biggest retail hardware chain store in Montreal. The next day he handed over the copy to the production manager, who looked it over. "Thanks, but we don't have any openings," he told Wagenaar. Tuned into CHOM a couple of days later, Wagenaar was surprised to hear his Pascal's commercial, word for word. The next day, he went back to confront the production manager. "What the fuck?" he said. "You stole my commercial!" Caught in something akin to copyright theft and perhaps intimidated by the agitated six-foot-seven Wagenaar seething over him, the production manager offered him a job.

Although they were off to a bit of a rough start, Wagenaar's relationship with the production manager proved very fruitful. After a short time in production, he worked the swing shift on CHOM, filling in for announcers. The same production manager fortuitously but inadvertently gave Wagenaar the idea for an on-air nickname that would stick for the rest of his career at the station. Seeing Wagenaar constantly ducking through the ancient doorways of the old Westmount home, he said, "Hey, you're too tall." For a very brief time at CHOM, there was an announcer called Robert Wagenaar, though barely anyone can recall who he was. But Tootall? Now that's the name that everyone remembers. Robert Wagenaar just kind of disappeared and Tootall took his place. That was 38 years ago.

Like most radio people, Wagenaar did some wandering before settling into the gig at CHOM. Very few stay at one station long enough to log the kind of seniority that Wagenaar now has with CHOM. It's CBC-quality longevity. Except for one year at CKGM-AM, Wagenaar's time at the station easily outstrips that of any Montreal radio personality – or Canadian one, for that matter – in either French or English. His is not yet an official Hall of Fame career (not that he's campaigning for the award, something other radio "lifers" have done), but he does have a star acknowledging his 35-year-plus radio career in the lobby of Bell Media's east-end Montreal headquarters, where CHOM relocated in 2012. (The star system began when Astral Media bought out Standard Radio, which owned CHOM, among other Montreal stations. Astral didn't have much time to work their celestial awards theme before Bell Media bought them out. Tootall is likely the last of the "lobby stars.") Alongside his star are two others: one for popular Québécois radio comedian and musician François Pérusse and another for award-winning radio sketch artists José Gaudet and Mario Tessier of Les Grandes Gueules (Big Mouths). For now, at least, he's satisfied with that.

Wagenaar's wandering spirit took him from the University of Regina, where he had helped set up the campus radio station, to Europe in search of a job at the pirate radio stations that were popping up in the mid-1960s in the United Kingdom and Europe. Pirate radio was akin to the free-wheeling style of the underground FM radio movement in the U.S., an exciting but illegal alternative to the staid, stiff-upper-lip monopoly of the BBC. Broadcasting from off-shore ships, stations like Radio Caroline, Radio London, and Radio Luxembourg drew millions of young listeners hungry for more than just an hour or two of BBC-produced rock radio shows. Pirate radio was rebel radio at its best, but the British government was not so amused, busting or bankrupting them with exorbitant fines. (The 2009 film *The Boat That Rocked*, released as *Pirate Radio* in North America, amusingly captures the whacky, willy-nilly, sink-or-swim world of pirate radio.) There was a certain renegade romance and danger to working for pirate radio stations, just the kind of adventure that attracted Wagenaar to the scene. It was a weird journey for the young radio enthusiast with no game plan. It was a search that had him coming close to getting aboard. In the end, alas, he had nothing but a few stories to share with friends back in Regina.

Back on familiar territory, he caught on with Top 40 station CJME-AM in Regina, while getting an early taste of the new experimental FM scene at CFMQ (also in Regina), programming music for one of the announcers. Back and forth between AM and FM was a fertile training ground for Wagenaar, who was laying the foundation for his versatility and flexibility, two qualities that would serve him well throughout his career. With a population of about 140,000 in the early 1970s, Regina was a small market town with not much radio maneuvering room for a young jock with a bad case of wanderlust and no fixed job agenda. He had two options: west or east. Vancouver, Toronto or Montreal. Vancouver seemed more accessible so that's where he headed, spending about five years in various radio-related jobs, including some hanging out at pioneer underground FM station CKLG. With colleague Brian Leboe on Vancouver Island, Wagenaar worked on a documentary on how killer whales communicate. Today it's called biomusic, but back in the late 1960s and early 1970s, it was hip to record whale sounds and throw in some musical accompaniment. (Think Mike Oldfield's *Tubular Bells II* with squeaky whale noises.) Leboe, whose middle on-air name at CHOM was "Major Buzz," regaled Wagenaar with his FM experiences. CHOM sounded like a cool place to work. "I knew all about CHOM from him," Wagenaar says. "So, I said, 'What the hell, I'll guess I'll go.'" It was as simple as that.

After the Pascal's incident secured him a pass inside the CHOM sanctum, Wagenaar barely spent much time in CHOM's production room and soon moved to doing various on-air shifts, filling in and making himself indispensable. CHOM was still progressive rock radio and he had plenty of freedom with the music he played, though there were creeping format changes designed to tighten up the station's playlist. "It wasn't exactly free-form when I started," he says. "It could be total chaos because you could have some really good people on the air and some people who were like 'What the heck? What's going on?' And CHOM was different from any other station in the sense that it was run by someone [Geoff Stirling] who was into Eastern mysticism and religions. No matter what kind of style of radio you have, it's a format. If it's free-form, it's a format. Everything's a format. I don't mind changing things around. I don't mind doing something else. I just adapt." That pretty well sums up the Tootall philosophy of radio, one that has kept him at the same station all these years while others have stomped out in a huff over format changes they disagreed with or couldn't adapt to.

In 1981, when CHOM management was playing around with various shift changes, Wagenaar was somewhat bent out of shape and accepted a job doing Top 40 at CKGM-AM. It was not a great year for Top 40 music. There was Dolly Parton's "9 to 5" in heavy rotation, along with maudlin rock hits like REO Speedwagon's "Keep on Loving You," Kenny Rogers' "Lady," and ABBA's "The Winner Takes It All." Even John Lennon had eased off the rock pedal with the dreary "Woman." All of those songs – and others like them – made *Billboard*'s Top 100 hits of 1981. If the 1980s sucked much of the punch out of Top 40 rock, Wagenaar had stumbled into the beginning of the declining years of Top 40 radio at CKGM-AM, and in North America. "Going to do Top 40 radio was no big deal for me," he says. "I'd done it in Regina. But things were changing at 'GM. They were losing numbers, starting to go down." AM radio was a performance for Wagenaar, an "art form" he was comfortable with. "You have to be tight on AM. You watch some of the old guys work, whoa! Hitting every post. The voice modulated properly. No heavy-duty content, but fast radio."

Tootall (born Robert Wagenaar) has logged more hours and years behind the mic at CHOM than any other Montreal radio announcer, he's one of only three honorees in Bell Media's current Montreal headquarters.
Courtesy of Tootall.

Although he was less than impressed with the AM music of the new decade, he hardly sat back on cruise control. At CKGM, he talked program director Robert G. Hall into a two-hour Canadian content show called *Made in Canada*. He'd interview big rock acts in town, like Randy Bachman of Bachman-Turner Overdrive or Montreal's heartthrob singer Gino Vannelli; he'd even broadcast Montreal-based rock bands live in concert. His show was a big factor in fulfilling the station's CRTC Canadian-content regulations, not to mention giving struggling bands some much-needed publicity and airtime. That type of show was unusual for AM radio, which was tightly formatted. But Wagenaar was breaking new ground and after that one-year AM gig, he went back across the street to CHOM, taking the *Made in Canada* concept with him. "It was a great time for Canadian music because in the late 1980s the scene just exploded," he says. He was swamped by Canadian bands trying to get some airtime on *Made in Canada*. He figures that from 1987 to 2008, when the show ran on CHOM, he was getting about 300 albums a year, playing about 250 of them, interviewing dozens by phone or when

CHOM was a great ambassador of music in the community and Tootall
was an enthusiastic promoter of Canadian rock music. One
local high school won a contest for school spirit, earning them an
appearance by the Max Webster Band and Tootall and the station's
mascot of the day, Rocky Racoon.
Courtesy of Mark Sherman.

they were in town doing live concerts. He was one of the first to
introduce the Tragically Hip, Our Lady Peace, and the Tea Party to
Montreal – they were all just starting out. It was a feather in their
cap to get on Wagenaar's show. Both the Tragically Hip and the Tea
Party remain Montreal favourites. When he took stock of how many
Canadian bands he had featured on *Made in Canada* by 2008, the
numbers weighed in at well over 2,000. "In the 38 years I've been
at CHOM," Wagenaar says modestly, "there's not been a time when
we didn't have local bands on the air. From Harmonium and Beau
Dommage to Walter Rossi and others throughout the years, we've
always been supportive of local talent. In fact, the majority of stuff
we play today is local."

Wagenaar made more local-rock-band-scene impact when he
headed up CHOM's l'Esprit competition in 1989, an idea that was

hatched in 1978, the brainchild of station manager Craig Cutler and promotion director Mark Sherman. The contest was meant to be a showcase for Montreal bands: the winner received cash prizes, a chance to record, and an opportunity to play in front of big crowds. The first l'Esprit winner, Cinema V, played live at Tokyo's legendary Budokan, an indoor arena that held its first rock concert in 1966 with the Beatles. Later, artists like Cheap Trick and Bob Dylan recorded live albums there, setting a trend for big-name rock groups. *Live at Budokan* became synonymous with great live albums, and groups discovered a whole new audience and market in Japan. L'Esprit winners have come and gone, but a few have stuck around for the long haul. In 1999 Rubberman, with lead singer Jonas Tomalty, won l'Esprit. Although Rubberman has since dissolved, today Tomalty tours as Jonas and the Massive Attraction.

Current CHOM jock Jason Rockman is lead vocalist for Slaves on Dope, winner of the 1994 version of l'Esprit. Four albums and three EPs later, along with some personnel changes and the usual rock band pitfalls, Slaves on Dope is still kicking. He credits Wagenaar with giving Montreal bands like his a chance to see how far they could take their talent. "Tootall was the only guy in the city giving bands a chance. CHOM's reputation was built on that," he says. "He's got history with Canadian bands. I listened to his show for a long time. He always had his ear to the ground and that rubbed off on me. He's a huge influence." The veteran radio man and the rookie became fast friends when Rockman joined CHOM in 2009. Thanks to Quebec's enlightened minister-for-a-day program, Wagenaar officiated Rockman's wedding to wife Julia that same year. When it was time for new blood to take up the torch for Canadian music, Rockman picked up where Tootall left off. "I enjoy going home now," says Tootall, admitting age could be a factor. "There's other people picking up the torch, you know? Doing stuff. So, that's fine. It's always nice to see new up-and-comers. The business has to keep fresh."

On *Amped* his nightly show, Rockman unveiled a "Big Shiny New Song of the Week"; and also did live interviews, featuring the edgier side of the rock scene. Likewise, on Sunday nights Jay Walker keeps the Tootall *Made in Canada* spirit alive with his show *Montreal Rocks*, the focus being the local and international indie rock scenes. Though l'Esprit came to an end in 2003, many Montreal musicians have great "almost famous" stories to tell their children. Tootall and CHOM are at the centre of those stories.

Wagenaar has been around CHOM long enough to be part of almost all of its 46 years of history. He was part of the CHOM ghost exorcism. In 1985, when CHOM moved back to the west side of Greene Avenue, he witnessed the fire that destroyed the former CHOM HQ, fortunately minus the famous CHOM door, which had been removed and is on display at Bell Media's head office. He's seen dozens of announcers, program directors, and general managers come and go. He's adapted to numerous format changes and the ebb and flow of local, Canadian, and international rock music. He's still on the "island" after four ownership changes, from Geoff Stirling to Bell Media. In 1977, when Wagenaar debuted on CHOM, Fleetwood Mac's *Rumours* was the No. 1 album; Barbra Streisand and Kris Kristofferson starred in the movie *A Star is Born* with the single "Evergreen" in heavy AM rotation; Debby Boone's "You Light Up My Life" and ABBA's "Dancing Queen" topped the charts. The Sex Pistols, Elvis Costello, Billy Joel, Steely Dan, and Linda Ronstadt all had a good year. Cassette sales equalled that of the album, signalling the decline of vinyl. T. Rex's lead singer Marc Bolan died in a car crash. On the Canadian and Montreal rock scene, 1977 was a good year for Quebec group Boule Noir and former Beau Dommage member Michel Rivard. CHOM was still spinning some vinyl (now a novelty sideshow on FM radio) with albums by Canadian bands Chilliwack, April Wine, Rush, and Max Webster, who were all hot in 1977.

Today, 38 years after Wagenaar's first CHOM show, listeners can still hear some of those artists (minus Boone and Streisand) on his weekly noon-hour *Made to Order* show, a heavier version of the popular long-running *Electric Lunch Hour* show. "People ask me if I play my own music," says Wagenaar. "The attitude of some is that with corporate ownership in radio, we're told what to play. Hell, I don't dress corporately. I have nothing to do with the corporate side of the business. The question seems to be important to people, but

I just laugh and say, 'I play what I do.' And they can tune in every noon hour Monday to Friday and hear. I think the best way to do this job is to find a place where you like to hang out, have a good time, scenery, weather, go there and do it."

Wagenaar, has the kind of radio street cred that is rare in a business that routinely eats up and spits people out when ratings are low or ownership changes. Along with morning man Terry DiMonte, he remains the anchor of CHOM's morning-to-midday on-air lineup. There's a reason they go back to back on CHOM's current broadcasting schedule. When those two guys decide to hang it up or move on, CHOM will be left with some gaping holes to fill. Meanwhile, Tootall's got the star and a show to do. He's livin' the dream, hanging out for four hours a day doing what he loves. Regina must seem like light years ago.

Terry DiMonte: From Churchill to CHOM

Terry DiMonte had just finished a two-year stint at John Abbott College on Montreal's West Island. In Quebec's education system a compulsory two-year pre-university program known as CEGEP gives high school graduates time to figure out what to do with the rest of their lives. For many, it's on to university. For DiMonte it was: How do I get a job in radio? He was taking the requisite psychology and social studies classes, which gave him time to hang out at the college's radio station. There, he made several audition tapes which he sent out to a stack of radio stations in Montreal. It was the tried-and-true way to find a radio job.

Fortunately, he got a bite at CBC Montreal for a job as a booth announcer. At the interview he decided to ask the CBC employee, Karen Sorensen (more than 40 years later, he still remembers her name), to tell him straight up whether they thought his audition tape was any good. In her hand was the evaluation sheet by CBC's head announcer. "It basically said, 'Don't quit your day job,'" DiMonte says. (He has that sheet framed and hanging on a wall in his Montreal condo.) Sorensen was not nearly as harsh as the head announcer.

"There's something about this tape I like," she told him. "So, I'm going to send it to CBC Northern Services in Ottawa."

About six months later, he called his father to share some good news: he'd been hired by CBC in Churchill, Manitoba; population 1,300, not including the polar bears.

"Oh, that's great news," his father says. "Where is that?"

"I'm not sure," DiMonte says. "Newfoundland? Maybe out west?"

His father is a bit flabbergasted. "How can you accept a job when you don't even know where it is?"

"Because I don't care." This is not the correct answer, not the one his father wanted to hear.

"What about money?"

"I didn't ask." DiMonte would have licked the floors clean for 10 bucks a week, he wanted the radio job so bad.

There was, at this point in the conversation, a parental expletive. "You might be going there for five dollars a week."

"Dad, it's the CBC. They have a union. I didn't ask how much."

DiMonte was 19 and on a plane to Winnipeg, where he would then fly on to Churchill. It was 1977 and there were no roads in or out of town. There still aren't! You have to want it bad, and be young and a bit foolish.

In the DiMonte family's Verdun apartment, the radio was tuned to CJAD, the station of choice for English-language Montrealers, who were mostly interested in news, weather, sports, and announcers who delivered it all with calm, cool professionalism. There was a sprinkling of music but nothing that would cause its loyal listenership to turn the dial. In 1958, the year DiMonte was born, the neighbourhood was solidly blue collar. Neighbours knew each other, if not through the ubiquitous Verdun apartment-balcony and street culture, then through the noises that seeped through the paper-thin 1940s walls. You got to hear your neighbours at their best and worst.

Through the walls of the family's apartment came the sounds of a shrieking teenage girl, as she cranked up the volume of her parents' radio, which was tuned to the Dave Boxer show on CFCF. A

Beatles song had come on, precipitating the celebratory noise. This was not the kind of noise DiMonte was familiar with, certainly not the kind of reaction CJAD elicited. He remembers the sound of someone running through the typically long apartment hall-ways, as his teen neighbour ran from one end of her corridor to the other, then the screaming. He thought maybe there was some kind of emergency, though it happened quite regularly, coinciding with Boxer's 6 to 11 p.m. Top 40 show. "It's okay," said the teen's younger sister, responding to a concerned DiMonte. "It's just my sister going crazy when a Beatles record comes on." Boxer played the Beatles a lot, so eventually DiMonte adjusted to the daily outbursts. "I wasn't processing it this way at the time as a six-year-old kid, but when I think about it today, I think, 'Boy, that powerful little box on the kitchen counter.'"

DiMonte was intrigued by all the fuss one musical group could make and, at the tender age of six, he wanted in on the action. His mother ("God bless her," as DiMonte is fond of saying today) bought him one of those plastic portable Eaton's record players and one Beatles single, "She Loves You," which he proceeded to play the hell out of. Thus was born another Beatles fan. Then came the weekly re-cord-shopping trips with his mother to Woolworths in Verdun and more Beatles 45s, plus a pack of Beatles cards that came with a slice of gum whose flavour faded after a minute of chewing. In 1965, the DiMonte family moved from the busy urban feel of Verdun to the relative quiet of suburban Pierrefonds on Montreal's West Island. The move was quite the culture shock for seven-year-old DiMonte, but the family's three-bedroom bungalow, built by his father, meant DiMonte and his sister had their own bedrooms. Suburbia was in its frontier-town infancy in the mid-60s, not the same kind of place as his Verdun apartment where you got to hear your neighbour's business over the balcony or through the less than sound-proofed walls. Still, he had his trusty Eaton's turntable, a handful of Beatles singles, and now his very own transistor radio, complete with the hard, plastic earpiece for private listening.

The year the family moved to the West Island was the same year CFOX debuted its breakthrough Top 40 format. DiMonte had no idea that the CFOX studios were only a short distance from where he lived. But with his earpiece in, he discovered the sounds of Top 40 and jocks like Dean Hagopian and "Big Daddy" Bob Ancell and he could fill up on a steady diet of his favourite Top 40 hits. It was CFOX, then CKGM, that he grew up with. By the time DiMonte landed his first radio gig in Churchill, he had digested a number of radio styles and personalities through names like Paul Reid and George Balcan at CJAD, Dave Boxer at CFCF, and Ralph Lockwood first at CFOX then at CKGM, and Marc "Mais Oui" Denis at CKGM. "These guys were celebrities. Back then Montreal was the economic engine of the country," DiMonte recalls. "Vancouver was this tiny, rainy city, and Toronto, well, they were just trying to catch up. So, we were surrounded by these giants of the radio business. We thought at the time they were just radio announcers, but there was so much talent in town."

DiMonte has a soft spot for CJAD's legendary morning man George Balcan, whom he would hear over breakfast on his parents' kitchen radio, permanently tuned to CJAD. (Later, when DiMonte started at CHOM, he would get to know Balcan on a personal and professional level.) "I remember my parents being so pissed off when Balcan went to CFCF from CJAD [from 1973 to 1975, before returning]. I learned from them just how passionate people can be about their radio." When DiMonte took that passion to Churchill, his head was filled with an amalgam of radio voices from the golden-throated Paul Reid and the rock-steady George Balcan to the rollicking freestyle humour of Ralph Lockwood. All he had to do was find his own voice.

If the Pierrefonds of 1965 seemed like the end of the universe to a very young DiMonte, it was nothing compared to the isolation of a town founded on the muskeg of Hudson Bay and once considered an ideal spot for the British government to test their fledgling nuclear bomb program (they chose Australia instead.) In January, the month he arrived in Churchill, the days were short. The long nights meant many misery-laden letters and expensive phone calls back home to his parents. He'd already laid down a $200 deposit for his phone and, after too many calls to Montreal, they cut off his service. He lived alone with only his black and white TV as company.

"I cried for the first two weeks I was there," he admits. "My parents were very good about letters, and I got care packages from my mom. At one point she asked, if I was so miserable, why didn't I come home." That letter was pivotal, steeling his resolve to stick it out. He thinks maybe his mother was pulling some kind of reverse psych-out on him – a "curve ball," as DiMonte calls it. "I remember thinking to myself that [going back to Montreal] would be moving backwards. Why would I do that? I've come through all this quicksand and mud of trying to get here, and now I'm doing what I wanted to do and my mom's mentioning my old job [selling ball bearings] which I fucking hated." He wrote his mother back saying he was going to stick it out. In future letters, he dialled down the whining, using the substantial amount of downtime in Churchill to hone his radio skills, experimenting with different styles, taping and retaping himself in the CBC studios.

He left the winter darkness of Churchill, only to step back into it in Winnipeg as the all-night jock at CITI-FM, which was abandoning its square-head format for something more contemporary. DiMonte's circadian rhythms must have been seriously askew, but this was the motherlode compared to Churchill. This time he had a roommate, Jeff Hamilton, who was working at CKY-AM doing Top 40. Both were radio nerds who in their spare time listened to sound checks of some of the great U.S. jocks of the day like Charlie Tuna and Cousin Brucie. "We would pop these cassettes in and listen to them for hours," says DiMonte. "Those were the Drake format days, the pinnacle of Top 40 radio that still affects radio today. Those guys had to entertain in eight- to 20-second bursts. They all had big voices and they were nuts. We thought it was wildly entertaining."

Though both got their fill of the "boss jock" pioneers, DiMonte realized he didn't have the right stuff to be a fast-talking Top 40 DJ. While at CITI-FM, he took some cues from CKY's Don Percy, the so-called "Master of the Morning," who, with 58 years in radio, retired as a Hall of Fame broadcaster. Between Percy and his Montreal-radio role models George Balcan and Ralph Lockwood, DiMonte was finding his own style.

After a couple of years doing nights and the swing shifts at CITI-

FM, he graduated to the sweet afternoon drive shift, radio's version of a promotion. Then he made something of a risky, lateral career move. He was sweet-talked into joining a small independent record label, managing and promoting local bands. For the next three years he was out of the radio biz and into the much more unstable world of marketing music. Just two weeks into his new gig, DiMonte remembers having an epiphany while listening to CITI-FM on his way to a meeting. "I was stopped at a red light, looking at my car radio thinking, 'I don't belong here. I belong in there.' It was 3 o'clock in the afternoon and I'm supposed to be in there. It was a strange feeling, but I'm glad I did it when I did because, even though I was frustrated and thought radio was not going to take me anywhere, it was what I was meant to do." At first, things went swimmingly. He went on the road as a talent scout, eventually signing up-and-comers Streetheart, whose cover of the Rolling Stones song "Under My Thumb" got major airplay. Streetheart and the band Queen City Kids helped put DiMonte and partner Gene Martynek on the musical map of western Canada. Perhaps it was beginners' luck, but then things levelled off in their second year and the company barely broke even. "In the third year, it all went to shit," says DiMonte. "We went bankrupt and I went back to doing weekend mornings at CITI-FM. I wasn't a big enough prick nor was I a good enough liar, and both of those things are key elements to being successful in the music business."

A bit beaten down and nearly broke, DiMonte was welcomed back into the fold at CITI-FM. It was a tribute to the way DiMonte worked. The radio biz can be treacherous for those who burn their bridges when leaving a station. CITI liked what he had done for them and he had left no personal detritus behind. He also landed a golden summer gig on an all-night CBC show, *Night Lines,* based in Winnipeg, that featured independent and alternative Canadian music. DiMonte's time there was brief but enlightening, and the show would become a mainstay of CBC's Friday and Saturday night programming, running from 1984 to 1997. The cool thing about that CBC show was that it ran in all six time zones of the country so DiMonte could actually go home and catch himself on radio in Winnipeg. "I remember being so terrified," he says. "I had to get it out of my head that people in Newfoundland, the Yukon, were going to be listening. I did get over it, fortunately. It was absolutely fascinating. I loved it." Though the CBC assignment was short-lived, it served to flesh out his radio credentials. He was finding his way in radio. And someone took notice.

Radio consultant John Parikhal of Joint Communications, who had been brought into CHOM in 1979 to help change its format, was in Winnipeg offering his services to CITI-FM. Parikhal was impressed by DiMonte and knew CHOM was looking for someone who could take their morning show and shake the ratings up. Parikhal gave CHOM program director Rob Braide a call. "There's this kid in Winnipeg I like a lot," he told Braide. "You should try and make a new talent happen and I think you should give Terry a chance." As a premier radio consultant, Parikhal's word carried weight. It was a decision Braide never regretted. "Terry was just a natural," Braide says. "He's an easy communicator who did stuff [outside of his on-air CHOM duties] in his free time – a normal person who has an amazing intelligence and sense for the street. No question, he's the finest broadcaster I've ever worked with. And that's saying something."

When Braide called him, DiMonte had the same reservations he had had with the CBC show. "I told Rob that I had never done morning radio before," says DiMonte. "I wasn't sure how to approach it." Braide was empathetic. "That's okay," he told DiMonte. "We'll work together on it." With that reassurance, DiMonte headed back to his hometown. His mother was ecstatic.

Though he was essentially raised on an AM rock radio diet, DiMonte knew CHOM had almost 15 years on the Montreal FM rock landscape. He had known their sound and their evolution since the pioneering Pringle days. He was a dial hopper by habit but, after being out of touch with Montreal radio for six years, he was coming back to a station looking to boost its morning market share. He was replacing capable morning man Ron Able, another well-travelled jock who had made the transition from CKGM-AM to CHOM. It was not intended to be a Winnipeg-Montreal swap, but nevertheless Able was headed back to Top 40 AM at CKY in Winnipeg.

Rookie CHOM morning man Terry DiMonte, sporting his
Pierrefonds High School sweatshirt.
Courtesy of Patti Lorange.

Braide thought that DiMonte could use some company on the
morning drive shift, normally a one-man operation. In today's AM
and FM radio world, the morning show is invariably a team effort,
sometimes with as many as three hosts working together as an entertainment package. Braide was ahead of the learning curve when
he introduced DiMonte to Patti Lorange, who was doing triple duty
as the CHOM receptionist and performing on-air bits with Ron
Able, before becoming the morning and afternoon drive traffic reporter. (In its early free-spirited years, CHOM never took the traffic
reports very seriously. In fact, they only began with producer Daniel Feist improvising traffic reports as a prank during the morning
show, from the imaginary CHOM submarine's periscope, using a
thick German accent.)

It was Able who tagged Lorange "Peppermint Patti." Between
answering the phones, monitoring traffic (courtesy of the CJAD
helicopter) and contributing to Able's regular "Tabloid Trash" seg-
ment, she was a very busy 20-year-old. The CHOM submarine was

dry-docked after legitimate sponsors wanted their names tagged onto traffic reports. Also dry-docked was Lorange's post-secondary education plans: her 1981 summer gig became a full-time job and her post-secondary education was put on the back burner, where it has simmered ever since.

DiMonte and Lorange had chemistry from the moment they met. Any concerns Braide might have had evaporated quickly. For almost three years, DiMonte and "Peppermint Patti" Lorange took the CHOM morning show to new levels of popularity. Lorange introduced DiMonte around when he started in late 1984, taking him out at night to her gig as host of Concordia University's Comedy Nights and to some of her familiar Crescent Street haunts. In the morning, running on fumes, the two of them would come in with notes scrawled on cocktail napkins: people's birthdays, store openings, names of people leaving town – all gleaned from their nightly rounds. People would hear their names mentioned on his show and tell their friends. It was like old-style politicking; with Lorange as wingman, DiMonte was making a lot of friends. "He went from hardly anyone knowing him to a high-profile radio personality," says Lorange. "We were both young enough that we could handle the nightlife, given that we both had to get up a couple of hours after we got in." It wasn't a schedule they had to maintain long-term: after laying the foundation, the information came to them. Together, they'd won over their constituents.

In the beginning. program director Braide gave DiMonte free rein with occasional suggestions, as he warmed to the task. The spring 1984 CHOM morning ratings showed the station was making something of a dent in the drive-to-work morning time slot. DiMonte's warm, casual style suited Montrealers getting up at ungodly hours, hustling themselves (and their kids) along to their appointed duties, only to have rush-hour traffic test their patience. DiMonte thought he owed these people some conversation; he couldn't take his foot off the pedal. He knew a lot of people were tuning into CHOM to test drive him. His style was a hybrid of his radio listening history: part Balcan, part Lockwood, part CBC thrown in between the usual morning affirmations of news, sports, weather, and music. He even rattled the new format conservatives at CHOM when he talked over the musical intros of songs. This just wasn't done on CHOM. "Some people had some definite ideas of what should and should not be done on the air," he says. " 'Stop talking over the fucking intros,' they would tell me. Well, I'm a Top 40 kid. On morning radio, I think you have to have a constant presence. Time is very important. I took some flak from the old hippies, but Rob [Braide] backed me up."

Braide had made his way up the CHOM ladder from all-night announcer in 1977 to the afternoon drive shift, then co-music director and program director before finishing as general manager and vice-president of both Standard Broadcasting and Astral Media. Braide arrived at a time when CHOM was in the ratings doldrums. CHOM's slumping ratings even had management contemplating making CHOM into a disco music station, says Braide. Program director John Mackey apparently had all the necessary infrastructure in place. Fortunately, that was Plan B.

Plan A involved bringing in the consultants from Joint Communications, who recommended that CHOM implement the Abrams/Burkhart format (Lee and Kent respectively, both former U.S. DJs turned radio consultants), more commonly known as album-oriented rock, AOR in radio speak. The guru behind it all was Lee Abrams, who was the Bill Drake of his time. The similarity to Bill Drake, whose research of young AM radio listeners in the 1950s was considerably pithier than Abrams' "psychographics," was evident, with the two essentially coming to the same conclusion: Play all the hits, all the time (though, unlike the 1950s and 1960s when the 45s ruled, in the 1970s it was the album's turn). Program the AOR format, then wait for the listeners and advertisers to come. By the end of 1979, CHOM's fall ratings soared from moribund territory to major contender in the Montreal radio market with 648,000 listeners. The CHOM disco Plan B was filed away, dying the same death as the music itself. At the CHOM and CKGM 1979 Christmas party, the FM side was in a celebratory mood, while the AM side was considerably more subdued. After a decade of CKGM beating its FM brothers and sisters in the ratings, 1979 would mark a turning point.

As program director, Braide cooked up a one-hour weekly lunchtime show at CHOM called *The Electric Lunch Hour* that played hits from the 1960s and 1970s, a program move that irked management at CKGM-AM. *The Electric Lunch Hour* had some major staying power, lasting almost 20 years as a staple of CHOM's programming day. It remains one of Braide's major CHOM successes, the show outlasting his tenure at the station by a number of years. Braide's crowning CHOM career achievement, however, was his decision to bring in a young Terry DiMonte from Winnipeg to take over the all-important morning drive slot. Although DiMonte was not big-radio market-tested, it was a managerial move that paid off, one that Braide is especially proud of.

DiMonte did not disappoint. He settled into a sometimes quirky but spontaneous on-air style. Occasionally, he got up from the live mic, went to the studio door and yelled for someone down the hall. It was a calculated, spontaneous move that he thought added to the warmth of morning radio. Like all the parents out there who were yelling at their kids to get out of bed, DiMonte was acting out his morning man-as-parent role. "I thought I was painting a kind of picture for listeners," he says, though again there was some blowback from CHOM standard bearers. "I didn't want to do what everyone else was doing. I got the freedom to experiment and I think it helped in the presentation. It certainly helped change the ratings." Lorange loved DiMonte's David Letterman-style of broadcasting. "He would tap his pen, crumple paper, all when the mic was open," she says. "Or sometimes he'd be in the middle of a phone call as a song was ending. It all seemed spontaneous and natural." In fact, it was mostly a kind of calculated improvisation. "We never did any pre-planning for the show," Lorange says. "Terry was so good with the flow [of the program]. He was not the same guy at 5 a.m. as he was at 9 a.m. By 9 a.m. the engine was revving on all cylinders. And if one of us was struggling, the other would step in to help. We had chemistry and trust."

DiMonte's show made steady inroads in the competitive morning time slot. It didn't happen overnight, but after a few years with him at the helm and a tighter overall CHOM AOR format, the station crept closer to the No. 1 English-language radio spot in Montreal.

291

These were dynamic times for DiMonte – and the radio business. Six months after DiMonte started at CHOM, Geoff Stirling sold Maisonneuve Broadcasting to Toronto-based CHUM Ltd. The idea of working for the legendary Geoff Stirling was part of the allure for DiMonte. He never did meet Stirling, and was bent out of shape when he heard about the imminent sale, even before he went on the air at CHOM. (DiMonte still has the job-offer sheet with the Maisonneuve Broadcasting letterhead.) But he was in no position to voice his discontent. CHUM's reputation as something of a corporate behemoth had preceded it. The family-owned station was being gobbled up by the suits from Bay Street. But DiMonte's trepidation was unwarranted as CHUM Ltd. took a soft hands-on approach with CHOM. It was the beginning of a new era in radio, as conglomerates gorged themselves on smaller media outlets, eventually becoming much fatter than even CHUM Ltd. was.

That same year CKGM-AM, in an attempt to recapture the glory days of Top 40 morning radio, brought back Ralph Lockwood. DiMonte had worshipped Lockwood when he was at his peak during DiMonte's formative years in the suburbs. When he heard he'd be going head to head against his radio idol, he was "spooked." He thought he would get creamed in the ratings. CKGM-AM took out full-page ads in the Montreal *Gazette* and on billboards announcing Ralphie's return. "I thought, 'This is gonna kill us,'" says DiMonte. By this time both stations were back together in the original 1310 Greene Ave. building. His hero was just down the hall from the CHOM studios. It was intimidating. Lockwood had left Montreal in 1981 for the U.S. When he returned it was a very different Top 40 radio market. He tried to pick up where he left off, but neither the energy nor the audience was there for him.

"The impression I got from Ralph's second go-around," says DiMonte, "was that he was so talented and so good at it that things came easy to him in his heyday. I think he stopped working at it. I think he figured his name was big enough that all he had to do was come back."

With morning partner Patti Lorange serving as ambassador/ mentor and sidekick, and with management giving him just the right amount of latitude, DiMonte went from a scared-shitless first show to growing a solid following over time. He continued the CHOM tradition of making stars out of struggling rock acts that came through Montreal. The station had done it with the Police, Chris de Burgh, Genesis, and Styx, among many others. DiMonte recalls interviewing Styx lead singer Denis DeYoung, who told him the group had just come from a club gig in Chicago where they had played in front of about 250 people. In Montreal, they played before more than 10,000 at the Forum. Likewise for former Genesis lead guitarist Steve Hackett, who dropped by to be interviewed by DiMonte to promote his new group.

When fledgling rock musician Melissa Etheridge came to town as an opening act at Theatre St. Denis, DiMonte was blown away by her performance and asked her and the band out for drinks after the show. "Nobody knew who she was at the time," he says. "I was totally taken by her show. The next morning I played almost all of her album. The album had just come out and she hadn't had much reaction yet." On the tour bus to Toronto, Etheridge had CHOM-FM dialled in and heard almost all of her album on radio. Elated, she phoned DiMonte from Toronto to thank him. Thanks to the CHOM/DiMonte promotion, the next time Etheridge was back in town, she played her very first arena gig at the Forum in 1988. Her popularity in Montreal had enough depth that she was asked to be the last rock artist to play the Forum in 1996 before it was shuttered as a concert and hockey venue.

In 1987 Lorange left CHOM, disappointed by her salary and just a little restless to get out on her own. The dynamic duo split when she got an offer from CKIS-FM (now CJKR-FM) in Winnipeg to do the all-night show. It seemed like a good idea on paper, but she soon discovered the solo all-night shift wasn't for her. She rebounded when she switched to the morning show with the high-energy "Brother" (Bro) Jake Edwards, before coming back to CHOM and Montreal in 1990 to rejoin DiMonte and his new morning show partner, Ted Bird. Lorange picked up right where she left off, only now she was part of a morning threesome.

With Terry, Ted, and Patti, the show took on a new dynamic.

Lorange had broken some new ground as the female co-host on a popular FM Montreal radio station, and kept CHOM entertaining in the highly competitive drive-to-work market.

Ted Bird had come to CHOM via CFCY in Charlottetown, P.E.I., a brief stint at CKGM-AM and five career-building years doing sports and news at CFTR-AM in Toronto, the No. 1 Top 40 radio station in that city. Though his memory of time spent at CKGM-AM in Montreal was not part of his career highlight reel, he nevertheless accepted an offer to work with FM 96 (later changed to Mix 96) morning man Mark Burns – the same guy who had hired him at CKGM. It was here that Bird developed his role as a co-host, first with Burns, then more so with morning jocks Bruce Kenyon and Jeff Lumby. So, when Terry DiMonte's sidekick Peppermint Patti Lorange left for Winnipeg, Bird was interviewed for the morning news gig on CHOM. He remembers the meeting with DiMonte and program director Ian Maclean as a very casual kicking of the tires. "We opened a bottle of scotch, had a few drinks and just shot the shit," Bird says. "It was quite obvious right out of the gate that it was a good fit. We were the same age [26], we grew up in the same middle-class families, had similar interests and senses of humour. It was sort of like the brother you never met kind of thing." DiMonte had the leverage, the clout – and the co-operation of management – to be able to vet his potential hire. Years later at CHOM, Bird would encounter a similar situation, but with completely different results.

With CHOM morning ratings on the move, other Montreal stations made overtures for DiMonte's services, especially when news got out about his imminent contract renewal with new station owners Standard Broadcasting. This was the pre-agent and -lawyer period. So when Mix 96 (CJFM-FM) came calling in 1993, it was a direct-to-DiMonte call. With more money on the table, DiMonte left CHOM for the less edgy, smoother and older demographic of Mix 96. It was a big score for the station. Bird was part of the deal, but not Lorange, who was "hurt and thoroughly pissed off. Radio is like a boys' club," she says. Without the gentility of DiMonte and the quick wit of Bird, the next couple of years at CHOM were not career-satisfaction highlights for Lorange.

Replacing DiMonte was John Derringer, who came from Q107 in Toronto. Derringer did not endear himself to his new audience, announcing off the top that he hated the Montreal Canadiens. Listeners must have wondered if they'd heard him right. Announcers worth their salt switched sports allegiances whenever they moved into a new market, whether they meant it or not. Lorange found him mercurial, not nearly as steady and supportive as DiMonte. "I missed Terry," she says. Somehow, she tolerated the situation for almost three years, while Mix 96 reaped the benefits of disenchanted CHOM morning listeners. After a brief time with the saner and more DiMonte-like Ken Connors, Lorange decided Calgary was where she would settle down and start a family. She had seen the writing on the wall when CHOM embarked on *The Howard Stern Show* experiment in 1997, which lasted less time than Derringer, but started in a similar fashion with Stern going on an anti-French tirade on his first show. He was dumped a year later. It was not a proud chapter in the CHOM history book.

From 1988 to 1993, before both DiMonte and Bird left for Mix 96, it was stellar morning radio for CHOM listeners. At first doing just straight news, Bird would evolve his role with DiMonte into more of a partnership, providing the necessary morning wake-up levity. He broke out his imitation of hockey commentator Don Cherry, deliberately mispronouncing DiMonte's last name. Bird was Don Scary; he called DiMonte "Delmonaco," riffing on Cherry's reputation for mispronouncing and re-arranging the English language. The Don Scary bits were an immediate hit with listeners. Bird was so good at his Cherry imitation, even "the Don" himself called to say, "You do me better than I do me."

"DiMonte never knew what I was going to say, but he was the perfect straight man," says Bird, who still gets on-the-street requests to do his Cherry imitation. "We never did much pre-show planning. My role as being more than a news guy just kind of happened. There was an unspoken understanding between us. I think that's part of the reason it worked so well. We didn't over-think it; it just happened."

After Lorange came back from Winnipeg, the three years with Terry, Ted, and Patti – the first three-pronged FM morning show in Montreal – were an amusing ride-to-work for CHOM listeners. If they didn't catch the most comical moments, they could catch a 30-second audio highlight reel from that morning's show that the station used for promotional purposes. It was the only CHOM show that got promos in other time slots. "With the three of us there, I thought the show was absolutely at its peak," says Bird.

When Bird and DiMonte moved to Mix 96 in 1993, CHOM took a hit in their morning ratings, which was exactly what Mix 96 management had hoped for: a boost in the morning ratings on a station that was retooling itself as an adult contemporary music alternative to CHOM. The team of DiMonte and Bird had a loyal following and by now CHOM's early 1970s demographic had grown up. For the next five years, it was the *Terry and Ted Morning Show*, until DiMonte left to move into George Balcan's morning spot at CJAD. DiMonte was humbled by the move. Coming after Balcan's 30 years at the station, he was taking over the chair of one of his early radio heroes. "You don't replace Balcan," DiMonte says. "You follow him." Some ardent CHOM/DiMonte listeners looked at his move to mainstream AM radio as a kind of selling out, but for DiMonte this was a career trajectory that made sense. It was an easy fit for a guy who could easily change gears if he had to. He just had to keep being himself, though the busy CJAD morning show left little room for the shenanigans that he, Bird and Lorange were famous for. Bird joined DiMonte for a two-year stint as sports announcer. "For about 20 years I had people telling me how funny I was," says Bird. "For the two years at CJAD, they called in to tell me how funny I wasn't," he says.

For both DiMonte and Bird, the family-owned factor was important, but when they returned to CHOM in 2002, it was under the ownership of Standard Broadcasting, a bigger, new boss, with nowhere near the intimacy of the Stirling days or even CHUM Ltd. Standard Broadcasting was the largest privately owned multimedia company in Canada at the time, with 52 radio stations Canada-wide, before

296

When DiMonte left CHOM in 2007 for Q107 in Calgary, it was an emotional last show. But he would be back again five years later.
Courtesy of Montreal Gazette. Photo by John Kenny.

it was eventually sold to Astral Media in 2007 for $1.08 billion. The beginning of corporate ownership meant a change of chemistry in the front office, and that filtered down.

The chemistry between DiMonte and Bird continued to be good fare on radio, but artistic differences DiMonte had with a program director who insisted on weekly meetings to review his performance got under his skin. After enduring this for a time, DiMonte ran out of patience and left CHOM to take a job as morning man at Q107 in Calgary, where he eventually hooked up on air with pal Peppermint Patti. He had made plenty of friends in Montreal over the years and his departure from CHOM rated a cartoon by the *Gazette*'s editorial cartoonist Terry Mosher, better known as Aislin. Between the irascible program director and lagging contract negotiations, DiMonte was prepared to move on.

Bird soldiered on with new morning man Rob Kemp, then "Bad Pete" Marier. He added a couple of new bits, one with his new wife Danielle which he called "Revisionist History," where he skewered current trends of rewriting history to serve personal or political interests. The live phone bits he did with Danielle were a big hit, but an on-air slip of her tongue landed Bird in the program director's office. F-bombs were not CRTC-approved language, but it was the "Revisionist History" bit, along with Bird's objection to the hiring of a new news announcer, that brought things to a boiling point. It was a power struggle that Bird lost. Later, he would explain his departure from CHOM on his blog.

> CHOM and most of the rest of the country's radio stations have been acquired by corporations who jettisoned the majority of the creative people in favour of bean counters beholden only to shareholders. The impact was swift, enormous, and predictable. By the time I left CHOM, it was about as much fun as working at the Soviet Ministry of Agriculture. No disrespect to Soviet farming apparatchiks, but that's not what I signed up for.

Bird had backed himself into a corner: his defiance of management came back to haunt him even though he thought he had a sure-fire fit for himself doing mornings at sports radio TSN 990. When TSN 990, which would then change frequencies to 690, was included in the Bell Media sale in 2012, he became a casualty after just 16 months on the job. Management has a long memory. Bird is now back on radio as morning host at a new station, the Jewel 107.7, serving the Montreal off-island communities of Hudson, St. Lazare, and Vaudreuil, back under the umbrella of a family-owned radio – a survivor at the tender age of 56.

In Calgary, DiMonte was given a five-year contract with Q107, the Eagle (owned by Corus) – time enough to make an impression and build an audience in the city's radio market. Corus, however, never went out of its way to promote DiMonte's arrival in the city, so it fell to him (and Peppermint Patti for a time) to generate a local following. Unfortunately, the numbers never did meet his expectations. In Montreal, meanwhile, new owners (Astral) kept one eye on CHOM's ratings and the other on DiMonte's in Calgary. They realized they'd made a mistake in letting him go in 2007 and sent program director Martin Spalding out to Calgary to make DiMonte an offer, despite the fact there were almost 18 months left in his five-year contract. DiMonte was flattered, but not flattered enough to jump at the opportunity to come back to his hometown and the station that had made him a fixture on Montreal morning radio. Unlike his 2007 contract negotiations with CHOM, this time he had legal counsel look closely at the offer. He wanted, and was given, more creative control, including being able to have a say in who his morning team would be. He didn't want a repeat of his acrimonious relationship with management, and so, with more than a year to go on his contract (an escape clause in his Q107 contract let him off the hook for six months of that), he agreed to return to CHOM.

Astral made the announcement six months before DiMonte would do his first show back at CHOM in January 2012. Montreal had plenty of time to anticipate his arrival and DiMonte used the time to re-acquaint himself with the city and his myriad of contacts and friends who welcomed him back with open arms. Speculation and rumours about a DiMonte/Bird reunion abounded, but this was not going to happen. The aging but dedicated CHOM listeners who were still around were a sentimental crowd, but DiMonte's January 9, 2012, CHOM debut was with former Virgin Radio afternoon host Heather Backman at his side. (As part of ongoing employment cuts by Bell Media, Blackman was let go in January just weeks after celebrating five years as DiMonte's co-host.)

In November 2014, DiMonte celebrated 30 years as a morning man in radio: November 5, 1984, was his first show on CHOM-FM. Now, with a five-year contract with Bell Media, DiMonte will be pushing 60 by the time his contract expires. His hero, George Balcan, logged 35 years as the CJAD morning man. DiMonte's career won't be about sticking around just to beat that number, like some sort of flamed-out athlete who doesn't know when to let go. As long as he can drag his ass out of bed at 4 a.m. every morning, and still love it, he'll have more miles yet left to travel.

Rocket Radio on Wheels

My "Radical" Years; Top 40 on the Decline

By the beginning of the '70s, CFCF and CFOX were not the Top 40 contenders they once were. Dave Boxer's Top 40 reign was up in 1968 and CFOX's No. 1 fortunes changed for the worse when CKGM went Top 40 in 1970. The Baby Boomers were now out of high school and either working or pursuing a post-secondary education. With newfound purchasing power, a stereo system was a necessity. The trend was away from 45s to albums, though Top 40 radio continued to be the place where, if the single was hot, then the album sold more.

As an arts student at Loyola College in Montreal, I grew my hair and wore bell-bottom jeans. Though still living at home, I spent more time away smoking dope and plotting the revolution on a friend's apartment couch. The student unrest in the U.S. spilled onto campuses in Canada, though the issues were different. The most infamous of all student-led activism was the so-called Sir George Williams University Computer Riot that began in late January of 1969 with the occupation of the university's Hall Building ninth-floor computer lab, until 14 days later when the administration called in the Montreal Riot Squad. Hundreds of students protested alleged racist treatment of black students by assistant professor of biology Perry Anderson. The occupation made for great national TV theatre as protesting students tossed thousands of computer punch cards out the ninth-floor campus windows and set fire to computers, causing about $2 million in damage. Two months later, 10,000 demonstrators marched through Montreal to the gates of McGill University. Dubbed by the press as the "McGill français" demonstration, they wanted the bastion of English education, which had an estimated three percent francophone students, to be more French. Even the conservative Jesuit-run Loyola College (soon to become part of Concordia University in a merger with Sir George Williams University in 1974) was not immune to the revolutionary fervour of the day. The non-renewal of the contract of physics professor Dr. P.S. Santhanam became the rallying point for student discontent in early 1970 and a five-day occupation of the college's administration building eventually ended with another appearance by Montreal's Riot Squad. I supported the cause, but I was hardly a ground-level activist. It was all about power to the people – John Lennon's song said so – and sticking it to The Man.

I had my own show at Radio Loyola, playing over speakers set up in the college's cafeteria and lounges. This was the closest I got to actually working in radio. In my fourth and last year at Loyola College, I rented a semi-basement apartment for $70 a month. Top 40 radio on my beat-up AM radio was still keeping me company, though I occasionally "borrowed" my mother's German-made AM/FM radio to listen to CHOM, the hippest new station in town. Any thoughts I had about going into radio were dampened by a lack of confidence – and the requisite radio voice – and after graduating and a couple of trips to Europe postponing adulthood, I took a job selling carpets. I had a B.A. in sociology; carpets were not my area of expertise. It was time to figure out what to do with my adult self. So, I went back to school.

In the mid-70s I was enrolled at McGill University's Faculty of Education in a one-year program designed for students who couldn't figure out what to do with their B.A. degrees. The next year, in 1974, I got a job teaching high school, hardly a quiet time in Quebec's dynamic public-sector union history. My starting salary was $8,200. I was on strike three times in my first nine years on the job and bought my first car, a used, ugly-orange 1968 VW Bug – and a stereo system for my one-bedroom apartment. The dial on the car's AM radio was

301

tuned into 980 CKGM. In my apartment it was either an album on the turntable or CHOM-FM. By the time I got married and started a family in 1984, Top 40 radio in Montreal was on the wane, displaced by the stereo power of FM. Miraculously, CKGM hung on for years after the last of its legendary Top 40 DJs, Ralph Lockwood, left the station in 1988 for good. The station would go through a number of format incarnations: Lite Rock, Less Talk, Favourites of Yesterday and Today, and Oldies 990, before becoming a sports talk radio station. (In the eyes of the CRTC, the station's call letters are still CKGM.) But by the end of the 1980s and into the '90s, listeners had lost track of its format changes, though die-hard Boomers liked the Golden Oldies format. CHOM, meanwhile, is still a vibrant part of the Montreal radio scene after 40-plus years on the air.

I became mostly respectable, married, then had one daughter, but after 27 years as a high school teacher, I ran out of gas and patience and launched a career as a freelance journalist, a job with about as much security as Top 40 DJ. Though listening habits have changed over the years with online streaming, and digital and satellite radio, according to a recent CRTC report, Canadians spend an average of 16 hours per week listening to AM and FM radio. And radio is still the main delivery vehicle for new music. Today, the Boomer crowd is more likely to have their radios tuned into CBC or NPR, though I'm sure I'm not the only 60-something who likes to occasionally blast a good Stones tune in the car.

Some summer days with windows open, you can hear me coming for miles, the volume cranked up, the car my own little rocket-radio world on wheels. I remember the halcyon days of Top 40 radio with great fondness and decided it was about time to pay tribute to the people who were such a significant part of my formative years, playing the music I still listen to today. We grew up together. It was the least I could do.

ACKNOWLEDGEMENTS

The idea for this book occupied a part of my brain for many years before I finally got into gear and actually began to write. Thanks to Simon Dardick of Véhicule Press, who appreciated the era of radio that I wrote about, this book is now a printed page reality.

Thanks to graphic designer David Drummond of Salamander Hill Design for a cover that pops like the music of the 60s and 70s.

Special thanks to freelance editor Licia Canton, whose diligence and dedication helped me pare the book down to a more manageable publication size, and to her husband Dominic Cusmano who leaned in to read and proffer advice. And my appreciation to Geri Newell, who brought my interviews to life from the tape recorder to the page.

If it was not for former CKGM-AM DJ Marc "Mais Oui" Denis and his "The 98 CKGM Super 70s Tribute" web site, getting this whole project off the ground would have been much more difficult.

To my "tech" guy and friend, Michael Hayes, and Ryan Hayes of Sparrow Digital, who offered more than just electronic help.

Terry Mosher helped me plant the seed with Véhicule Press.

And thanks to the many who dug deep into their personal archives for photos and personal stories: radio memorabilia buffs Dan Kowal, Don Major, and Ted Brennan; Allan Nicholls, Bob Burgess, Al Birmingham, Jurgen Peter, Denis Grondin, Patti Lorange, Oko Shio, DKD, Bob Gillies, Tootall, Dean Hagopian, Louise "Corky" Van Guelpen, Rachel Irwin, Eric Pressman, Pip Wedge of the Canadian Communication Foundation, Mark Sherman, Ian MacLean, Alex Taylor, Roy Kerwood, John Cosway, and Patricia Desjardins, who all facilitated my photo/memorabilia and information search. While virtually harassing some for photos, I was reminded by one, "Hey, it was radio, man." Radio historians and authors Martin Melhuish and Garry Moir were inspirations.

To all the DJs, news and traffic reporters, radio management people, musicians, and radio historians, who dipped back into their

305

50-plus-year-old memory banks to provide me with the meat of this book, a major tip of the hat. And last, but not least, thanks to premier concert promoter – a DJ at heart – Donald Tarlton (a.k.a. Donald K. Donald), who has seen the radio and rock 'n' roll business from more angles than a professional billiards player.

.

311

315